Historical Problems
Studies and Documents

Edited by
PROFESSOR G. R. ELTON
University of Cambridge

8
THE ROYAL SUPREMACY
IN THE ELIZABETHAN CHURCH

In the same series

THE ROYAL
SUPREMACY
IN THE
ELIZABETHAN
CHURCH

Claire Cross
University of York
Author of 'The Puritan Earl'

LONDON: GEORGE ALLEN AND UNWIN LTD
NEW YORK: BARNES AND NOBLE INC.

GENERAL INTRODUCTION

The reader and the teacher of history might be forgiven for thinking that there are now too many series of historical documents in existence, all claiming to offer light on particular problems and all able to fulfil their claims. At any rate, the general editor of yet another series feels obliged to explain why he is helping one more collection of such volumes into existence.

One purpose of this series is to put at the disposal of the student original materials illustrating historical problems, but this is no longer anything out of the way. A little less usual is the decision to admit every sort of historical question: there are no barriers of time or place or theme. However, what really distinguishes this enterprise is the fact that it combines generous collections of documents with introductory essays long enough to explore the theme widely and deeply. In the doctrine of educationalists, it is the original documents that should be given to the student; in the experience of teachers, documents thrown naked before the untrained mind turn from pearls to paste. The study of history cannot be confined either to the learning up of results without a consideration of the foundations, or to a review of those foundations without assistance of the expert mind. The task of teaching involves explanation and instruction, and these volumes recognize this possibly unfashionable fact. Beyond that, they enable the writers to say new and important things about their subject matter: to write history of an exploratory kind, which is the only important historical writing there is.

As a result, each volume will be a historical monograph worth the attention which all such monographs deserve, and each volume will stand on its own. While the format of the series is uniform, the contents will vary according to need. Some problems require the reconsideration which makes the known enlighteningly new; others need the attention of original research; yet others will have to enter controversy because the prevailing notions on many historical questions are demonstrably wrong. The authors of this series are free to treat their subject in whatever manner it seems to them to require. They will present some of their evidence for inspection and help the learner to see how history is written, but they will themselves also write history.

G.R.E.

AUTHOR'S NOTE

Since Elizabethan Englishmen did not use it I have tried in this book to avoid entirely the word 'Anglican' with its inevitable anachronistic overtones of nineteenth century ecclesiastical controversies. 'Puritan', an equally ambiguous and equivocal word, has proved on occasions to be indispensable, though whenever possible I have substituted a more precise term. It did become current in the second part of the sixteenth century and referred then to those zealous Englishmen, clerical and lay, who strove by all legal means for the further Protestant reformation of the national church. Contemporaries did not consider Separatists, much less Anabaptists, to be Puritans as they had abandoned the concept of one comprehensive church for all Englishmen in favour of exclusive assemblies of the elect; and, guided by the recent definitions of Professor Basil Hall and Dr Patrick Collinson,[1] I have attempted to employ the word in its more restricted Elizabethan sense.

All Latin phrases have been translated and in the documents words in italics show where this has been done: square brackets indicate emendations or additions. The title of a book, given in an abbreviated form in a footnote, appears in full in the bibliography: where no place of publication is shown London should be assumed. The spelling of all Elizabethan English has been modernized including the titles of books. The initials B.M. and P.R.O. throughout stand for the British Museum and Public Record Office.

I should like to thank Lord Verulam and the governing bodies of Corpus Christi College, Cambridge, the Inner Temple, London, Trinity College, Cambridge, Hertfordshire County Record Office and the Huntington Library, San Marino, California for allowing me to consult and publish documents 29, 30, 31, 39, 40, 46 and 48. Dr Collinson and the Editor of the *Bulletin of the Institute of Historical Research* kindly gave me permission to reproduce document 46, and the Honorary Secretary of the Somerset Record Society to reproduce document 48.

Dealing with a topic like the royal supremacy about which so much has already been written, I am more than usually beholden to the historians who have gone before me: I hope I have acknowledged my indebtedness adequately in the text and footnotes. There are, how-

---

[1] B. Hall, 'Puritanism: the Problem of Definition', G. J. Cuming, ed. *Studies in Church History*, II, pp. 283–296. P. Collinson, *The Elizabethan Puritan Movement*, 1967, pp. 13–15, 22–28.

ever, three historians I must mention by name for without their work this book could never have been compiled: I am under an especial obligation to the late Professor Norman Sykes for first introducing me to the Elizabethan church, to Sir John Neale for all his research on Elizabethan Parliaments and to Dr Collinson both for his scholarship on Elizabethan Puritanism in general, and for his generous criticism of this essay in particular. I am also most grateful to the Editor of this series for his encouragement and advice. Lastly I should like to thank the President and Fellows of University College, Cambridge who, by granting me an honorary Visiting Fellowship for Easter Term, 1968, provided congenial surroundings in which to write.

CLAIRE CROSS

August 1968
Department of History
University of York

CONTENTS

INTRODUCTION

Introductory

'The prince alone is the person in the world to whom God hath committed the seat of justice, and they only to execute the duty of it to whom it is committed, at whose hands God will require it. . . . The minister is appointed for another defence where horsemen and chariots will do no good. They may hinder the minister and make him forget his duty, they cannot profit him in his office and function. He must frame the heart, upon which you cannot yet set a crown; and edify the soul, which flesh and blood cannot hurt.'[1]

'Her highness' pleasure is that from henceforth no bills concerning religion shall be preferred or received into this House, unless the same should be first considered or liked by the clergy.[2]

'Surely this was a doleful message, for it was as much as to say, "Sirs, ye shall not deal in God's causes; no, ye shall in no wise seek to advance his glory. . . ."

'I do surely think, before God I speak it, that the bishops were the cause of that doleful message; and I will show you what moveth me so to think. I was, amongst others, the last Parliament sent unto the bishop of Canterbury, for the articles of religion that then passed this House. He asked us why we did put out of the book the articles for the homelies, consecrating of bishops and such like. "Surely, sir," said I, "because we were so occupied in other matters that we had no time to examine them how they agreed with the word of God." "What," said he, "surely you mistook the matter, you will refer yourselves wholly to us therein?" "No, by the faith I bear to God," said I, "we will pass nothing before we understand what it is, for that were but to make

---

[1] Edward Dering to William Lord Burghley, November 3, 1573. Quoted in P. Collinson, *A Mirror of Elizabethan Puritanism: the Life and Letters of 'Godly Master Dering'*, 1964, p. 25.

[2] May 22, 1572. *Commons Journals*, II, p. 97.

you popes; make you popes who list," said I, "for we will make you none. . . ." [1]

These two extracts, the first from a letter by the famous Protestant preacher, Edward Dering, the second part of a speech by the equally famous parliamentarian, Peter Wentworth, epitomize the double dilemma the monarch faced in exercising the royal supremacy within the Elizabethan church. On the one hand the queen encountered the theoretical predicament of the lay headship. Both Catholic and Protestant ecclesiastics in differing degrees objected to a lay person wielding authority over the church, for they argued that a minister owed primary allegiance not to his earthly sovereign but to God. This constituted a largely clerical problem. On the other hand, the monarch had to solve a practical problem. From the beginning of the reign royal apologists devised a simple division of labour. They maintained that the queen could quite properly rule over the church in jurisdictional matters; doctrine she would leave to be determined by the clergy: but the complexities of Tudor politics did not allow a monarch's actions to fit into these neat categories. Elizabeth almost immediately after her accession came under attack on two fronts, from clerics of very different beliefs concerned for the autonomy of the church, and from laymen eager for a voice in deciding upon church policy. A lay head, she yet tried to restrain lay intervention in the government of the church. She held that the royal supremacy meant royal rule of the church through the clergy, and to a certain extent sustained this interpretation until her death; but she could not prevent zealous laymen from asking why, if a layman could be the head of the church, laymen in general could not participate in its government. Increasingly as time went on radical clergy supported the laity's claim and in practice Elizabeth found herself powerless to control laymen who took the reform of their local churches into their own hands, although she did stop a further national reform of the church by Parliament. The documents in this book have been chosen to illustrate this twofold problem; firstly to demonstrate the theoretical difficulties which arose when a layman claimed to be supreme over the church, and secondly to show some of the practical difficulties met by the queen when she attempted to exercise this royal supremacy.

[1] Speech by Peter Wentworth, February 8, 1576. S. D'Ewes, *A complete journal . . . of the House of Lords and House of Commons throughout the whole reign of Queen Elizabeth*, 1693, pp. 238, 239–240.

The Royal Supremacy
in Theory

I. PROLOGUE

THOSE who supported or attacked the idea of the royal supremacy in 1558 had experienced a generation of rapid change and were by no means theorizing in a void. Henry VIII had been the innovator;[1] Edward VI, having inherited the sovereignty over the church asserted by his father, used it to establish a fully Protestant church in England; Mary had renounced these powers and recognized anew the authority of the pope. Obviously Catholics hoped that Elizabeth might be persuaded to follow her sister's example and keep England within Catholic Christendom. It is less often realized that a body of articulate Protestants disliked the ecclesiastical experiments of Henry VIII almost as much as did the Catholics. Anthony Gilby, who had gone into exile soon after Mary's accession, and had eventually migrated with John Knox to set up an English Calvinist church in Geneva, in 1558 attacked Henry VIII with surprising virulence (Doc. 2). He did not see Henry as the defender of the faith but as a wild boar destroying the Lord's vineyard, preventing his true ministers from fulfilling their labours, killing his saints. Henry had indeed cast out the pope, but then had made himself a lay pope in his place. Not even the government of Edward VI had allowed a thorough Protestant reformation; the king's servants had permitted the plundering of the church to continue, they had censored the free preaching of the gospel and failed to establish Protestant discipline. Protestants of Gilby's type hoped for a monarch who would finally pull down the pope's usurped supremacy and then abdicate from the ecclesiastical sphere completely, giving all power to the godly ministers.

Catholics felt as strongly as the more radical Protestants that the royal claims to headship over the church bordered upon the

[1] For a detailed discussion of Henry VIII's view of the royal supremacy see J. J. Scarisbrick, *Henry VIII*, 1968.

sacrilegious. By 1558 educated Catholics recognized, as with some exceptions they had not recognized during Henry VIII's reign, that a lay headship constituted the first move in the admission of heresy into England. They remained faithful to their belief that the church should be ruled by Christ and his vicar, St Peter, and by the bishops of Rome, the successors of St Peter. A lay ruler who attempted to exercise jurisdiction reserved for the clergy alone plainly transgressed the divine law and this power, wrongfully obtained, could have no shred of legality. Bishop Scot, speaking in the first Parliament of Elizabeth when Catholic prelates could still take their seats in the Lords, put the case for the conservatives (Doc. 4). A wiser man than Gilby, he did not comment directly on the extent of royal authority, but he did not hide his opinion that Parliament, a body composed largely of laymen, had no powers to legislate in matters concerning religion. The truths of religion never changed and must be passed down entire from one generation to another; but, he argued, one Parliament could undo the acts of its predecessor, and he therefore concluded that parliamentary intervention in matters of religion automatically brought an end to Catholic certainty. However great were the divisions between them, Catholic and radical Protestant theologians at least united in upholding the exclusive rule of the clergy in the church.

Catholics and some Protestants also held in common a further objection to Elizabeth's assuming the royal supremacy over the church in the same form as her father had exercised it. Since Catholic theologians could not accept that a layman could rightfully have jurisdiction over the church, for a laywoman to pretend to have such a power seemed a mere absurdity. That a woman might attempt to become the head of a Protestant church caused some zealous Protestants equal disquiet. While Mary Tudor was still alive John Knox wrote that both divine and natural law prohibited a woman from bearing civil rule over men: he refused even to contemplate that God would allow a woman any authority within the church (Doc. 1). As long as Protestants in England and Scotland suffered under the government of Catholic women, Mary Tudor and Mary of Guise, such an assertion may have proved acceptable to the godly, but the accession of Elizabeth entirely altered the situation; now it was upon a woman that English Protestants pinned their hopes. Knox's apparently unshakable arguments required urgent refutation, and while still in exile John Aylmer, the former tutor of Lady Jane Grey, wrote in Elizabeth's defence (Doc. 3). God, he believed, could work through the weakest of his creatures, even through a woman. If he sent the English a woman to rule over them, they must in obedience submit to his will. In order to counter the zeal of the Protestant radicals he found it necessary to return to the medieval concept of the two spheres. Divines had exceeded their office and had confusingly mingled the ecclesiastical and civil; they ought now to forbear from meddling in the secular world. Yet this was a far from conclusive argument since it could equally well be employed against the pretensions of lay rulers in regard to the church. Aylmer had also to consider the even more daunting problem of justifying the rule of a woman in the church for which English history provided no precedent at all. He replied by dividing ecclesiastical government into two parts, spiritual ministry and formal jurisdiction. The New Testament, he agreed, clearly excluded women from the spiritual ministry but he proceeded to argue that in exceptional cases a woman could act as an overseer in the church. This subsequently became the standard Protestant defence of Elizabeth's position throughout the reign.

In the weeks before Parliament defined the royal supremacy which the queen should exercise, the objections of her fellow monarchs to the Henrician form of supremacy may well have counted far more with Elizabeth than the opinions of divines, whether Catholic or Protestant. Philip II wasted no time theorizing on the extent of kingly authority; instead he told Elizabeth, when it appeared that she had resolved to imitate her father, that he alone could control the papacy. If she denied the pope's power in England, then he would withdraw his restraining influence, and the pope would at once declare the queen illegitimate and release her subjects from their allegiance (Doc. 5). While in his own dominions Philip had not hesitated to withstand papal injunctions, by not fearing to resurrect the ancient spectre of the pope's power to depose secular rulers, he brought into the open the final argument against the royal supremacy which Catholics in England had not yet dared publicly to discuss. By early in 1559, with this intervention from Spain, most of the chief theoretical objections to the idea of the royal supremacy and the counter arguments in its support had emerged in embryo to be elaborated in infinite detail as the reign progressed.

II. THE ACTS OF SUPREMACY AND UNIFORMITY

One of the main functions of the first Parliament of Elizabeth which assembled on January 25, 1559, was to re-establish formally the queen's authority over the English church. Professor Neale has suggested that the government intended that this Parliament should merely assert the queen's supremacy; an act to redefine Protestantism in England could more conveniently and appropriately await a later Parliament by which time the Marian Catholic bishops would have been displaced and Convocation have been able to take a full part in the discussion of doctrine. The government aimed at achieving a policy of reformation by gradual stages in order to lessen the chance of disturbances in the country and, even more vital, give as little offence as possible to the Catholic powers on the continent. In their very different ways both the House of Lords and the House of Commons from the beginning set out to frustrate the government's wishes. The lords spiritual to a man refused to consider recognizing Elizabeth as supreme head of the church. If the queen and her advisers had hoped, and there is evidence that they had, that with judicious handling the Marian bishops would behave as the Henrician bishops had done and remain loyal to the queen rather than to the pope, they miscalculated gravely. The Commons, on the other hand, contained a vociferous and powerful group of active Protestants some of whom had actually been exiles; of these, many associated themselves closely with the exile clergy. These men would be content with nothing less than an immediate and permanent settlement of Protestantism in England. Early in the Parliament they made their influence felt by raising the question whether the Parliament was a legally valid one since the writs of summons had left out the royal title of supreme head. They went on to call for an act to prescribe the doctrine of the English church in addition to the act for the royal supremacy. Some of the radicals undoubtedly favoured the English service book which Knox had used at Geneva, and not even the more conservative Coxians at Frankfort had observed the second Prayer Book of Edward VI in its entirety. So for them to call just before Easter for the restoration of religion as it had been in the last year of Edward VI could be seen as an attempt at a compromise. It seemed, nevertheless, that the queen would end the Parliament before any religious settlement could be achieved. The news of the successful completion of the peace negotiations with France may have caused her to decide to continue the session until after Easter; she may also have been swayed by the Protestants in the Commons. At all events a marked change in the government's attitude came about: when the queen dissolved Parliament after Easter, it had passed not only the act of supremacy but also the act of uniformity based on the second Prayer Book of Edward VI.[1]

The act of supremacy which set out the exact position of the monarch in the church, together with the act of uniformity which defined the doctrine of the church, proved to be the keystones of the Elizabethan religious settlement. Outwardly the act of supremacy looked back to the reigns of Henry VIII and Edward VI (Doc. 6). As

---

[1] J. E. Neale, 'Elizabethan Acts of Supremacy and Uniformity', *English Historical Review*, LX, 1950, pp. 304–332. J. E. Neale, *Elizabeth I and her Parliaments, 1559–1581*, 1953, pp. 33–84. P. Collinson, *The Elizabethan Puritan Movement*, 1967, pp. 30–35. J. V. P. Thompson, *Supreme Governor*, 1940, pp. 1–15, 43–69.

far as might be, it restored to the crown those ecclesiastical powers which Henry VIII had enjoyed at the end of his reign; it revived the legislation passed in Henrician Parliaments against the pope, and repealed all the ecclesiastical legislation of Mary. It once again recognized the monarch as being formally supreme over the English church and as having the right to delegate his authority to commissioners. The act required that all ecclesiastical persons should take an oath accepting the royal supremacy, and this enabled the government at last to deprive Catholic clerics who refused the oath and replace them with Protestants. It adjudged a matter to be heretical which could be so defined only by the authority of the scriptures or of the first four general councils. The most obvious difference between the Elizabethan act of supremacy and that of Henry VIII was that Elizabeth received the title not of supreme head but of supreme governor. Edwin Sandys thought the queen in not styling herself supreme head had bowed to the susceptibilities of the more radical Protestants, voiced by Lever (Doc. 8): Jewel went even further and believed she had conscientious objections to accepting a title contaminated by antichrist (Doc. 10), although it seems more likely that Elizabeth took this step to win over her Catholic subjects. The Protestant clerics united in considering that the change in title made no practical difference in the queen's powers (Doc. 9), but subsequent historians have suggested that they may not have grasped the full implications of the change.[1]

Professor Elton has pointed out that Elizabeth's supremacy was markedly less ecclesiastical than her father's. Henry VIII had seen himself as a lay bishop within the church in direct imitation of the Emperor Constantine: although never attempting to exercise the priestly function, Henry strove to appear as more than a layman. By designating herself as supreme governor, Elizabeth renounced the semi-ecclesiastical element contained in the Henrician supremacy; she did not aspire to rule her churchmen as if she were one of them, but disciplined the ecclesiastical body from outside. In addition, Elizabeth's supremacy depended upon Parliament to an extent to which her father's had never done, even though throughout her reign Elizabeth hotly contested this fact. Henry VIII had claimed that his headship over the church formed an intrinsic part of his kingship; any English king was by divine permission head of the English church, a right which the pope had unjustly usurped in recent centuries. The Reformation Parliament in its act of supremacy only recognized this headship, and then went on to lay down penalties for those who refused to acknowledge it. While Henry VIII lived, the royal right to rule over

---

[1] G. W. Prothero, *Select Statutes*, 1913, pp. xxx–xxxi. F. W. Maitland, 'Elizabethan Gleanings: Supremacy and Uniformity', *English Historical Review*, XVIII, 1903, pp. 517–532.

the church depended upon the king alone, not upon the king-in-Parliament. Events during Edward VI's and Mary's reigns considerably modified this proposition. The Edwardian act of uniformity could be read as giving the liturgy and ceremonies of the church parliamentary sanction. Parliament had described, in the second act of uniformity, the first Edwardian Prayer Book as having been set forth 'by authority of Parliament'. Mary had had to work through Parliament in order to bring about the reconciliation with Rome since only Parliament could repeal the penalties imposed in the earlier supremacy acts. Parliament could well now be seen as participating in the exercise of the royal supremacy, and to this extent the 1559 act had to admit the change. The Elizabethan act of supremacy stated that powers over the church enjoyed by Henry VIII should be restored to the crown 'by the authority of this present Parliament'. The queen's right to delegate her authority to commissioners was also essentially parliamentary. Ultimate authority over the church now rested in the queen in Parliament.[1]

The spiritual peers in the Lords unanimously opposed the act of supremacy: Convocation which met alongside Elizabeth's first Parliament, having been given this lead by the Marian bishops, showed itself no less hostile to any attempt to deny the pope's authority over the English church or to introduce any Protestant innovations. Consequently, while Protestant divines were consulted, Convocation, the formal organ of government of the English church, could not be allowed any part in the Elizabethan settlement. This fact together with the old revulsion against a lay supremacy and against a woman's attempting to rule over the church gave Catholics from the beginning of the reign an opportunity to undermine the royal supremacy. The queen found it necessary to define the theoretical extent of the royal supremacy twice within a decade of the passing of the act of supremacy and in particular to deny, in answer to the insinuations of the Catholic pamphleteers, that she aspired in any way to exercise spiritual powers. In the fifth year of her reign Parliament passed an act 'for the assurance of the queen's royal powers'. After the Northern Rebellion had shown that an appeal to Catholic sympathies could still awake a response among conservatives, the government issued 'a declaration of the queen's proceedings since her reign' in which the queen's powers in ecclesiastical affairs were stated most explicitly. After asserting that the queen claimed no rights over the church which her predecessors had not enjoyed for generations and very specifically denying that she did 'either challenge or take to us (as malicious persons do untruly surmise) any superiority to ourselves to define, decide or determine any article or point of the Christian faith and religion, or to change any

[1] G. R. Elton, *The Tudor Constitution*, Cambridge, 1960, pp. 333–335.

ancient ceremony of the church from the form before received and observed by the Catholic and Apostolic church, or the use of any function belonging to any ecclesiastical person, being a minister of the word and sacraments in the Church,' it continued:

'But that authority which is yielded to us and our crown consisteth in this; that, considering we are by God's grace the sovereign prince and queen next under God, and all the people in our realm are immediately born subjects to us and our crown and to none else, and that our realm hath of long time past received the Christian faith, we are by this authority bound to direct all estates, being subject to us, to live in the faith and the obedience of Christian religion, and to see the laws of God and man which are ordained to that end to be duly observed, and the offenders against the same duly punished, and consequently to provide that the church may be governed and taught by archbishops, bishops and ministers according to the ecclesiastical ancient policy of the realm, whom we do assist with our sovereign power etc. An office and charge as we think properly due to all Christian monarchs, and princes sovereigns, whereby they only differ from pagan princes that only take care of their subjects' bodies without respect to the salvation of their souls, or of the life hereafter to come.'[1]

Despite the large phrases describing the government and teaching of the English church as being by archbishops, bishops and ministers, the civil authority could not hide the fact that in the first instance the doctrine and the ritual of the church had been established by act of Parliament. The act of uniformity no more than the act of supremacy had been sanctioned by Convocation, even though it dealt with the doctrine of the church. Parliament repealed the statute of Mary which had withdrawn the second Prayer Book of Edward VI, revived the same book with certain modifications, and enjoined its use throughout England. The act prescribed punishments for anyone, whether clerical or lay, who spoke in derogation of the new form of service, or failed to attend church on Sundays and holy days (Doc. 7). That Elizabeth consented to the adoption of the second Prayer Book of Edward VI, when all the indications are that she would have preferred the more conservative Prayer Book of 1549, points to the strength of the Protestant pressure group both inside and outside Parliament. The most Protestant Prayer Book the English church had ever had came again into use, and yet, so fast had been their progress, this represented a considerable concession on the part of the exiles who would have wished for a book purged of all traces of popery. Before

[1] W. E. Collins, *Queen Elizabeth's defence of her proceedings in Church and State*, Church Historical Society, LVIII, 1899, pp. 42-43.

the uniformity bill became law it seems that the queen herself insisted on two changes, both probably intended to conciliate Catholic sympathizers. Two sentences were added to the communion service as it stood in the second Edwardian Prayer Book: 'The body of our Lord Jesus Christ which was given for thee, preserve thy body and soul unto everlasting life,' and 'The blood of our Lord Jesus Christ, which was shed for thee, preserve thy body and soul unto everlasting life.' These insertions made it possible for men to use the Prayer Book and still believe in the real presence of Christ at the eucharist, an alteration which would have found favour with many Protestants as well as Catholics. Protestants reacted quite differently to the second change. The queen had substituted for the clause in the Edwardian act of uniformity which had merely enjoined upon the clergy the wearing of the surplice the ambiguous rubric which directed that such ornaments and vestments as had been in use in the second year of Edward VI were to be retained.[1] Sandys, in the optimism of the moment, interpreted this to be merely a measure to save vestments and ornaments from physical destruction: he could not conceive that they would ever be imposed upon conscientious Protestants (Doc. 8). The Vestiarian Controversy subsequently proved how wrong his assumption had been. In the meanwhile, the queen soon made it clear to the new Protestant bishops that she wanted the established church to appear as like the old church in its outward form as it possibly could. Probably this accorded with her personal inclinations but she had also a political motive behind her action. She hoped to disturb as little as was necessary the mass of her subjects who still followed the old ways in religion, and, even more important, to minimize the differences between the English church and the Catholic continental churches. When the Privy Council sent the French ambassador and his train to visit Parker at Canterbury in 1564, the archbishop took immense pains to impress upon them the queen's concept of the church. Having explained to the French that the English church still kept set prayers and days of abstinence, used 'reverent mediocrity' in its common prayer and sacraments, that it preserved a hierarchy in church government and had music in its services, he drew the gratifying response 'that we were in religion very nigh to them'.[2]

Perhaps Elizabeth may have gone some way to persuade foreign visitors that the English church agreed with the Catholic church in the main essentials; she failed totally to deceive informed English Catholics. In Parliament and private letters, the Catholic bishops from

[1] Neale, *Elizabeth I and her Parliaments*, I, pp. 77–80. Collinson, *Puritan Movement*, pp. 33–36.

[2] J. Bruce and T. T. Perowne, eds, *Correspondence of Matthew Parker*, Parker Society, Cambridge, 1853, no. CLXIV.

the very beginning of the reign gave warning that they could not accept a form of Christianity which had no greater spiritual warrant than an act of Parliament. Under the authority of the act of supremacy during the summer of 1559, Elizabeth appointed royal visitors to inspect all the dioceses throughout England. Seeing these Protestant ecclesiastics and laymen at work in the south, Cuthbert Tunstal, the Catholic bishop of Durham, feared that soon they would reach his diocese to inflict similar damage on the church there. In his letter of protest to Cecil he made it plain that no Catholic bishop could any longer even passively assist in the royal policy.

'This shall be to advertise your lordship that albeit I would be as glad to serve the queen's highness and to set forwards all her affairs to her contentation as any subject in her realm, yet if the same visitation shall proceed to such end in my diocese of Durham as I do plainly see to be set forth here in London, as pulling down of altars, defacing of churches, by taking away of the crucifixes, I cannot in my conscience consent to it, being pastor there, because I cannot myself agree to be a sacramentary, nor to have any new doctrine taught in my diocese. . . .'[1]

Already the validity of the royal supremacy over the English church had emerged as the most hotly contended issue between the leading Catholic clergy and the defenders of the 1559 settlement.

III. THE ERASTIAN VIEW OF THE ROYAL SUPREMACY

The first apologists for the Elizabethan church, recalling how God in Old Testament times had employed pious monarchs to reform the church, looked with conscious approval at the powers of the lay magistrate within the English church. Like Erastus, they held that in a Christian state all jurisdiction, ecclesiastical and secular, belonged exclusively to the Christian magistrate, but, again like Erastus, they were far from teaching that the magistrate could impose whatever religious opinions he pleased and still expect obedience from his subjects.[2] John Jewel stands foremost among these early English Erastians: to a very considerable extent the arguments he put forward in 1562 to justify the crown's authority within the church retained their cogency throughout the reign. Later writers defending the royal

---

[1] Tunstal to William Cecil, August 12, 1559; P.R.O. SP 12/6/22.

[2] J. N. Figgis, 'Political Thought in the Sixteenth Century', *Cambridge Modern History*, III, 1907, pp. 736–769; and 'Erastus and Erastianism,' in Figgis, *Divine Right of Kings*, Cambridge, 1914. N. Sykes, *Old Priest and New Presbyter*, Cambridge, 1956, pp. 1–29. W. M. Lamont, *Marginal Prynne 1600–1669*, 1963, p. 155, 166.

supremacy explored his ideas in greater depth, they did not seriously modify them. Jewel composed his *Apology* expressly to answer the taunts of the Catholics that English religion had become a mere parliamentary religion and that Parliament had declared that the monarch possessed rights over the church which could legitimately be exercised only by a spiritual head, the pope.[1] In his controversy with Harding, the fact that the queen had chosen to be called supreme governor rather than head of the English church materially strengthened Jewel's hand. He maintained that the change of title had a real significance since by calling herself governor and not head Elizabeth had demonstrated that she intended to limit her influence in the church to jurisdictional matters. He distinguished sharply between the sphere of ecclesiastical jurisdiction, in which he considered the monarch had a God-given right to act, and the sphere of doctrine where the truths of religion were beyond human interference.

'Concerning the title of "supreme head of the church" we need not to search for scripture to excuse it. For first we devised it not; secondly we use it not; thirdly our princes at this present time claim it not. Your fathers, M. Harding, first intitled that most noble and most worthy prince, King Henry the Eighth, with that unused and strange style, as it may well be thought, the rather to bring him into the talk and slander of the world.

Howbeit, that the prince is the highest judge and governor over all his subjects whatsoever, as well priests as laymen, without exception, is most evident . . . by the whole course of the scriptures, and by the undoubted practice of the primitive church. Verily the prince . . . had both the tables of the law of God evermore committed to his charge; as well the first, that pertaineth to religion, as also the second, that pertaineth to civil government.'[2]

Christ alone could be the head of the church; the church remained free to proclaim the truths it had received from him but in England, in matters of government, the English clergy recognized no superior to the English monarch (Doc. 11). Jewel made frequent comparisons between the powers of the English crown and the powers Constantine had exercised in the church once Christianity became the official religion of the Roman empire. Repeatedly, as Elizabeth's reign proceeded, defenders of the royal supremacy drew parallels between the ecclesiastical authority of the queen and that of the eastern emperors. The Old Testament provided further examples of godly monarchs, and from there Jewel derived the idea of the monarch as a

[1] W. M. Southgate, *John Jewel and the Problem of Doctrinal Authority*, Cambridge, Mass. 1962, pp. 32–33.

[2] J. Ayre, ed. *Works of John Jewel*, IV, Parker Society, Cambridge, 1850, p. 974.

nursing mother (Doc. 12). As a nurse Elizabeth would cherish and watch over the English church, safeguarding its ministers in their divinely appointed work.

When he came in detail to defend the exercise of royal authority within the church Jewel found himself in something of a predicament.[1] As a churchman he believed that the English church formed part of the universal church and taught universal truths, yet in upholding the royal supremacy he had also to accept that the ministers who proclaimed these truths were appointed by the crown, and, in the last instance, held their benefices at the pleasure of the monarch. He attempted to prove that in doctrinal matters the clergy retained their independence while the monarch in matters of ecclesiastical jurisdiction remained the supreme governor. 'Touching the knowledge of God's word and cases of religion, certain it is the king is inferior to a bishop.'[2] The prince had no authority to execute the priestly office, to preach or minister the sacraments, as Elizabeth herself explicitly acknowledged in the declaration of the queen's proceedings in 1569.

Jewel lived at a time when Protestants had already begun to feel themselves under attack from the greater might of Rome; the English monarch seemed the surest bulwark between the English church and the papacy and consequently he saw his chief duty to lie in supporting to the uttermost the monarch's ecclesiastical authority within its jurisdictional limits. Adopting the conventional thesis that the monarch received his powers direct from God, he went on to argue that the godly monarch had the positive obligation to see that the ministers duly performed their offices. A prince had a moral right to supervise the reformation of the church in his own dominions. Since in a Christian commonwealth no division between church and state could exist, as ideally the prince and clergy were together striving to perform the commands of God, therefore the magistrate had the right to judge in ecclesiastical causes. As Alexander Nowell, the dean of St Paul's, explained in 1566, the prince had authority

'. . . to oversee that the bishops and clergy do these their offices so peculiarly by God's word to them appointed, diligently and truly, according to the rule of God's word, to command them to do their duty, to admonish them being therein slack, to reprehend them offending, depose or deprive them, being incorrigible; yea, and to punish all others that will in any wise impeach bishops, or other ecclesiastical ministers in their offices.'[3]

---

[1] Southgate, *John Jewel*, pp. 201–206. J. E. Booty, *John Jewel as Apologist of the Church of England*, 1963, pp. 189–195.

[2] *Jewel's Works*, IV, Parker Society, p. 675.

[3] A. Nowell, *A Reproof*, 1566, p. 23v. Quoted in Booty, *John Jewel*, p. 195.

Because he believed that the well being of the church depended upon the protection of the monarch, Jewel could scarcely at the same time express fears about royal interference. He had to hope that the monarch would be content to be guided by his spiritual advisers, but he had no means of laying down limits to royal power. He emphasized and re-emphasized the obedience all subjects must show to their godly prince. The right religion held by the prince constituted in effect the justification for obeying the monarch in all things. Yet where the monarch was not godly, as in Scotland, Jewel preached no such unqualified obedience: 'the queen of Scotland ... is obeyed of her subjects so far as is convenient for godly people to obey their prince'.[1]

In England, however, Jewel thought that the right of a subject to disobey his prince was an academic one since the settlement of religion in 1559 had been based upon a general consent. He transformed the Catholic allegations of English religion being a mere parliamentary religion into a main theme of his defence of the English church. Religion had been defined in England only after open debate in Parliament and long consultation with divines. He thought of Parliament as a body of Christians, both lay and clerical, representing the whole Christian commonwealth in a way in which Convocation, which represented the clergy alone, could not do. Erastian defenders of the Elizabethan church never lost sight of this idea, and at least in the earlier part of the reign the bishops welcomed the support of Parliament and in 1566 actually petitioned the queen to allow Parliament to confirm the Articles of Religion (Doc. 13). In 1571 the queen did permit the passing of an act to confirm the Thirty-nine Articles, and supporters of the royal supremacy could look upon this as an instance of the supreme body of a Christian commonwealth, the queen in Parliament, declaring fundamental truths of religion. In their respect for the queen's religious authority in Parliament some of these Elizabethan theories approach claims made for general councils of the church in the fifteenth century.

Jewel seems genuinely to have believed that the English church, protected by the royal supremacy, would be left completely free to perform its spiritual functions. Just as he tended to idealize the constitutional position of the church within the Elizabethan state, so in an appendix to the *Apology,* perhaps written by Archbishop Parker, there appeared an idealization of the existing government of the English church in which the church seemed to be operating quite independently of its royal governor. After having explained that the English church was divided into the provinces of Canterbury and York the writer showed how a hierarchy which had developed in the late medieval period could be made to function with virtually no adapta-

[1] *Jewel's Works*, III, Parker Society, pp. 172–173.

tion in a church reformed. He asserted that in England only learned priests, such as could instruct their flocks, became bishops and went on to give a rose coloured picture of the church from the cathedrals down to the individual parish churches.

'Everyone of the archbishops and bishops have their several cathedral churches, wherein the deans bear chief rule, being men specially chosen both for their learning and godliness, as near as may be.

These cathedral churches have also other dignatories and canonries, whereunto be assigned no idle or unprofitable persons, but such as either be preachers, or professors of the sciences of good learning.

In the said cathedral churches upon Sundays and festival days the canons make ordinarily special sermons whereunto duly resort the head officers of the cities and the citizens, and upon the worken days thrice in the week one of the canons doth read and expound some piece of holy scripture.

Also the said archbishops and bishops have under them their arch-deacons, some two, some four, some six, according to the largeness of the diocese; the which archdeacons keep yearly two visitations, where-in they make diligent inquisition and search both of the doctrine and behaviour as well of the ministers as of the people. They punish the offenders; and if any errors in religion and heresies fortune to spring, they bring those and other weighty matters before the bishops them-selves.

There is nothing read in our churches but the canonical scriptures, which is done in such order as that the psalter is read over every month, the New Testament four times in the year, and the Old Testa-ment once every year. And if the curate be judged of the bishop to be sufficiently seen in the holy scriptures, he doth withal make some exposition and exhortation unto godliness.

And for so much as our churches and universities have been wonder-fully marred, and so foully brought out of all fashion in time of Papistry as there cannot be had learned pastors for every parish, there be prescribed unto the curates of meaner understanding certain homilies devised by learned men which do comprehend the principal points of Christian doctrine; as of original sin, of justification, of faith, of charity, and such like, for to be read by them unto the people.

As for common prayer, the lessons taken out of the scriptures, the administering of the sacraments, and the residue of service done in the churches, are every whit done in the vulgar tongue which all may understand.'[1]

---

[1] J. Jewel, *Apology*, 1564, sig. [Q VIII]-R II. For attribution to Parker see J. E. Booty, ed. *An Apology of the Church of England*, Ithaca, New York, 1963, p. xlvi.

This passage reveals the innate conservatism of the defenders of the established church: nowhere does the writer suggest that a reformed church, placing a new emphasis on preaching, could be better served than by canons attached to a now inadequate number of cathedral churches, or that some dioceses were indeed so large as to prevent a godly bishop exercising a pastoral guidance over his clergy and lay people. Nevertheless, in spite of an evident failure to take into account existing need, the philosophical justification of the royal supremacy as it was discharged in the church and indeed of the present state of the church itself continued to be offered without abatement throughout the reign and apparently still continued to find acceptance.

Although Jewel in his *Apology* had set out to prove that the English church was a true church despite Catholic assertions to the contrary, and although he had only incidentally provided a rational defence of the royal supremacy, yet subsequent writers remained content to extend the points he had made: they did not on the whole see any need to develop a new form of defence. Again and again they applied the text from Isaiah to the English church: 'Thou shalt suck the breast of princes; kings shall be thy foster fathers, and queens thy nursing mothers.' In part two of his book, *The True Difference between Christian Subjection and Antichristian Rebellion*, 1585, Thomas Bilson vindicated the queen's supreme power to command for truth within her realm.[1] As well as likening Elizabeth to the religious monarchs of the Old Testament, Bilson also made the conventional comparison between Elizabeth and Constantine: as Constantine had dealt in causes ecclesiastical, so could she. He reiterated the argument that the queen's supremacy lay solely in the sphere of ecclesiastical jurisdiction: 'the scriptures be superior to princes, and yet they supreme: the sacrament be likewise above them, and yet that hindereth not their supremacy . . .'. 'We make no prince judge of faith.'[2] Bilson deliberately proceeded to elaborate the defence of the royal supremacy which certain Jesuits had charged Jewel with not adequately discussing in the *Apology*, yet again he did little more than fill out Jewel's earlier observations.

'This then is the supreme power of princes which we soberly teach and you [the Jesuits] so bitterly detest: that they be God's ministers in their own dominions, bearing the sword, freely to permit, and publicly to defend, that which God commandeth in faith and good

[1] For a discussion of Bilson and Bridges see C. Morris, *Political Thought in England: Tyndale to Hooker*, Oxford, 1953, pp. 117–121. And also W. M. Lamont, 'The Rise and Fall of Bishop Bilson', *Journal of British Studies*, v, 1966, pp. 22–32.

[2] T. Bilson, *The True Difference between Christian Subjection and Antichristian Rebellion*, 1585, pp. 133, 166, 173, 213.

manners, and in ecclesiastical discipline to receive and establish such rules and orders as the scriptures and canons shall decide to be needful and healthful for the church of God in their kingdoms. And as they may lawfully command that which is good in all things and causes, be they temporal, spiritual or ecclesiastical, so may they with just force remove whatsoever is erroneous, vicious or superstitious within their lands, and with external losses and corporal pains repress the broachers and abettors of heresies and all impieties; from which subjection unto princes, no man within their realms, monk, priest, preacher nor prelate is exempted; and without their realms no mortal man hath any power from Christ judicially to depose them, much less to invade them in open field, least of all to warrant their subjects to rebel against them.'[1]

Bilson wrote his book as Jewel had done in an attempt to answer Catholic criticisms of the royal supremacy. Thomas Cooper confronted different assailants in his *Admonition* where he concentrated on replying to Puritan attacks upon the church: there he extended another aspect of Jewel's *Apology*; the obedience owed by the subject to the monarch. In a discussion about the degree to which church lands belonged to the crown Cooper agreed that the clergy should be subject to all civil taxation but went on to claim that the magistrate, being godly, would not ask anything of the clergy not in accordance with the will of God and the furtherance of the gospel. This led him to a consideration of the obedience all subjects should render to the state. He concluded that a prince ought to be obeyed in all things which were not against the will of God: what God commanded a Christian prince could not forbid; what God forbade a Christian prince could not command; but in external matters where God had given no precise commandments there a prince might rightfully intervene. If in these external matters a prince acted unjustly the subject must suffer passively: only if a prince interfered in a subject's duty to God need he not obey, but even then he must not actively resist (Doc. 14).

The influence of Jewel upon subsequent defenders of the Elizabethan church can clearly be seen in Hooker, who, no less than Bilson or Cooper, was indebted to Jewel for theories first set out in the *Apology*.[2] Hooker indeed began his dedication of his first book of *The Laws of Ecclesiastical Polity* with the now almost obligatory comparison between the queen and the godly warriors of the Old Testament: as

---

[1] Bilson, *True Difference*, p. 256.

[2] C. S. Lewis, *English Literature in the Sixteenth Century Excluding Drama*, Oxford, 1954, pp. 451–463. C. Morris, *Political Thought in England*, pp. 172–198.

F. J. Shirley, *Richard Hooker and Contemporary Political Ideas*, 1949, especially chapter VI. C. J. Sisson, *The Judicious Marriage of Mr. Hooker and the Birth of the Laws of Ecclesiastical Polity*, Cambridge, 1940.

C

in ancient times the Jews had fought under the banner of God and of their captain Gideon so all the churches in England should proclaim in gratitude for their liberation, 'By the goodness of Almighty God and his servant Elizabeth we are' (Doc. 15). Like Jewel, Hooker essentially regarded Elizabeth as the guardian of the English church against the machinations of the papacy. Under the benevolent protection of the crown the English church remained free to govern itself: still for Hooker, as for Jewel, the advantages of having the queen on the church's side far outweighed the dangers which might arise from royal interference. He continued to put forward the convenient assumption that in a state which had provided for the right reformation of religion the interests of church and state would inevitably coincide. To devise a curb against monarchical pretensions did not occur to him precisely because in an ideal world a godly monarch could not have conceived of governing except to the best advantage of the church.

Hooker's celebrated simile in which he likens the Elizabethan church and state to different sides of an equal sided triangle again stemmed from the identification which Jewel had also made of church and state. Because of the passing of time which saw the emergence of separating Protestants as well as of separated Catholics, Hooker must have been even more conscious than Jewel that some Englishmen indignantly rejected the idea that by a mere accident of birth they were willy nilly members of the English church; nevertheless, he clung to the ideal of unity upon which he could at least hope England would model itself.[1] Since in theory all members of the commonwealth automatically enjoyed membership of the national church any separation between the civil and ecclesiastical power was artificial. Again following Jewel, Hooker emphasized the parallel between the power of Elizabeth and that of the Christian emperors within the Eastern church. As church and state formed one single whole the monarch could exercise authority within the church in the same manner as she heard civil causes, appoint bishops, summon councils, exactly as the emperors had done. Yet in so doing the queen no more than the Eastern emperors attempted to fulfil priestly functions: in spiritual matters ecclesiastics had complete freedom to declare the ancient truths of the faith.

The theory of the royal supremacy set out by Hooker included a justification for persecution. Since a monarch's highest obligation lay in securing his subjects' salvation, untrue religion must be extirpated from the land and its purveyors banished. For the honour of God and for the sake of national unity he thought all Englishmen ought to join in public worship. Yet Hooker never came near to teaching that the

[1] C. Russell, 'Arguments for Religious Unity in England 1530–1650', *Journal of Ecclesiastical History*, XVIII, 1967, pp. 201–226.

subject must hold in religion what the state professed, merely because the state professed it. Rather, just because he emphatically believed that the truths of religion were eternal and outside the reach of human manipulation, he could not concede that in certain circumstances the Christian ideal might be deflected by political necessity. If Hooker had withheld from the monarch the right to suppress religious error, he would have implied that in practice the godly magistrate could not distinguish between truth and falsehood: and this would have destroyed his entire case in favour of a national church.[1]

Yet while, because of his great respect for tradition and because of his sincere belief that the Elizabethan age was an age of singular religious enlightenment, Hooker can clearly be seen like Jewel as an apologist for the royal supremacy as expressed in the act of 1559, this very conservatism and respectful caution caused him to become an implicit critic of the existing régime. The royal supremacy which Hooker defended in 1593, (the date by which he had almost certainly completed Book Eight in its present form,) was not the royal supremacy the queen considered she exercised.[2] Elizabeth maintained that the act of supremacy had declared her authority to rule the church through her bishops and through Convocation. Archbishop Whitgift, under whom Hooker served, evidently also thought in terms of a dual form of government under one supreme governor: in civil affairs the monarch ruled, advised by the Council and by Parliament; in ecclesiastical affairs the same monarch ruled, but advised by the bishops and by Convocation. He wrote: 'the archbishop doth exercise his jurisdiction under the prince and by the prince's authority. For, the prince having the supreme government of the realm in all causes and over all persons, she doth exercise the one by the lord chancellor, so doth she the other by the archbishops'.[3] Very signally, and in spite of his obvious regard for his royal and ecclesiastical superiors, Hooker failed to adopt this interpretation of the royal supremacy and instead set out the right of Parliament to legislate in ecclesiastical matters. Having shown that membership of the church and of the state were coextensive he argued in Book Eight that the king in Parliament was the very essence of all government on which the whole state depended. What concerned all should be consented to

[1] J. W. Allen, *History of Political Thought in the Sixteenth Century*, 1928, pp. 232–235. A. P. D'Entrèves, *Medieval Contribution to Political Thought*, Oxford, 1939, pp. 117–142.

[2] R. A. Houk, ed. *Hooker's Ecclesiastical Polity, Book VIII*, New York, 1931, p. 87. P. Munz, *The Place of Hooker in the History of Thought*, 1952, especially chapter III.

[3] J. Ayre, ed. *The Works of John Whitgift*, II, Parker Society, Cambridge, 1852, p. 246.

by all. Convocation represented the clergy alone, but Parliament, in particular Parliament together with Convocation, represented the commonwealth, and the whole Christian commonwealth should participate in the making of ecclesiastical law, not merely the clergy:

'Till it be proved that some special law of Christ hath for ever annexed unto the clergy alone the power to make ecclesiastical laws, we are to hold it a thing most consonant with equity and reason that no ecclesiastical laws be made in a Christian commonwealth without consent as well of the laity as of the clergy, but least of all without consent of the highest power' (Doc. 15).

It is ironic that this, the most comprehensive and intellectually satisfying of the justifications of the Elizabethan supremacy, should be so much at odds with the political realities of the 1590s. Hooker defended the royal supremacy for those very characteristics which Elizabeth disliked most. He did not see the royal supremacy as one of the mysteries of kingship, did not consider it to be inherent within the royal power: potentially his belief that all authority in the church and in the state depended on voluntary consent could undermine monarchy itself. It can be no accident that Book Eight of the *Laws of Ecclesiastical Polity* did not come to be published until 1648. Dr Munz indeed has suggested that by 1593 Hooker had reached a philosophical impasse. He wished to defend the national church of which he was a most loyal member; but, should his complete defence appear, it would immediately be seen to clash with the interpretation of the royal supremacy held by Elizabeth and by some of the most influential leaders of the church, Whitgift, Bancroft, Saravia. Hooker had no great difficulties in preparing Books One to Five for the press: in these he described his scheme of the different types of law in the universe, and maintained against the Catholics that the English church was a true church, against the Presbyterians that it was a reformed church, in answer to their assertion that God had laid down a unique form of church in the New Testament. He died in 1600 in the midst of reconstructing Book Six in which he intended to deny the necessity of the office of a lay elder in the church. Even if he had lived many more years he would have been unable to revise Books Seven and Eight in a way which would have been philosophically acceptable to himself. Book Seven dealt with episcopacy; Book Eight with the exercise of the royal supremacy: to please the queen and her ecclesiastical advisers Hooker would have had to abandon his cherished concept of the royal supremacy being founded upon general consent and expressed by the approbation of the queen in Parliament. He could not go against his conscience in this way, and therein lay his tragedy. Yet although Book Eight was not published in the Elizabethan period Hooker had written his version of it by 1593, and it constitutes the fullest apology for the royal supremacy ever produced during the reign by the Erastian defenders of the English church.[1]

IV. THE CATHOLIC REJECTION OF A LAY SUPREMACY

Throughout Elizabeth's reign the leading Catholic thinkers remained impervious to these philosophical arguments of the defenders of the royal supremacy, even when voiced in the conciliatory tones of Hooker. Bishop Scot had set out the Catholic objections to the very idea of a royal supremacy over the church when Parliament had been discussing the supremacy bill in 1559 (Doc. 4), and essentially Elizabethan Catholic intellectuals never modified his arguments. On the passing of the act of supremacy the Catholic bishops refused to take the prescribed oath acknowledging the queen's authority over the church and were deprived of their sees. The state placed most of them under house arrest and they had little further opportunity of questioning the government's religious policy publicly, although Feckenham, the last abbot of Westminster, was drawn into a disputation with his custodian, Robert Horne, the new bishop of Winchester, who published the controversy in order to clear himself of aspersions of not being a whole hearted supporter of the royal supremacy.[2] On the silencing of the Marian bishops a number of Catholic scholars, imitating their Protestant predecessors in Mary's reign, went into voluntary exile on the continent, and a powerful school of Catholic pamphleteers rapidly grew up at Louvain.[3] Thomas Harding, one of the leading English scholars there, wrote an answer to Jewel's *Apology* as soon as it appeared: refusing absolutely to concede that a lay ruler could exercise jurisdiction over the church he paid no attention to the distinction Jewel made between matters of jurisdiction and matters of faith. He stated adamantly that the English Protestants had made the lay magistrate the supreme pastor of the church in all spiritual causes, and this could only be seen as an 'enormity' by all good Catholics (Doc. 12). Thomas Stapleton, another learned Oxford scholar who similarly migrated to Louvain, elaborated Harding's theme.[4] In the *Counterblast*, published in 1567, he went so far as to claim that the oath attached to the Elizabethan act of supremacy elevated royal pretensions over the church to an even higher degree

[1] Munz, *Place of Hooker*, chapter III.

[2] M. R. O'Connell, *Thomas Stapleton and the Counter Reformation*, New Haven 1964, pp. 154–183.

[3] P. McGrath, *Papists and Puritans under Elizabeth I*, 1967, pp. 60–63.

[4] M. Richards, 'Thomas Stapleton', *Journal of Ecclesiastical History*, XVIII, 1967, pp. 187–199. O'Connell, *Stapleton*, pp. 150–151.

than had been attempted by either Henry VIII or Edward VI. In addition to the major stumbling block, that the new monarch pretending authority over the church was a woman, he implied that the taking of the oath logically meant that the government could prescribe whatever form of religion best suited its purposes with no reference at all to divine truths. Stapleton dismissed the queen's declaration in the Injunctions of 1559 (Doc. 28) that she would take upon herself no powers over the church which her father and brother had not exercised with the assertion that injunctions cannot limit an act of Parliament, and maintained that the act of supremacy implicitly denied the spiritual authority not only of the pope but of general councils. Religion in England henceforth would be defined by English laymen with no reference to the rest of Christendom.

'Where then was this lesson of late when laymen only, by act of Parliament, took upon them to teach the whole clergy? Did not then less men than kings, queens and princes (who may not, you say now, claim or take upon them this kind of spiritual government and rule to feed the church with God's word) take upon themselves to feed all the realm with such doctrine as it pleased Parliament to allow; the Parliament, I say, of laymen only, not one bishop amongst them, you being neither by the law of God . . . neither by the law of the realm any bishops at all?'[1]

William Allen attached himself to this group of scholars in Louvain during his first years in exile; then, in 1568, he left the university there to establish his seminary at Douay for the training of priests for the English mission. In his *True, Sincere and Modest Defence of English Catholics,* (1584), he explained in its most complete and succinct form the attitude of orthodox Catholics towards the royal supremacy (Doc. 17). Like the Catholic exiles who had written earlier he would permit of no distinction being made between royal jurisdiction within the church, which its apologists claimed the crown could rightly enjoy, and the spiritual affairs of the church, in which the monarch did not interfere. No such separation could be made, he said, and all royal authority over the church was illegitimate. That Elizabeth claimed to be supreme governor, not supreme head made no practical difference: for propaganda purposes in company with many other Catholic pamphleteers Allen repeatedly referred to the queen as 'supreme head', thus emphasizing for Catholics the monstrous fact that a woman should have been given this dominion. Once the monarch had been declared supreme in both spiritual and temporal affairs, he alleged, all sorts of heretical ideas which for the time being might seem attractive to him could find entrance to the kingdom. The supreme governor-

[1] Stapleton, *Counterblast*, pp. 404–405, quoted in O'Connell, *Stapleton*, p. 193.

ship, whatever the queen and its defenders might say, made the king
and the priest one; the queen in practice did invade the sphere of
priestly authority. If other monarchs followed Elizabeth's example
national churches professing their own national forms of Christianity
would spring up all over Europe and a united Christendom would no
longer exist.

This then was the classic Catholic teaching concerning the royal
supremacy. Had Catholic theologians done no more than thunder
forth censures against the established church then its Erastian
defenders might have continued to have had difficulty in presenting a
convincing case against their contention that the state encroached upon
the realm of the spirit. The publication of the bull *Regnans in excelsis,*
however, in February 1570 translated the controversy into a different
and far more dangerous sphere. In the bull in the traditional language
of the medieval papacy Pius V declared that he, as the undoubted
successor to St Peter, possessed plenary authority over the church.
This authority Elizabeth, the so called queen of England, had infringed
by seizing the kingdom and usurping the place of supreme head over
the English church. As a follower of Calvin, she had driven out
Catholics recently restored by Mary and demanded an oath of
obedience from all her subjects to her supremacy over the church.
In consequence of these wicked actions the pope excommunicated
her, deprived her of her right to her kingdom and released her subjects
from their allegiance (Doc. 16).

To English Protestants this papal pronouncement seemed finally to
reveal the secret designs of the enemy: hitherto Catholic opponents
of the royal supremacy had not explicitly advocated treason as the
pope now appeared to be doing. Recently writers have pointed out
what the wording of the bull tends to obscure, that the pope was
acting to cope with a particular political development in England, the
Northern Rebellion of the late autumn of 1569, and that the bull did
not result from long deliberation.[1] The pope wished to give immediate
aid to the English rebels and, apart from sending money to England,
the only other way he could help them was by this assurance that they
committed no sin by taking up arms against Elizabeth. Even this
declaration came too late: the rebels had been crushed before the bull
was promulgated. Pius V apparently did not consider what the effect
of the bull would be if the English rebellion failed: he did not consult
with Catholic powers before issuing it, nor take pains to make it known
to them, much less, later in 1570, appeal to a Catholic state to carry

[1] A. O. Meyer, *England and the Catholic Church under Elizabeth,* 1967 reprint,
pp. 73–89. P. Hughes, *The Reformation in England, III,* 1954, pp. 272–276.
McGrath, *Papists and Puritans,* pp. 69–72. T. Clancy, 'English Catholics and the
Papal Deposing Power', *Recusant History,* VI, 1961–2, pp. 114–140.

out the bull on his behalf and invade England to remove the queen from the throne. He certainly behaved as if the bull were intended to be no more than a gesture of encouragement and a justification of an internal rebellion should it have succeeded. Nevertheless, contemporaries did not take account of the bull's intentions but of its wording. As it stood it gave the Elizabethan government abundant grounds for considering all Catholics potential traitors, and logically it now became virtually impossible for their apologists to argue, at a time when the pope clearly seemed to be attempting to overthrow the queen, that English Catholics owed allegiance to the pope in spiritual matters, but to Elizabeth in temporal matters. Some of the exiled intellectuals in fact welcomed this state of open warfare. The Jesuit, Robert Parsons, subsequently went to the full limits in justifying the right of the pope to depose secular monarchs when he wrote in *Elizabethae Angliae Reginae*, published in 1592:

'Tis certain we must believe it, and it is the opinion of all divines and lawyers, that if any Christian prince fall from the Catholic faith, and would have others to follow him, he himself thereby doth forthwith, both by divine and human law, though the pope do no way censure him, fall from all his authority and dignity, and his subjects are freed from all their oaths of allegiance which they swear to him as a lawful prince; and so they may, nay and ought, (if they have force enough to overcome) pull him down from the throne as an apostate, heretic, a forsaker of Christ and an enemy to the commonwealth.'[1]

In England, however, the Catholic laity resorted to all possible stratagems to escape this inexorable conclusion. They wanted to remain obedient both to the pope and to the queen and could not comprehend why this should not be as feasible in the realm of ideas as it was in the realm of politics.

The rebellion of 1569 together with the bull of 1570 aroused very considerable prejudice against Catholics in England which found immediate expression in anticatholic legislation.[2] The Commons in 1571 indeed tried to pass a bill compelling all subjects to receive communion in the national church once a year; the queen refused to sanction it, but gave her assent to an act which made it high treason to say that she was not the lawful queen or that she was a heretic or schismatic. Another act passed in the same year prohibited the bringing in of bulls from Rome. These acts proved to be of no avail against

---

[1] Quoted in Clancy, *Recusant History*, VI, p. 131.

[2] McGrath, *Papists and Puritans*, chapters VI, VIII, X. For a very useful summary of penal legislation and its local implementation see note by H. Aveling, *Catholic Record Society*, LIII, Miscellanea, pp. 291–307.

the entry into England of an increasing number of seminary priests trained at Douay: in 1580 Campion and Parsons arrived in England, the first Jesuits to come on the English mission, and Campion declared his eagerness to defend the truths of Catholicism against all comers. His brag achieved considerable publicity; his trial in 1581 on a charge of treason commanded still more attention since the government had great difficulty in proving him guilty under the treason statute of 1352. This demonstration of the insufficiency of the medieval treason laws to secure the conviction of Catholic priests resulted in the passing of a new law in the Parliament of 1581 'to retain the queen's majesty's subjects in their due obedience.' Now any priest who persuaded an Englishman to recognize the spiritual authority of the pope could be judged guilty of high treason. The new act instituted a fine of £20 a month for non-attendance at church in addition to the 12d weekly fine laid down in the act of uniformity. In 1586 Parliament amended this act so that a recusant, once convicted, would automatically be required to continue paying the monthly fine into the Exchequer until due certification came in of his conformity: failure to pay entitled the state to confiscate two thirds of a recusant's property. Since priests still entered the country and still found protection with the Catholic laity, in 1584 Parliament passed a further act against Jesuits and seminary priests which ordered all such priests to leave the country within forty days, and decreed that any who remained, or in future came into the country, should be guilty of high treason. The last major act against Catholics appeared in 1593 when in the act against popish recusants Parliament barred any convicted recusant from travelling five miles from his dwelling house without licence.

Few historians would now dispute that at least from 1570 Catholics endured a real persecution for their religion in England. Between 1577 when the first priest was hanged, drawn and quartered and the end of the reign 189 Catholics were put to death, most, but by no means all of them being priests.[1] In addition many Catholics were imprisoned and because of the noisome conditions in prison, a considerable number died there. The records of the Northern High Commission (Doc. 34) and the surviving assize records make it clear that the government tried to force into conformity not only Catholic gentlemen of influence but totally insignificant laymen who could never have posed any threat to the state. Father Walker has now shown that the government did not systematically levy the £20 a month fine from all wealthy Catholics, but used it rather as a deterrent. Nevertheless, some Catholic landowners, chosen to be a warning to their fellows, like Ferdinando Paris of Norfolk, John Sayer of the North Riding of Yorkshire and John Townley of Lancashire regularly paid

[1] P. Hughes, *Rome and the Counter Reformation in England*, 1942, p. 246.

the monthly fine for over twenty years.[1] Few of these lay Catholics behaved in an overtly hostile way towards the Elizabethan state, yet the government always contended that they were punished for their treasonable activities, not for their religious beliefs. As the 1581 act stated, any priest who withdrew an Englishman, or any Englishman who allowed himself to be withdrawn 'from the religion now by her highness' authority established within her highness' dominions to the Romish religion, or ... to promise obedience to any pretended authority of the see of Rome ... shall be to all intents adjudged to be traitors, and being thereof lawfully convicted shall have judgement, suffer and forfeit as in case of high treason.'[2]

Because of the bull of 1570 and the growing amount of legislation directed against priests and the practice of their religion by the laity, Catholic apologists from 1570 onwards had to attempt to answer the charge that all Catholics were potential traitors. William Cecil's pamphlet, *The Execution of Justice in England*, 1583, and William Allen's reply, *The True, Sincere and Modest Defence of English Catholics*, 1584, illustrate the Catholic predicament particularly clearly.[3] In his propaganda tract intended primarily for continental readers Cecil set out the official government case that Catholics in England were persecuted not for their religion but for treason. He insisted that the missionary priests entered England committed to overthrowing the government by force. He cited the Northern Rebellion and the invasion of Ireland in 1579 by certain English Catholic exiles as firm evidence of papal support for political action against the English government and maintained that all the missionary priests who had come into the country in the 1570s and 1580s, despite their assertion that they were concerned solely with matters of religion, in fact instructed English Catholic laymen on the excommunication of the queen and their duty to take up arms against her at the first practical opportunity. In an attempt to prove that the government harried priests for their traitorous activities alone Cecil instanced Elizabeth's lenient treatment of the Marian higher clergy; they had on conscientious grounds refused the oath of supremacy, but because in civil matters they pledged their allegiance to the queen they had been permitted to live out their days in retirement notwithstanding their heterodox religious views. He contrasted these Marian loyalists with the new missionary priests who professed allegiance to the crown neither in matters of religion nor politics, and worked clandestinely for the destruction of the state.

[1] F. X. Walker, 'The Implementation of the Elizabethan Statutes against Recusants, 1581–1603', Unpublished London Ph. D. thesis, 1961.

[2] *Statutes of the Realm*, IV, pt. I, pp. 657–658.

[3] Both these two books have been recently reprinted in R. M. Kingdon, ed. *Cecil, Execution of Justice; Allen, Modest Defence*, Ithaca, New York, 1965.

Catholics had now allowed their religious convictions to influence their political actions and he called for a return to the way of thinking current at the beginning of the reign when, he asserted, Catholics distinguished between their private religious beliefs and their obedience to the state. So long as a subject outwardly obeyed the law to which the whole country had assented in Parliament he was allowed freedom of conscience in religious matters, but the state could not permit these religious convictions to be expressed in political actions.

Allen in his *Modest Defence* brought out very quickly to refute the government's insinuations used Cecil's argument that the government persecuted not for religious but for political reasons to prove the Machiavellian nature of the new state. Mary had persecuted out of her concern for her subjects' eternal salvation; no such ethical motives inspired the present government which paid attention solely to the security of the state. He then proceeded to argue that English Catholics had been persecuted, condemned and executed for matters of religion alone since the state had made matters of conscience, such as denying that the queen was head of the church, treason. Catholics could not be proved to be traitors under the old treason laws, only under the new laws passed since 1558, as the trial of Edmund Campion had showed, when the government had to fabricate evidence that Campion had conspired against the English state at Rome and Rheims in order to secure his conviction. Allen contended that English Catholics, both priests and laymen, had right up the time he wrote accorded the queen proper obedience in civil affairs in spite of the papal bull of 1570:

'We never procured our queen's excommunication; we have sought the mitigation thereof; we have done our allegiance notwithstanding; we have answered, when we were forced unto it, with such humility and respect to her majesty and council, as you see; no man can charge us of any attempt against the realm or the prince's person.'[1]

Yet just as Cecil had put his case against Catholics with very considerable distortion, for the government did persecute Catholics for religious reasons, and the most that it could prove against Campion was that he was a potential, not an actual traitor, so Allen's *Modest Defence* has been shown to be equally devious.[2] Allen did not end his book with his illustration of the shallowness of the government's pretence of believing all Catholics to be traitors. Instead he went on to discuss the right of the pope to depose heretical rulers. He stated quite openly that he thought that the pope possessed this

[1] Kingdon, ed. *Allen, Modest Defence*, p. 127.

[2] G. Mattingly, 'William Allen and Catholic propaganda in England', *Travaux d'Humanisme et Renaissance*, XXVIII, Geneva, 1957, pp. 325–339.

power in certain circumstances but suggested, at the very time when he himself was deeply involved in negotiations with Rome and with Spain to overthrow the English government by force, that the question of the implementation of the papal bull of 1570 was merely hypothetical, and the Elizabethan government had no plausible grounds to concern itself about so remote an eventuality. He made much play with the fact that his own students in their seminary course had been strictly instructed to separate religion and politics: they had not even been allowed in their academic disputations to discuss the papal deposing power for fear of giving offence to the queen. Professor Mattingly has demonstrated the extent to which Allen indulged here in special pleading. While appearing to explain away the queen's excommunication he provided a convenient summary of the contents of the bull of 1570. Though seeming to condemn them, he advanced arguments which in the future could be used by missionary priests and their supporters in England if they were called upon to execute the bull of deposition. The missionary priests may indeed have been forbidden to discuss politics with their flocks, but only temporarily. In his *Memorial* which he wrote as plans for the Spanish invasion matured Allen revealed his true intentions: 'we have now (although many have been recently deported) almost three hundred priests in the households of noblemen and men of substance and we are daily sending others, who will direct the consciences and actions of the Catholics in this affair when the time comes'.[1] The *Modest Defence*, ostensibly intended to allay the government's fear of Catholic treachery, in the event gave good reasons for those suspicions. Allen succeeded in producing a moving description of Catholics, who merely wanted the spiritual exercise of their religion, being persecuted by a materialistic government, which unworthily imputed political motives to their religious aspirations. Significantly, he did not even try to argue in an explicit apology for English Catholics that these Catholics could be anything but hostile to the concept of the royal supremacy as expressed in the act of 1559.

Allen believed in complete sincerity 'there is no war in the world so just or honourable, be it civil or foreign, as that which is waged for religion, we say for the true, ancient, Catholic Roman religion'.[2] This constituted the fighting faith of the English clerical exiles, stated most unequivocally by the Jesuits. Robert Parsons, who did not die till 1610, never wavered in his opinion that the suffering Catholic people in England could only be relieved, and the true faith restored, by the armed intervention of a Catholic power. Priests actually trying

---

[1] Quoted by Mattingly in 'William Allen', p. 336. And see J. Bossy, 'The Character of Elizabethan Catholicism', *Past and Present*, xxi, 1962, pp. 39–59.

[2] Kingdon, ed. *Allen, Modest Defence*, p. 160.

to find a means of living under a Protestant government became increasingly less able to sympathize with the exiles' schemes for invasion. Most Catholic laymen seem no more to have wanted a Spanish occupation of England than did their Protestant neighbours. Their desire to prove that a man could be a good Catholic and a loyal subject caused some modifications to be made in the Catholic teachings on the pope's supremacy, modifications, however, which never won the approval of Elizabethan Jesuits or of most of the Catholics in exile. Fairly soon after the contents of the bull of 1570 became known in England some Catholics began to question the extent of the papal deposing power.[1] John Bishop in *A Courteous Conference with the English Catholics Roman*, written about 1574, put forward the thesis that the pope possessed no earthly sovereignty and therefore could not depose princes or release subjects from their temporal allegiance; he could operate solely in the sphere of spiritual censures. In a conference with John Reynolds in the Tower in 1584 John Hart, then still a secular priest, was reported to have denied the temporal power of the pope. Another priest, Thomas Wright, attacked the Spanish claim to be the instrument of the papal deposing power and the demand which many of the Catholic exiles made that all English Catholics should welcome a Spanish invasion. These seem at first to have been isolated individuals but their number increased later in the 1590s. These Catholics attributed the intensity of the persecution in no small degree to the continuing papal policy of working for the restoration of Catholicism in England by force of arms: they pointed out to their fellow Englishmen on the continent that the promulgation of the bull *Regnans in excelsis* by calling forth retaliatory measures from the English government had disastrous consequences for Catholics within England. Although they did not deny that the pope had the right to depose princes, they argued that he had been wrong to exercise this right in the circumstances which existed in England in 1570.

In answer to a royal proclamation issued in 1591 which described the 'great troubles pretended against the realm by a number of seminary priests and Jesuits sent and very secretly dispersed in the same to work great treasons under a false pretence of religion' Robert Southwell, the Catholic poet, composed *An Humble Supplication to Her Majesty* (not, however, published till 1600). First he made the conventional assertion that priests were not traitors in the accepted sense of the word; the way in which treason had been defined in the new treason laws would have made even the saints of the church traitors:

[1] T. Clancy, 'English Catholics and the Papal Deposing power', *Recusant History*, VI, 1961–2, pp. 205–227; VII, 1963–4, pp. 2–8.

'Yea, if to be a priest made by the authority of the see of Rome, and present within your majesty's dominions be a just title of treason; if they that relieve, harbour or receive any such be worthy to be deemed felons: then all the glorious saints of this land, whose virtue and doctrine God confirmed with many miracles, were no better than traitors, and their abettors felons.'

Then, most interestingly, he, a priest, went on to express the emotional loyalty towards the English state in a time of war which the Armada crisis had shown the Catholic laity widely shared with Protestant Englishmen: 'we do assure your majesty that what army soever should come against you, we will rather yield our breasts to be broached by our country['s] swords, than use our swords to the effusion of our country's blood'.[1]

The debate over the extent of allegiance owed to the pope and allegiance owed to the crown became public in the Appellant Controversy which in the last years of the reign split the ranks of the priests on the mission in England and left the general body of English Catholics divided at the accession of James I.[2] The conflict between national feeling and the international claims of the papacy, intensified by the jealousy between the secular priests and the Jesuits, first appeared among the priests imprisoned at Wisbech in 1595: it reached its height when in 1598 Clement VIII appointed Blackwell to be archpriest over the English clergy and he began discriminating actively in favour of the Jesuits. The English government exploited the discords and 1601 actually aided a group of secular priests, the Appellants, in their remonstrance to the pope against the actions of the archpriest. The apparent benevolence of the Elizabethan government led some of the more optimistic priests among the Appellants to believe that, despite all the years of persecution, toleration for Catholics might be achieved in England. In 1602 Bluet, an Appellant, urged the pope to negotiate with Elizabeth: 'if I who am a worm and no man could prevail so much with the queen, what might not your highness do, with the aid of the most Christian King, towards obtaining consolation for English Catholics?'[3] Another Appellant, Watson, though less hopeful concerning the English government's intentions, could still stress the duty English Catholics owed to their queen in civil matters and confess their failings therein in previous decades. 'We ought to have carried ourselves in another manner of course

[1] R. C. Bald, ed. *Robert Southwell, An Humble Supplication to her Majesty*, Cambridge, 1953, pp. xxi–xxii, 29, 35.

[2] McGrath, *Papists and Puritans*, pp. 253–299. A. O. Meyer, *England and the Catholic Church*, chapter IV, and criticism by J. Bossy, p. xxvii.

[3] Quoted by McGrath, *Papists and Puritans*, p. 293.

towards her, our true and lawful queen, and towards our country, than hath been taken and pursued by many Catholics, but especially by the Jesuits.'[1] While in practice the actual number of secular priests in opposition to the Jesuits may never have been great, the government let it be known that, although it would never consider tolerating Jesuits, in certain circumstances secular priests might be acknowledged to be loyal English citizens. A proclamation of November 5, 1602, banished all Jesuits from the country but permitted priests who swore allegiance to the queen to stay in England, though not to continue their missionary activities. Such was the feeling among some of the priests that thirteen did swear the oath in which they recognized the pope to be the successor of St Peter and that he had

'. . . as ample, and no more authority or jurisdiction over us and other Christians, than had that apostle by the gift and commission of Christ our Saviour; and that we will obey him so far forth as we are bound by the laws of God to do: which, we doubt not, but will stand well with the performance of our duty to our temporal prince.'[2]

Only a small minority of the priests made this explicit acknowledgement of the spiritual authority of the pope and the temporal authority of the queen: their attitude reflected more accurately that of the Catholic laity many of whom throughout the reign had doggedly asserted their civil loyalty. Yet even taking this concession to its furthest limits it implied merely that certain priests had attempted to define the pope's powers in temporal affairs: none had disputed his right as the spiritual head of the Catholic church on earth. Whatever the relatively small qualifications made in the debate over secular allegiance, thinking Catholics were no more prepared at the end of Elizabeth's reign, than they had been at the beginning, to admit the lawfulness of the royal supremacy over the English church.

V. THE QUALIFIED ACCEPTANCE OF THE ROYAL SUPREMACY BY PRESBYTERIANS AND SEPARATISTS

If criticism of the royal supremacy had been confined to Catholics and Catholic sympathizers, the task of the defenders of the royal supremacy would have been a relatively easy one, but the idea of the royal supremacy came under attack not only from the Catholic conservatives but also from the Protestant radicals. Neither Presbyterians nor Separatists absolutely repudiated the royal supremacy as Catholics did, yet both to a varying extent very decidedly wanted

---

[1] W. Watson, *A Sparing Discovery of our English Jesuits*, 1601, quoted by McGrath, *Papists and Puritans*, p. 292.

[2] Quoted by McGrath, *Papists and Puritans*, p. 298.

to restrict the royal prerogative in ecclesiastical matters. From the moment of Elizabeth's accession some Protestants felt that she might be usurping powers over the church which belonged to Christ alone, as the debate over the exact meaning of the queen's title revealed (Doc. 8). As long as the reform of the English church seemed to be going ahead, Protestants concealed their unease, but as soon as the bishops began to restrain this reform protests began anew, and in the criticism of the persecuting ways of the bishops the exercise of the royal supremacy indirectly began again to be disputed. The attempt in 1566 to compel all clergy to wear the surplice when ministering at any service let loose the pent-up resentment of the radicals at the tardy progress of reformation in England. In this very year John Bartlett dared to write in *The Fortress of Fathers*:

'The lordship of bishops now exercised over both the rest of the clergy and over the lay people hath no ground in the word of God. Christ is only the head of his mystical body which is the church as the prince or chief magistrate is the head of the politic body of his realm and country. The supreme magistrate is bound to obey the word of God, preached by Christ's messengers, and he is also subject to the discipline of the church. Neither the prince nor any prelate hath any authority by the word of God to make any ecclesiastical law or rite, to bind men's consciences in pain of deadly sin to keep them.'[1]

In Geneva Beza now preached unreservedly against episcopacy as a valid form of church government in a way in which Calvin himself had never done and certain English ministers who preferred rather to resign their livings than to wear the 'antichristian' surplice appealed to him for aid. Beza without any qualification came down on the side of the English radicals. 'The papacy was never abolished in that country, but rather transferred to the sovereign', he informed Bullinger who with his fellow ministers at Zurich had shown much more sympathy for the English bishops, several of whom had been their guests. Beza attacked 'the assumed power of the bishops': in England, 'just the same as under the papacy, they have in the place of a lawfully appointed presbytery their deans, chancellors, and archdeacons'. No reformed discipline had yet been devised; instead, the queen ruled all. 'Whatever it may please the queen's majesty, with the sole concurrence of the archbishop of Canterbury to establish, alter or take away, with respect to the rites of the church it shall forthwith be considered as having the force of law.'[2]

Zealots who had not had the privilege during the Marian exile of

[1] Quoted in Collinson, *Puritan Movement*, p. 115.

[2] H. Robinson, ed. *Zurich Letters*, II, Parker Society, Cambridge, 1845, no. LIII.

observing the operation of a fully reformed church in Geneva, or had not the means now to make a pilgrimage there, still had a chance of learning from the Calvinist churches in England which had been set up not only in London but in Canterbury, Norwich, Southampton and Sandwich. They envied the liberty the foreign refugees enjoyed to establish a fully reformed church polity while the authorities attempted to force them into conformity.[1] 'It seemeth rightful that subjects natural receive so much favour as the churches of national strangers have here with us,' Thomas Earl wrote, 'but we cannot once be heard so to obtain. This with them: they an eldership; we none. They freely elect the doctor and pastor; we may not. They their deacons and church servants with discipline; and we not.'[2] Dr Collinson believes that direct contact with the foreign reformed churches in England led English radicals to demand that the government of the English church should be modelled on the Genevan system before Thomas Cartwright set out the design of a Presbyterian church in his lectures at Cambridge. The two young clerics who drew up the *Admonition to the Parliament* came from among the discontented London radicals who had been associating with the French church in London, not from Cartwright's Cambridge followers.

The *Admonition*, published when Parliament was still sitting in 1572, but intended as an appeal to the Elizabethan laity at large, rather than to an exclusively parliamentary audience, for the first time displayed the virtues of a Presbyterian church system to the public (Doc. 18). After illustrating in some detail the popish abuses yet remaining in the English church, Field and Wilcox made a direct attack on the powers of bishops. For autocratic bishops should be substituted a godly seigniory, for patronage as then exercised the congregational calling of ministers. By their graphic descriptions of the corruptions in the English church they hoped to shock their contemporaries into demanding further reform. Travers more soberly in *A Full and Plain Declaration of Ecclesiastical Discipline* showed the way in which these reforms should be carried out (Doc. 20). He considered the only permissible form of church government to be by pastors, doctors, elders and deacons, each with their precise duties, a system laid down in the New Testament which could never be changed. A magistrate had the duty to restore this form of church government, to preserve and maintain it, but should not rule in ecclesiastical matters, for even kings and the highest magistrates were subject to those whom the Lord had set over them.

---

[1] P. Collinson, 'The Elizabethan Puritans and the Reformed Churches in London,' *Proceedings of the Huguenot Society of London*, xx, no. 5, 1964, pp. 528–555.

[2] Quoted in the above article, p. 539.

D

Thomas Cartwright, regarded by contemporaries as the intellectual leader of the English Presbyterians, did not enter the controversy over the government of the English church directly till 1573 when he wrote his first *Reply* to Whitgift's *Answer to the Admonition*.[1] In the tortuous works of Whitgift, where he first quoted whole paragraphs of Cartwright before going on to confute them, the ideal Presbyterian church emerged. Cartwright somewhat disengenuously emphasized that he called not for the destruction of the English church but for its reformation. Comparing the commonwealth and the church to the twins of Hippocrates which stood or fell together he maintained that the state could only benefit from a further reform of the church. The English church must be reconstructed on the apostolic model and nothing which had been abused by Rome should be retained in it. God, who had given detailed instructions for the building of the Temple in the Old Testament, had laid down the essentials for a true church in the New Testament, and Presbyterianism constituted the only possible form of church government in accordance with God's word. He held that in general the ceremonies in a reformed church should be as unlike as possible to those kept in the antichristian Roman church, and he directed his main criticism against the popish hierarchy still in power in England. In a true church the only permissible superintendents were presbyters, and all presbyters were equal. In spiritual affairs the church must be autonomous and all discipline exercised by the ministers and elders alone. Presbyteries and synods should replace the old pre-reformation courts, the relics of antichrist. Christ alone was the head of this church, of which the magistrate could not be more than a respected member.

Cartwright seems scarcely to have written with the intention of undermining the royal supremacy, although the government soon recognized the threat that he and his supporters posed to the established church. He constantly professed his loyalty to the queen and assigned the monarch some authority in his Presbyterian system, though significantly less than Elizabeth already possessed. In civil matters a subject must obey the magistrate, but the magistrate must also govern in accordance with the laws of God. The civil ruler had the special duty of protecting the church but had not the power to interfere in its government. He conceived of the monarch exercising authority at the behest of a national synod. As in the medieval church, the ruler should impose civil disabilities to supplement the ecclesiastical penalties of excommunication and, also as in the medieval church, could in exceptional cases become liable to the penalties of excom-

---

[1] A. F. S. Pearson, *Thomas Cartwright and Elizabethan Puritanism*, Cambridge, 1925, pp. 58–121. D. J. McGinn, *The Admonition Controversy*, New Brunswick, 1949, pp. 3–147. J. V. P. Thompson, *Supreme Governor*, pp. 169–174.

munication himself.[1] The revolutionary implication of Cartwright's teaching came out most forcibly in his metaphor of the house and its hangings (Doc. 21). Whitgift refused to accept that God had prescribed any one form of church government for all time and maintained that in a monarchical state a hierarchical form of church government was the most appropriate. Cartwright would have nothing to do with this Erastian reasoning. He vehemently attacked the idea that the church must be framed according to the commonwealth: rather, the commonwealth must be modelled on the true form of church government. With justification Whitgift contended that this argument would overthrow a prince's authority and compared Cartwright's declaration on the necessity of a prince subjecting himself to the church with the autocratic teaching of the papacy.[2]

Other defenders of the English church immediately seized on the political implications of Cartwright's tenets in order to discredit him. In 1573 Bishop Sandys reported to Zurich that rash young men sought to destroy the whole ecclesiastical polity and held that the civil magistrate had no authority in ecclesiastical matters (Doc. 19). Twenty years later Bancroft summed up the revolutionary potential of Presbyterianism:

'Cartwright and some others with him do affirm . . . that all kings (as well heathen as Christian) receiving but one commission and equal authority immediately from God, have no more to do with the church the one sort than the other, as being in no respect deputed for church officers under Christ otherwise than if they be good kings, to maintain and defend it. And secondly, that as God hath appointed all kings and civil magistrates his immediate lieutenants for the government of the world in temporal causes, so Christ, as he is mediator and governor of his church, hath his immediate officers to rule in the church under him, and those they say are no other than pastors, doctors and elders, to whom they ascribe as large authority in causes ecclesiastical.'[3]

Elizabethan herself realized as fully as any of her subjects the diminution of the royal prerogative Presbyterianism could effect. 'Let me warn you', she wrote to James VI in 1590,

'. . . that there is risen, both in your realm and in mine, a sect of perilous consequence, such as would have no kings but a presbytery,

---

[1] A. F. S. Pearson, *Church and State: Political Aspects of Sixteenth Century Puritanism*, Cambridge, 1928.

[2] *Whitgift's Works*, I, Parker Society, p. 32.

[3] R. Bancroft, *A Survey of the Pretended Holy Discipline*, 1593, p. 205, quoted in S. B. Babbage, *Puritanism and Richard Bancroft*, 1962, p. 35.

and take our place while they enjoy our privilege with a shade of God's word, which none is judged to follow right without by their censure they be so deemed. Yea, look we well unto them. When they have made in our people's hearts a doubt of our religion, and that we err, if they say so, what perilous issue this may make I rather think than mind to write.'[1]

While Cartwright undoubtedly held a less exalted opinion of the royal prerogative than did the queen herself, and in this respect fully deserved her strictures, he yet gave a qualified support to the idea of the royal supremacy and he never departed from the idea of the necessity of a state church. The difference on this point between the Presbyterians and the Separatists is very marked. Cartwright constantly taught that reformation in the church could only come through the agency of the civil magistrate; he directed all his energies towards persuading the queen to countenance further reform; without the magistrate's permission in theory he would take no action. The Separatists, however, would wait for no one and abandoned the whole concept of the need of church reform to attend upon the magistrate's pleasure. In so doing, almost by accident, they also abandoned the idea of a national church. Separating churches came into existence well before individual Separatists devised a philosophical justification to rationalize their separation. In London some Protestant house churches from Mary's reign persisted under Elizabeth and the attack of the bishops upon nonconformity at the time of the Vestiarian Controversy seems to have added to their strength, as it did to the incipient Presbyterian demand for a complete alteration in church government. Indeed, it has proved quite impossible to make a distinction between Presbyterians and Separatists in this early period: they were united in their demand for the overthrow of the popish hierarchy and its replacement by the rule of doctors, pastors and elders, and historians of Congregationalism have been disconcerted to find the same radicals appearing sometimes as Separatists, sometimes as nonseparating Presbyterians.[2] Nevertheless, fairly soon after the strife over the surplice, some Separatists had begun to think of themselves

---

[1] J. Bruce, ed. *Letters of Queen Elizabeth and King James VI*, Camden Society, First Series, XLVI, pp. 63–64.

[2] A. Peel, *The First Congregational Churches*, Cambridge, 1920. See also C. Burrage, *The Early English Dissenters in the Light of Recent Research 1550–1641*, 2 vols Cambridge, 1912, especially vol. I, chaps 2–4. P. Collinson, 'The Godly Aspects of Popular Protestantism in Elizabethan England; *Past and Present*: Conference Papers, July 7, 1966. H. G. Owen, 'A Nursery of Elizabethan Nonconformity 1567–72', *Journal of Ecclesiastical History*, XVII, 1966, pp. 65–76 and Owen, 'The Liberty of the Minorities: a Study in Elizabethan Radicalism, *East London Papers*, VIII, 1965, pp. 81–97.

as a distinct group. As early as 1571 the London church to which Richard Fitz ministered proclaimed its difference:

'Therefore according to the saying of the Almighty our God [Matt. XVIII. 20.] "where two or three are gathered in my name, there am I," so we a poor congregation whom God hath separated from the churches of England and from the mingled and false worshipping therein used, out of the which assemblies the Lord our only Saviour hath called us, and still calleth, saying, "Come out from among them, and separate yourselves from them, and touch no unclean thing, then will I receive you, and I will be your God and you shall be my sons and daughters, saith the Lord" [2 Cor. VI. 17–18]. So as God giveth strength at this day we do serve the Lord every Sabbath day in houses, and on the fourth day in the week we meet or come together weekly to use prayer and exercise discipline on them which do deserve it. . . .'[1]

A very small number of Separatist churches consequently existed before Bishop Freke's attempt to enforce conformity and abolish the exercises in Norwich drove Robert Browne and Robert Harrison into open Separatism, yet these men still seem to have been the first logically to have vindicated their actions.[2] The title of Robert Browne's first work, *A Treatise of Reformation without Tarrying for Any*, describes exactly these Separatists' intention: they would proceed with the further reform of the church, come what may (Doc. 22). Once a minister had seen the light and become informed of the details of the fully reformed church he must lead his flock, 'be they never so few', to the realization of this ideal, or be responsible for their eternal damnation. 'Often have I heard the kings and princes should wait what the Lord should say unto them by the mouth of prophets and priests, but never the contrary, that the prophets or any ministers should wait what God should say to them by the mouth of magistrates, except you mean by their mouth their sword.'[3] These new self-conscious Separatists, like Fitz's congregation a decade earlier, had gone on deliberately to establish their independence:

'We have our Churches planted, the unclean separate from the clean, all open abominations of antichrist expelled, and our poor flocks

---

[1] Quoted in Peel, *First Congregational Churches*, p. 33.

[2] Collinson, *Puritan Movement*, p. 204. A. Peel, *The Brownists in Norwich and Norfolk about 1580*, Cambridge, 1920.

[3] 'A Treatise of the Church and the Kingdom of Christ', in A. Peel and L. H. Carlson, eds. *The Writings of Robert Harrison and Robert Browne*, 1953, p. 56. There is some disagreement about whether Robert Harrison or Henry Barrow was the author of this treatise, see L. H. Carlson, ed. *The Writings of Henry Barrow 1587–90*, 1962, pp. 69–70.

redeemed from his iron yoke and governed by the due order of Christ's government, and we have the keys of outward binding and loosing, without borrowing them from any antichristian court. . . .'[1]

Robert Browne knew very well that for taking reform into their own hands the Separatists would be accused of disobedience to the civil magistrate. He defended himself by saying that although in secular matters a subject owed obedience to the secular ruler his primary allegiance must be to God. Until then, English ministers, by waiting for the magistrate's permission before taking up ecclesiastical reform, had wickedly elevated the magistrate's authority to thrust out Christ. Magistrates might aid the reformation of the church, but only in their civil capacity, as by restraining the enemies of reform to free the ministers for their godly undertaking. Magistrates themselves had not the authority to be prophets, priests or spiritual kings. They might not compel religion or force the godly to submit to an ungodly ecclesiastical domination. If the magistrate was Christian, Browne maintained, he would submit to the church; if he was not, he asked why the salvation of men's souls should depend upon his decision (Doc. 22).

Whether he realized it or not, Browne had gone far towards denying the royal supremacy altogether. Other Separatists drew out the implications of his theory.

'Where the chiefest and highest ecclesiastical authority is in the hands of antichrist, there is not the church of Christ, for Christ hath given authority to his own servants, but in the churches of our ministers, the lord bishops, deans, chancellors, commissaries, and such like, being the pope's bastards, have greater and chiefer authority than they, and exercise authority over them and they suffer that yoke: therefore they have [not] the church of Christ among them.'[2]

Browne did not persist for long in his separation and in 1585 was reconciled to the established church: Harrison died, probably in 1585, when ministering to his Separatist congregation at Middelburg, and this church in the Netherlands dispersed; but a new generation of Separatist leaders now came forward in England to perpetuate their teachings.[3] In 1587 Henry Barrow and John Greenwood were arrested for having set up Separatist conventicles and were examined at various times before the High Commission, the major charge against them being that they did not recognize the royal supremacy. When asked on March 24, 1589, whether he believed the

---

[1] *The Writings of Harrison and Browne*, p. 52.
[2] *The Writings of Harrison and Browne*, p. 32.
[3] C. Burrage, *The True Story of Robert Browne*, Oxford, 1906.

queen had supreme authority to govern the church in causes ecclesiastical, Barrow answered:

'I think the queen's majesty is the supreme governor over the whole land, and over the Church also, both of bodies and goods; yet I am persuaded that she ought not to make or impose other laws over them than Christ hath made and left in his Testament, and that the prince ought most carefully, above all other, to revive and enquire out the laws of God which are commanded in his word, and can make no new.'[1]

He refused to answer whether in general the ecclesiastical laws established by authority be permissible or not, but said that certain of the laws were ungodly and contrary to God's word. 'Being asked whether the congregation may reform abuses in the church, if the queen or magistrate do refuse or delay to the same, saith, that the church need not to stay for the prince in the reforming of any abuse, but may reform it, though the prince say no.' John Greenwood most explicitly denied the royal supremacy as defined in the act of 1559. Examined on the same day as Barrow he allowed himself none of Barrow's legal equivocations. To the question whether the church in England constituted a 'true established church' he replied: 'The whole commonwealth is not a church.' When interrogated specifically on the royal supremacy he granted that Elizabeth was 'a supreme magistrate over all persons to punish the evil and defend the good' but he went on to make a quite clear distinction between secular and sacred affairs. The queen was not supreme in ecclesiastical causes: 'Christ is only head of his church, and his laws may no man alter.' He pursued his objection to its logical end and refused to take the oath of supremacy, saying that in his conscience he could not approve 'the order and government with all the laws in the church as it is now established'.[2] The Separatism of Barrow and Greenwood cost them their lives: for publishing seditious matter to the defamation of the queen's majesty, which had been made a felony punishable by death under the statute of 23 Elizabeth, they were executed in April 1593.

Although even by the 1580s little outwardly distinguished the Separatists from the Presbyterians, and Separatists were as convinced as Presbyterians that the only divinely appointed form of church government was by doctors, pastors and elders, yet on this question of the authority of the magistrate within the church a fundamental difference emerged: the Separatists had virtually come to deny the magistrate's authority in the church altogether; the Presbyterians, with

---

[1] *Writings of Henry Barrow*, pp. 206–207.

[2] L. H. Carlson, ed. *Writings of John Greenwood 1587–1590*, 1962, pp. 25–28.

their quite different concept of the church never reached this conclusion. Partly by force of political events the Separatists had felt themselves driven to contract out of Elizabethan civil society, and the migration of Browne and Harrison with their flock to the Netherlands symbolized their repudiation of the English state. The Brownists, because of the hostility of the greater part of society, had become explicit sectarians: their gathered churches existed only for the godly minority; the elect had separated themselves out from the unregenerate. Cartwright and his followers, on the other hand, while they criticized the abuses remaining in the English church as vocally as the Separatists, refused absolutely to abandon the idea of a state church. To this end, the establishment of a fully reformed church, the monarch for them was still an essential instrument, even though they did not accord Elizabeth as much power over the church as she enjoyed under the act of supremacy. Cartwright believed just as firmly as Hooker that as by birth men were members of the English state so equally by birth they became members of the English church. Since knowledge of election is reserved to God alone, men on earth could not, and should not, anticipate the separation of the regenerate and the unregenerate which belonged to Christ and his angels.[1]

The exclusiveness of the Separatists had the effect of making Cartwright and the Presbyterians appear more and more in the guise of defenders of the established church. Cartwright's writings in the 1580s certainly took on a very different tone from his forthright denunciations of the previous decade. Barrow recognized this change in attitude and directed his bitterest invective not at the bishops and their supporters who, to his way of thinking, were irredeemably antichristian but at the Presbyterians who had once set their hands to the plough but had now turned away from their God given task. The Presbyterians, he complained, blamed all on the magistrate, and remained passive:

'If it were in them, it should not [remain]; they wish for reformation and sigh for it daily, yea, they pray with tears both publicly and privately for it, and as far as it lieth in them they seek it by all means. They sue to the Parliaments for it; and seeing it cannot be obtained, they persuade all men to have patience until it may please God to turn the prince's heart, and in the mean time to rest contented with this measure of God's truth and freedom they have....

They have but conceived chaff and brought forth stubble. First where find they that either our Saviour Christ or his apostles sued to Parliaments or princes for the planting or practising of the gospel; and whether the word itself, if it be faithfully taught, be not of power

---

[1] A. Peel and L. H. Carlson, eds *Cartwrightiana*, 1951, pp. 71, 73.

both to tack princes in the net and to bind them in chains and fetters? Then if princes resist or neglect, where [do] they find the faithful ought to rest in their defaults and disorders until God change the princes's heart?'[1]

Admonitions such as this caused Cartwright, because of his belief in the necessity of a national church, to assert that the English church, despite its manifold imperfections was still a church of God:

'Where, therefore, there is no ministry of the word, there it is plain that there are no visible and apparent churches. It is another part of the discipline of our Lord, that the rest of the body of the church should obey those that are set over them in the Lord. Wheresoever, therefore, there is no obedience of the people given to the ministers that in the Lord's name preach unto them, there also can be no church of Christ, but where these two be, although other points want, yea, although there be some defect in these, that neither the ministers do in all points preach as they ought, nor the assemblies in all points obey unto the wholesome doctrine of their teachers, yet do they for the reason above said retain the right of the churches of God.'[2]

It must surely have been because of this qualified support for the established church, and for the exercise of the royal supremacy within the church, that Cartwright came out from his examinations before the High Commission and long imprisonment relatively unscathed whereas Barrow and Greenwood went to their deaths. In the interests of religion the Separatists could contemplate the overthrow of society: when made to face the alternative of obedience or social anarchy, the Presbyterians waited on the prince's will; a national church meant more to them than a reformed but exclusive sect.

VI. QUESTIONING OF THE ROYAL SUPREMACY BY CLERGY WITHIN THE CHURCH

In the end Elizabethan Presbyterians never separated from the established church. There were others within the church far less radical than they, who did not object in principle to the government of the church by bishops so long as godly men were chosen to be bishops, who yet became increasingly uneasy as the supreme governor seemed to be failing to act as a nursing mother to the church. The first Convocation of Elizabeth's reign to sit after the exclusion of the Marian Catholics showed in 1563 how many Protestant clergy wanted moderate reforms to continue. Convocation received numerous peti-

---

[1] *Writings of Henry Barrow*, p. 64.
[2] *Cartwrightiana*, p. 54.

tions advocating practical improvements, that the poverty of livings be relieved, abuses in patronage prevented, lectureships and grammar schools attached to cathedrals. In addition other petitions called for changes with doctrinal implications: some wanted popish ceremonies like persistent bell ringing to be abandoned, marriage to be permitted at any time of the year, only those who could give an account of their faith to be allowed to stand as godparents. The lower house of Convocation rejected by one vote the Six Articles which asked that all holy days except Sundays and the principal Christian feasts be abrogated, divine service be read by the minister facing the people, that the sign of the cross at baptism be optional, kneeling at communion be left at the discretion of the ordinary, that the wearing of the surplice (and not vestments) be sufficient at all services, and that organs be removed.[1] Apparently Elizabeth and her clerical supporters would not distinguish between the practical and the doctrinal changes the more zealous Protestants wanted. It could not be very long before they began to question whether the queen in fact performed the duties of a godly monarch towards her church.

All over England Protestant ministers, burning to fulfil their divine commission to preach the gospel to the unenlightened masses, felt disappointed in their monarch who shared none of their sense of urgency.[2] They believed passionately that without abundant preaching true faith could never be established in England, yet the queen, the protector of the church, seemed oblivious of the scandal of an insufficient, nonpreaching clergy. Edward Dering represented this kind of minister. In his famous sermon delivered before the queen in February 1570 (Doc. 23) he did not ask for changes in the government of the church, merely for a spiritual reformation. Impropriations and sequestrations still remained as in the medieval church; patrons irresponsibly exercised their rights of patronage; ministers inadequate on both moral and intellectual grounds continued to be appointed to livings. He called upon the queen herself to rebuke her bishops and oversee personally the reformation of the church. This appeal Elizabeth either would not or could not understand; her failure to sympathize with the pastoral zeal of the godly, both clerical and lay, led ultimately to a common sense of frustration with the operation of the royal supremacy, though few Protestants, not in high office, would face the fact that the queen did not want further reform. They directed their antagonism against the queen's advisers, in this case chiefly the bishops.

[1] J. Strype, *Annals of the Reformation*, I, 1725, pp. 315–325. W. P. Haugaard, *Elizabeth and the English Reformation*, Cambridge, 1968, pp. 52–78.

[2] P. Collinson, *A Mirror of Elizabethan Puritanism: the Life and Letters of 'Godly Master Dering'*, 1964.

This disillusionment was not confined, at least in the first half of
the reign, to the lower clergy. Many of the exiles, who had returned
to England on Elizabeth's accession and had accepted leading positions
with the firm intention of creating a thoroughly reformed church, had
to recognize that the queen, more than any other one single person,
stood between them and further reform. Their godly prince in practice showed little sign of willingness to be instructed by her clergy.
The former exiles, now bishops, constantly struck a defensive note
in their letters to their friends in Zurich.[1] Under the given political
circumstances the English church was the best church they could hope
to have: an insufficiently reformed church was infinitely preferable
to not having a reformed church at all. Many leading churchmen must
have shared Whitgift's belief that the government of the church
should be based upon the form of government existing in the state:
while Zurich enjoyed an aristocratical church government, an
English church government could only be monarchical (Doc. 21).
Even at the top of the hierarchy this consciousness of defects remaining in the church persisted for a surprisingly long time. When
Edwin Sandys, in succession bishop of Worcester, London and lastly
archbishop of York, made his will in 1588, he still found it necessary
to disassociate himself from abuses as yet uncorrected in the church.

'... Concerning rites and ceremonies by political constitutions
authorized amongst us. As I am and have been persuaded that such
as are now set down by public authority in the church of England
are no way either ungodly or unlawful but may with good conscience
for order and obedience sake be used of a good Christian; for the
private baptism to be ministered by women I take neither to be
prescribed nor permitted. So have I ever been and presently am
persuaded that some of them be not so expedient for this church
now, but that in the church reformed, and in all this time of the
gospel (wherein the seed of the scripture hath so long been sown)
they may better be disused by little and little than more and more
urged. Howbeit, as I do easily acknowledge our ecclesiastical policy
in some points may be bettered, so do I utterly mislike, even in my
conscience, all such rude and indigested platforms as have been more
lately and boldly, than either learnedly or wisely preferred, tending
not to the reformation, but to the destruction of this church of
England. . . .'[2]

Sandys accepted that 'a large Christian kingdom' could not have

---

[1] *Zurich Letters*, First Series.

[2] Borthwick Institute, York. Chancery wills, November 26, 1588. Preamble
printed in J. Ayre, ed. *Sermons of Edwin Sandys*, Parker Society, Cambridge,
1841, pp. 446–449.

the same sort of ecclesiastical government as would be suitable in 'a small private church'. He contented himself with giving an account of his stewardship despite the political limitations he had been forced to observe, and seems not to have questioned the actual working of the royal supremacy further. Matthew Parker, rather unexpectedly, considering his great personal devotion to Elizabeth, at the end of his life allowed his conjectures on the same subject to range somewhat more widely (Doc. 24). The queen had always impressed upon him throughout the sixteen years of his archiepiscopate that she wished him and his fellow bishops to act on their own responsibility. Even when a command originated with the queen she preferred it to be issued under Parker's name and she refused to give royal confirmation to episcopal orders likely to be unpopular, such as the Advertisements of 1566. Yet when bishops did genuinely act on their own initiative the queen was more than likely to question or even countermand their decisions. In his last letter to Burghley Parker recalled how he had recently completed a visitation of the diocese of Winchester which he had carried out at the request of the bishop there. In the Winchester diocese both Catholic and Protestant dissenters flourished, and he had used some severity to enforce that conformity which accorded with the queen's will. Immediately complaints had been made to those councillors known to sympathize with Puritans and the result had been that the queen had publicly rebuked Parker for his proceedings; and yet he had merely been performing his duties as primate.

Parker considered that part of his office lay in advising the queen on appointments to be made within the church. He had tried to the best of his ability to establish uniformity in the church, and now the see of Norwich was vacant where in the past under Parkhurst considerable latitude had been given to nonconformists. Understandably Parker hoped the queen would appoint as the next bishop a firm supporter of the 1559 settlement and suggested three candidates who he considered could bring order to the diocese. The queen chose none of them; as Strype commented: 'but neither had the archbishop his desire now, any more than formerly he used to have, for Goodman succeeded not, hindered, I suppose, by Leicester's means. . . .' Not only had the queen never paid much attention to Parker's recommendations for the filling of high posts in the church throughout his period of office; she had also interfered in appointments which were directly within his gift. In May 1573 a notorious case had occurred when Parker made Bartholomew Clerk dean of the Court of Arches. The queen had objected very forcibly to his appointment, having a candidate of her own for the post, and she had brought strong pressure on

Parker to dismiss Clerk, but in this instance Parker had stood his ground and Clerk had kept his office.[1]

Practical experience of the royal supremacy, the occasions on which the queen had disregarded his advice, the other occasions when she had intervened with little warrant, caused Parker now to question the 'supreme government ecclesiastical' which the queen had once told him, under her, he enjoyed. He obviously felt that the queen had exceeded her powers as supreme governor, but he had not the temerity to attempt to define what these powers were. Perhaps he thought that the queen had been exercising authority which should not be exercised by any layman: he certainly believed that Cecil had overstated the monarch's authority in the Injunctions of 1559 which said that 'the queen's power within her realms and dominions is the highest power under God, to whom all men, within the same realms and dominions, by God's laws, owe most loyalty and obedience, afore and above all other powers and potentates in earth' (Doc. 28). Parker went no further than to say vaguely that the royal supremacy was less than stated in these Injunctions, greater than the Papists allowed. Probably he never defined even in his own mind what he thought the extent of the royal supremacy should be; at all events, his definition cannot be reconstructed now. The significance of his letter lies mainly in the fact that Parker, perhaps the most compliant of all Elizabeth's archbishops, should have thought of querying the queen's authority generally within the church.

A little more than a year later Grindal's explicit attempt to limit the queen's powers in ecclesiastical affairs followed Parker's indecisive murmurings concerning the royal supremacy. Where Parker only revealed his doubts in a private letter to Burghley, Grindal risked a public confrontation with the queen. Elizabeth's command to Grindal in 1576 to abolish the prophesyings in the southern province revealed more clearly than any one other of her acts the great gulf which divided the queen from her godly subjects clerical and lay alike over the actual form a national, Protestant church should take.[2] In 1575 Grindal had seemed an archbishop who could have commanded the support of virtually all who were working for a further reformation of the English church. The Protestant governing class respected him, as did all but a small minority of the godly ministers: in the deviousness of Elizabethan public life he had kept his reputation untarnished. When he had been bishop of London he had been seen to be no lordly prelate but a sober, 'primitive' bishop, after the pattern set out by Martin Bucer whom he had known in Edwardian Cambridge and whose

[1] J. Strype, *Life and Acts of Matthew Parker*, 1711, pp. 490–492.

[2] J. Strype, *Life and Acts of Edmund Grindal*, 1710, pp. 190–314. Collinson *Puritan Movement*, pp. 159–167, 191–201.

ideals he revered. He was a scholar not only of national but of international repute. The Protestant zealots expected him to proceed with moderate, practical reforms in the church and he seemed to be as eager to promote the reforms as they to ask. During his year of freedom he suggested that the popish Court of Faculties should be abolished and appointed a commission to look into the abuses of other archiepiscopal courts, the Courts of Audience, of Arches and the Prerogative Court of Canterbury, courts which had survived with very little change from the medieval church. During 1576 he also permitted the printing of the Geneva Bible for the first time in England, the only translation of the Bible of which godly Protestants wholeheartedly approved.

Grindal no longer demanded the strict conformity to the settlement of 1559 which Parker had tried to enforce: instead he actively encouraged Protestant preaching. Thomas Norton recorded that during Grindal's rule the bishops and the preachers and other good men 'loving the peace of the church' agreed to 'join together against the Papists, the enemies of God and her majesty, and not spend themselves in civil wars of the church of God'.[1] On all sides there seemed to be a new readiness to increase the amount of preaching, to improve the quality of the men coming into the ministry, to introduce a godly discipline, to exercise a stricter surveillance over Papists. Grindal wished to employ scrupulous ministers within the church to win them to conformity by this means rather than to compel them by persecution. Had he had an opportunity of realizing his plans he might have built up the sort of church the governing class so much desired, based on an alliance between the gentry and the preachers. It seemed that at last bishops were about to renounce all prelatical ambitions and become preaching fathers in God. Grindal's clash with the queen prevented the fulfilment of any of these hopes.

Elizabeth shared none of the ideals the godly cherished for the church. She had consistently disapproved of the prophesyings, or preaching exercises, wherever she had come across them. The basis of her dislike of them was largely political, for she saw them as harbourers of Presbyterianism, and Presbyterianism as the foe of monarchy. On receiving Elizabeth's order to prohibit the exercises, Grindal first wrote to the other bishops in the province of Canterbury to get their verdict on the prophesyings. Then, when the generally favourable reports had come in, he addressed his reasoned protest to the crown (Doc. 25). He told Elizabeth that he would willingly put the exercises under stricter episcopal supervision and reform them in necessary details but, believing with all his mind that they fostered learning and preaching in a sadly deficient body of clergy, he said

---

[1] Quoted in Collinson, *Puritan Movement*, p. 165.

that he could not in conscience order them to cease. Instead he begged the queen to grant two petitions:

'... that you would refer all these ecclesiastical matters which touch religion, or the doctrine and discipline of the church, unto the bishops and divines of your realm, according to the example of all godly Christian emperors and princes of all ages.

... that, when you deal in matters of faith and religion, or matters that touch the church of Christ, which is his spouse, bought with so dear a price, you would not use to pronounce so resolutely and peremptorily, *as from authority,* as ye may do in civil and extern matters.'

This was the nearest any Elizabethan churchman came to setting a limit upon the royal supremacy. Grindal and Elizabeth disagreed in essence over who should determine what the ultimate good of the church should be. The queen had actually told the archbishop that she considered it would be better for the church to have fewer preachers: Grindal believed with equal conviction that the church could be re-invigorated only through plentiful preaching, and that the exercises did much to stimulate this preaching. He dared to stand against the queen in defence of the freedom of the church. At the time the queen seemed to triumph. She sequestered Grindal from his see and sent out royal letters direct to the southern bishops commanding them to end the prophesyings. At one stage she even intended to deprive Grindal but the privy councillors and the bishops almost to a man shielded the archbishop. The queen's advisers persuaded her to ask for Grindal's resignation instead and in the event he died in 1583 still in office. The queen had to recognize the fact that her supremacy did not extend to the deposing of ecclesiastics on a matter of conscience. She had, however, made it abundantly clear that no churchman in future would be likely to be able to carry out any proposals for church reform of which she personally did not approve.

Grindal's sequestration because of a matter so near to the hearts of convinced Protestants as the necessity for plentiful preaching made it possible for many of them to remain faithful to their ideal of a godly bishop right up until the Civil War in spite of the actions of the later Elizabethan bishops and even of the Laudians. With Grindal's death their trials began, for the appointment of John Whitgift as archbishop marked the beginning of the reaction against the Protestant enthusiasts. Once again the archbishop with the support of the queen attempted to compel radical Protestants to conform. Whereas Grindal had consciously tried to lead his clergy like a primitive pastor, Whitgift treated his delinquent ministers as though they were errant scholars and he still the authoritarian master of Trinity. Resentment flared up anew against persecuting prelates and encouraged the growth of hostility to episcopacy as such. Partially at least to counter the taunts of the radicals, voiced with a new vigour in the popular tracts of Martin Marprelate, a movement grew up within the church which placed a far greater emphasis on the powers of bishops. This in its turn provided ardent Protestants with additional reasons for considering episcopacy as a form of church government to be papistical and positively antichristian: they also did not fail to point out that the new claims being made in support of episcopacy could threaten the royal supremacy itself.

Elizabeth's first generation of bishops had concerned themselves remarkably little with theoretical definitions of their office.[1] It seemed to them a matter of common sense and the best way for the preservation of discipline that there should be divisions of rank within the clerical body and that the highest rank should be that of a bishop. They clearly did not believe that bishops formed a separate order within a Protestant church, and to free themselves from the medieval Catholic assumptions in relation to episcopacy many English Protestants would have preferred to have called the new bishops superintendents: even Hooker for his part cautiously defined a bishop as being a 'principal ecclesiastical overseer'.[2] Protestants considered that a bishop just like any other minister had been called to his office in the church by God, but this in no way prevented them also willingly recognizing that the jurisdictional powers of bishops, in exactly the same way as the powers of any civil officer, derived from the crown. A statement made by the chancellor of the bishop of London only a few months before Richard Bancroft preached his sermon at Paul's Cross indicates the attitude of most Elizabethans towards episcopacy:

'The bishops of our realm do not . . . nor may not, claim to themselves any other authority than is given them by the statute of the 25 of King Henry the VIII, recited in the first year of her majesty's reign, neither is it reasonable they should make other claim, for had it pleased her majesty, with the wisdom of the realm to have used no bishops at all, we could not have complained justly of any defect in our church.'[3]

Whitgift in his contest with Cartwright made very modest claims

[1] P. Collinson, 'Episcopacy and Reform in England in the later Sixteenth Century', *Studies in Church History*, III, Leiden, 1966, pp. 91–125. N. Sykes, *Old Priest and New Presbyter*, chaps. I and III. E. T. Davies, *Episcopacy and the Royal Supremacy in the Church of England in the Sixteenth Century*, Oxford, 1950.

[2] R. Hooker, *Works*, III, Oxford, 1888, p. 147.

[3] Quoted in Babbage, *Puritanism and Richard Bancroft*, p. 29.

for episcopacy. In reply to Cartwright's assertions that God had appointed Presbyterianism and no other form of church government he reiterated that the Bible laid down no one form of government. 'It is plain that any one certain form or kind of external government perpetually to be observed is nowhere in the scripture prescribed to the church.'[1] Although in Book Seven of *The Laws of Ecclesiastical Polity* Hooker appeared to have placed a greater emphasis on episcopacy for the well being of a church, in the books published in his own life time he did not advance beyond Whitgift's argument, and indeed made it his main logical proposition to refute the claim that Presbyterianism existed by divine right.[2] The unwillingness of the earlier apologists for the Elizabethan church settlement to answer Presbyterian claims with counterclaims for the divine right of episcopacy reveals the depth of their Erastianism. Not until about 1589 do defenders of episcopacy seem publicly to have begun to move over to a more positive, and higher, standpoint.[3] Bancroft's assertions on February 9, 1589, sounded relatively moderate (Doc. 26). Although he emphasized that bishops formed a superior order with respect to government in the church, he did not state that episcopacy alone was sanctioned by God's will, only that it had been in continuous use ever since the time of the apostles. He omitted, however, to make the by now almost customary statement that the precise form of church government constituted a matter indifferent. Reading the Paul's Cross sermon in isolation it is difficult to understand why Knollys should have responded to it so violently (Doc. 27). His worries that 'the covetous ambitions of clergy rulers' would threaten the royal supremacy and that bishops would proceed to base their authority upon higher grounds than from the queen seem scarcely justified. Yet Knollys by no means stood alone in his apprehension of episcopal ambitions, nor was Bancroft the only ecclesiastic making higher claims on behalf of bishops. At the same time as Knollys wrote his personal letter of protest to Burghley, this anonymous syllogism, referring to a sermon recently preached by John Bridges, circulated among the Protestant zealots.

'Major. Whosoever doth maintain that any subject of this realm hath superiority over the persons of the clergy, otherwise than from and by her majesty's authority, doth injury to her majesty's supremacy.

[1] Sykes, *Old Priest and New Presbyter*, p. 7.

[2] Hooker, *Works*, III, 1888, p. 209. But see also R. A. Houk, *Hooker's Ecclesiastical Polity, Book VIII*, pp. 73–76.

[3] W. D. J. Cargill Thompson, 'Anthony Marten and the Elizabethan debate on episcopacy', in G. V. Bennett and J. D. Walsh, eds. *Essays in Modern English Church History in Memory of Norman Sykes*, 1966, pp. 44–75.

E

Minor. The preacher upon Sunday, the 12th of January, 1588[/9] maintained that the bishops of this realm had superiority over the inferior clergy, otherwise than by and from her majesty's authority, namely by *divine right*.

Conclusion. Ergo, the preacher therein did injury to her majesty's supremacy; unless he can better expand this saying than I can imagine.'[1]

Events proved that the Protestants' fears merely anticipated claims on behalf of episcopacy which came apace in the 1590s. In his Latin work, *De Diversis Ministrorum Evangelii Gradibus*, published in 1590, Saravia, a Dutchman beneficed in England, held that bishops were necessary in any church and that episcopal government was the best form of church government and of divine authority. Bishops had been instituted by God, and confirmed by apostolic tradition. He even went so far as to deplore the loss of episcopacy by the reformed churches of the continent. Matthew Sutcliffe in *A Treatise of Ecclesiastical Discipline*, 1591, argued that episcopacy had come into being through Christ's specific command, and emphasized the continuity of episcopal government from the time of the early church without a break until the sixteenth century. Yet again in 1593 Thomas Bilson in his book on *The Perpetual Government of Christ's Church* stated that episcopacy derived from the apostles themselves and therefore must of necessity be retained in the church. He answered the Presbyterian claim of divine institution with a specific and exactly similar claim for episcopacy. Bancroft himself in 1593 in his *Survey of the Pretended Holy Discipline* no longer forbore to say what he had refrained from saying in 1589, that episcopacy owed its institution directly to God. Out of this developed the seventeenth-century doctrine of episcopacy by divine right.[2]

Wisely the Elizabethan high churchmen never precisely defined the extent to which a bishop derived his powers directly from God and mediately through the supreme governor. Bancroft contented himself by suggesting that while episcopacy had been instituted by God, and that God called a man to this office, yet at the same time a bishop received the human jurisdictional rights attached to his actual office in the English church through the monarch. Episcopacy existed both by divine right and by permission of the crown and these two aspects of episcopacy could not be sundered. Potentially, however, as the Protestant zealots saw, the theory of episcopacy by divine right could well become a means for the clergy, reacting against Erastianism, to

---

[1] J. Strype, *Life and Acts of John Whitgift*, 1718, pp. 292–293. Strype does not make it clear who actually preached this sermon on January 12th: it was in fact by John Bridges. I owe this point to the kindness of Dr Cargill Thompson.

[2] Sykes, *Old Priest and New Presbyter*, ch. III.

throw over the authority of the monarch and escape from the control of the laity in general. Knollys could with considerable right declare that 'by claiming of the said superiority of government first and principally from God's own ordinance, and not principally and directly from her majesty's grant nor from her supreme government' the supporters of the new concept of episcopacy had fallen under the penalty of *praemunire*.[1] The queen chose to pay no attention to these allegations of Protestant enthusiasts: she had at last schooled her bishops into becoming pillars of the monarchy, but, as events in the seventeenth century proved, when a monarch no longer acted as a protector to the church, bishops, by appealing to their divine institution, felt permitted to abandon their dependence upon the crown. The idea of the divine origin of episcopacy could emancipate the clergy from the Erastian interpretation of the royal supremacy.

[1] Quoted by Cargill Thompson, 'Anthony Marten', *Essays in Modern Church History*, p. 44.

The Royal Supremacy in Practice

In an age so pragmatic as the Elizabethan one it is not surprising that the powers which apologists claimed for the crown as the supreme governor of the English church and the actual authority exercised by the queen within the church did not exactly coincide. In spite of her own declarations and the pious hopes of her clerics that in ecclesiastical matters the queen would be guided by her clergy, Elizabeth repeatedly on her own initiative interfered in questions of faith and doctrine, albeit mainly in a negative way. Nominally the guardian of the church, she felt no compunction in plundering its estates and permitting favoured lay subjects to follow her example. Only in matters of clerical jurisdiction did the queen allow her clerics any semblance of independence, and here the laity checked a possible resurgence of clerical power which the considerable development of prerogative ecclesiastical courts might have foreshadowed during the reign. Elizabethan laymen implicitly believed that the royal supremacy meant the government of the church by the crown and Parliament. Neither the queen and her churchmen, nor the governing classes in Parliament, succeeded in converting the other to their particular interpretation. In practice a *modus vivendi* rather than a compromise resulted: at Westminster the queen acted as though she were the untrammelled head of the church and normally made a point of ruling through her higher clergy; in the localities the nobility and gentry, even certain town corporations, assuming without question that some share in the direction of the church belonged to them as the governing élite, in so far as they had the power, went ahead with the reformation of the local church.

I. ROYAL INTERVENTION IN THE CHURCH

While she may have scrupled to take the title of supreme head and adopted instead that of supreme governor, in practical matters Elizabeth always presumed that she possessed ultimate control over the church. Again in practice, she does not seem to have made any distinction between jurisdictional matters and matters of faith and doctrine which defenders of the royal supremacy so carefully distinguished in theory. There can be no doubt that she took a personal interest in her powers over the church, she perhaps influenced the development of the established church more than any subsequent monarch, and yet her interest was curiously dilatory and spasmodic. So long as the church appeared quiescent and to be inculcating the habit of obedience among her subjects, the queen tended to allow ecclesiastics considerable freedom to rule the church in their own way; the moment, however, anything was done which offended her susceptibilities or seemed to infringe her prerogative she did not hesitate to intervene in person.

During the period between the passing of the acts of supremacy and uniformity to which the queen gave her assent on May 8, 1559, and the consecration of Matthew Parker as archbishop of Canterbury on December 17, 1559, no formally instituted Protestant episcopate existed, and the queen had no choice but to appear openly as the supreme governor of the church. The royal Injunctions of 1559 which she issued on her own authority to both the clergy and the laity show that when forced by the occasion the queen believed herself to be fully empowered to pronounce in ecclesiastical matters (Doc. 28). By the Injunctions the government intended to plant 'true religion' in England; it instructed the clergy on the necessity for preaching, on the form in which to conduct services, on the books to provide in their parish churches, how to behave, and even on the studies they were to pursue if under the degree of M.A. All clergy had both to recognize and teach that the queen in England was supreme in both civil and ecclesiastical causes. These Injunctions, which provided a standard of discipline which lasted for the whole of the reign were not in fact particularly novel. The injunctions up to and including number xxviii follow the Injunctions of Edward VI of 1547 with a few significant deviations.[1] Injunction xxix indicates the degree to which the government saw the clergy now as beholden to the state in all aspects of life: it grudgingly permitted the clergy to marry, but only after prospective clergy wives had been approved by the bishop of the diocese and by local justices of the peace; the archbishop himself had the oversight of the future wives of bishops. The Injunctions reveal the extent of lay penetration into ecclesiastical affairs: at least at this stage in her reign the queen made no attempt to work with her ecclesiastics alone; she needed lay cooperation, as the subsequent royal visitation further emphasized.

[1] See H. Gee, *The Elizabethan Clergy and the Settlement of Religion 1558–1564*, Oxford, 1898, pp. 46–65, where both sets of Injunctions are compared.

The Injunctions of 1559 together with the royal visitation of the same year illustrate how the monarch had taken over the jurisdictional powers previously belonged to the pope.[1] The main purpose of the visitation was to tender the oath of supremacy to the clergy and to impose both the Prayer Book and the royal Injunctions throughout England. For this purpose the government divided the country into several districts and assigned each district particular sets of visitors: in every commission the laity seem to have outnumbered the ecclesiastics, though it may well be that the clergy carried out the bulk of the work. In the north, for which the visitors' report survives, although the commission named fourteen men as visitors, most of the work seems to have fallen on Sir Thomas Gargrave, vice president of the Council in the North, Sir Henry Gates, Henry Harvey, D.D. and the Marian exile and future bishop, Edwin Sandys; and of these four, Sandys and Harvey seem to have been the most energetic. They began work on August 22, 1559, and ended their visitation late in October. In the south other commissioners carried out similar visitations at exactly the same time. Jewel wrote to Peter Martyr on August 1st that he was about to set out on 'a long and troublesome commission for the establishment of religion through Reading, Abingdon, Gloucester, Bristol, Bath, Wells, Exeter, Cornwall, Dorset and Salisbury'. Back in London by November 'with a body worn out by a most fatiguing journey', he reported that they had deprived popish priests from their offices. He expressed particular concern over the 'wilderness of superstition' which 'had sprung up in the darkness of the Marian times' and implied that he and his fellow commissioners had cast out the 'votive relics of saints, nails with which the infatuated people dreamed that Christ had been pierced, and I know not what small fragments of the sacred cross' which they had found all over the area.[2] The zeal her commissioners displayed in extirpating relics of popery exceeded the queen's intentions: for the sake of social order she probably wanted the common people to be disturbed as little as possible. Herein lay Elizabeth's difficulty: at this period in her reign she just had not the ecclesiastics who could understand and execute her policy. The exiles, her allies against Rome, thought of nothing less than the establishment of the form of Protestantism which they had experienced on the continent. With the consecration of Parker, however, the queen secured at the head of her episcopate a man more attuned to her own way of thinking. From the beginning of 1560, normal episcopal administration could

---

[1] Gee, *Elizabethan Clergy*, pp. 41–130. H. N. Birt, *The Elizabethan Religious Settlement*, 1907, pp. 120–252.

[2] *Zurich Letters*, I, nos XVI, XIX.

be resumed, and from this time onwards the queen invariably worked through her bishops and normally refrained from openly acting in ecclesiastical matters upon her royal prerogative. Yet this apparent withdrawal behind her bishops by no means signifies that from 1560 the queen no longer personally intervened in ecclesiastical affairs.

Elizabeth's private religious opinions seem to have been those of a conservative Protestant. If she had been free to choose she might perhaps have favoured the creation of a Lutheran church in England, but no one form of religious orthodoxy seems to have appealed to her independent way of thinking. She had firm predilections of her own and never felt confined to follow the teaching of any Protestant leader. Prejudice and policy combined in her actions. Whereas her churchmen kept their eyes fixed on the state of the English church and in their single-mindedness demanded reform, they frequently failed to grasp the fact that the queen could never disregard the general European political situation. This held especially true for Elizabeth during the first decade of her reign when the country was particularly weak and in need of continental allies. What to some of her zealous ecclesiastics seemed to be almost inexplicable acts, wilfully hindering the reformation of the church, made far more sense in the wider European context.[1]

In the matter of the exact nature of rites and ceremonies to be retained in the English church, royal prejudices coincided with the need to conciliate foreign powers. In 1559 the royal visitors, probably contrary to the queen's wishes, had been busily casting out all traces of Rome from the churches they inspected. During the ensuing winter the queen insisted that the crucifix, particularly offensive to zealous Protestants, should remain in her own chapel and provoked an immediate crisis with her newly consecrated bishops. 'This controversy about the crucifix is now at its height,' Jewel informed Martyr on February 4, 1560. 'Whatever be the result I will write to you more at length when the disputation is over; for the controversy is as yet undecided; yet, as far as I can conjecture, I shall not again write to you as a bishop. For matters are come to that pass that either the crosses of silver and tin, which we have everywhere broken in pieces, must be restored, or our bishoprics relinquished.'[2] Sandys, three months later, wrote even more outspokenly about the nature of the clash between the supreme governor and her episcopate:

'The queen's majesty considered it not contrary to the word of God, nay, rather for the advantage of the church, that the image of

---

[1] Collinson, *Puritan Movement*, p. 29. For a radically different interpretation see Haugaard, *Elizabeth and the English Reformation*.

[2] *Zurich Letters*, I, no. XXIX.

Christ crucified, together with Mary and John, should be placed, as heretofore, in some conspicuous part of the church, where they might more readily be seen by all the people. Some of us thought far otherwise, and more especially as all images of every kind were at our last visitation not only taken down, but also burnt, and that too by public authority: and because the ignorant and superstitious multitude are in the habit of paying adoration to this idol above all others. As to myself, because I was rather vehement in this matter, and could by no means consent that an occasion of stumbling should be afforded to the church of Christ, I was very near being deposed from my office, and incurring the displeasure of the queen. But God, in whose hands are the hearts of kings, gave us tranquility instead of a tempest, and delivered the church of England from stumbling blocks of this kind: only the popish vestments remain in our church, I mean the copes: which, however, we hope will not last very long.'[1]

The queen had decided to compromise: she kept the crucifix in her own chapel but realized that, in the face of her bishops' hostility, Catholic images could not be restored in parish churches. Nevertheless, the royal stand brought favourable foreign reactions for which the queen must have hoped: Throckmorton reported from France that the Guise 'made their advantage of the cross and candles in your chapel, saying you were not yet resolved of what religion you should be.'[2] Until at least the papal excommunication of 1570 Elizabeth could continue to let foreign Catholics think that she was not irretrievably committed to Protestantism, much to the distress of her Protestant ecclesiastics.

The queen appreciated Catholic ceremonial: its retention in the royal chapel and to a much more limited extent, in cathedrals may also have impressed some Catholic foreign visitors in the earlier part of the reign. Her attitude to the marriage of the clergy, however, can scarcely be justified by pleading similar motives of interest of state. In her first Parliament she refused to allow a Commons' bill for the reviving of the Edwardian act for the marriage of priests to go forward. As Sandys remarked to Parker, the queen would wink at the practice, but not establish it by law: this would have the affect of bastardizing their children (Doc. 8). In fact, the royal Injunctions of 1559 went rather further than this and explicitly permitted the clergy to marry, provided the bishop and neighbouring gentry first approved their prospective wives, but the queen never overcame her dislike of married clergy and proceeded to try to modify the concession very soon after granting it. Having heard of the offence given by the

[1] *Zurich Letters*, I, no. XXXI.
[2] Quoted in Collinson, *Puritan Movement*, p. 35.

presence of wives, children and their nurses, in 1561 she issued another injunction forbidding any cleric to live with his wife and family in any college or cathedral close (Doc. 30). In addition, she also spoke so slightingly of clerical marriage to Parker that he feared she might be about to prohibit it entirely. Yet, as Parker unhappily reminded Cecil, clerical marriage was fully in accord with the gospel of Christ and the practices of the early church (Doc. 31). Again the queen had provoked a crisis with her bishops who tried so hard to serve her in all obedience. Richard Cox in particular objected to married clergy being excluded from cathedral closes.

'In cathedral churches ye know the dean and prebendaries have large and several houses, one distant from another, and if their wives be driven out, I suppose ye shall seldom find in most of the churches either dean or prebendary resi[d]ent there.... There is but one prebendary continually dwelling with his family in Ely church. Turn him out, doves and owls may dwell there for any continual housekeeping.'[1]

As in the dispute over the crucifix the queen had to modify her demands: the ban on married clergy in university colleges remained, but she allowed married clergy to continue living in cathedral closes. Yet although the objections of committed Protestants proved too strong to permit the queen to take any further steps against married clergy she never allowed any further moves during her reign actually to sanction the marriage of the clergy under the statute law. Despite the eagerness of the clergy and the zealous Protestant laity for parliamentary legislation, no act reviving the Edwardian law in favour of married priests could gain the royal assent while Elizabeth remained queen. Not until 1604 did the first Parliament of James I officially permit clerical marriage.

The queen's desire for a decorous uniformity within the English church again lay behind the Vestiarian Controversy, although whether the queen herself actually caused the outbreak of the troubles in 1565 is more disputable.[2] Almost certainly the queen had had the clause inserted in the act of uniformity that 'such ornaments of the church and of the ministers thereof shall be retained and be in use, as was in the church of England, by authority of Parliament, in the second year of the reign of King Edward the Sixth...'. The reformers had not wanted it, and indeed Sandys thought that the former exiles would not have to wear vestments, 'but that they may remain for the queen' (Doc. 8). In practice during the early years of

---

[1] *Parker Correspondence*, no. CIX.

[2] Strype, *Annals*, I, 1725, pp. 459–463. Strype, *Parker*, 1711, pp. 151–173, 211–220. Collinson, *Puritan Movement*, pp. 69–70.

the reign most bishops had realized they could not enforce this rubric, partly because of the destruction of vestments during the royal visitation and partly because of general Protestant hostility to any form of clerical dress suggesting continuity with the Roman church. In consequence considerable diversity of practice resulted, and the more extreme Protestants came to object even to the surplice. There is no doubt that deviations from uniformity offended the queen and that the letter of January 25, 1565, echoed her sentiments in stating that 'variety, contention and vain love of singularity, either in our ministers or in the people, must needs provoke the displeasure of Almighty God, and be to us, having the burden of government, discomfortable, heavy and troublesome'.[1] Yet the letter itself may well have been instigated by Parker, not the queen, for when he was drafting it Cecil told the archbishop that the queen would be likely to be angry when she discovered there was such need of reformation. The letter proved not to be sufficiently authoritative for Elizabeth who altered the draft to command the bishops 'to use all expedition' (instead of 'good discretion') that 'hereafter we be not occasioned, for lack of your diligence, to provide such further remedy, by some other sharp proceedings, as shall percase not be easy to be borne by such as shall be disordered . . .' (Doc. 32).

The peremptory note of this letter precisely conveys the queen's intention that her wishes should be observed in the church. It also illustrates the weakness of the bishops at this time. Parker had no confidence at all that he would be obeyed unless he could show royal authority for his actions.[2] Yet having issued this public rebuke to the bishops for not having enforced uniformity the queen left them alone to shoulder the ensuing unpopularity when they attempted to make the nonconformist clergy wear the surplice. She would not even allow Parker's Advertisements, which prescribed the wearing of the surplice at all services, though entirely in accord with her inclinations, to go out with her formal authorization in March 1566. Elizabeth never showed much understanding of the practical difficulties of her bishops nor much sympathy for them in their labours, and, though she may have expected the laity to respect the clergy, she never concealed the fact that she believed them to be first and foremost the servants of the crown.

The queen's contempt for clerical scruples is nowhere more clearly revealed than in her treatment of Grindal for his refusal to prohibit the prophesyings. She had convinced herself that large gatherings of 'the vulgar sort of people' could only lead to political unrest and

[1] *Parker Correspondence*, no. CLXIX.
[2] *Parker Correspondence*, no. CLXXV.

paid not the slightest attention to Grindal's plea that the exercises, reformed and under strict episcopal supervision, were indispensable for improving the education of the clergy. When Grindal failed to take action she issued her command to ban the prophesyings direct to all the individual bishops in the province of Canterbury with the scarcely veiled threat that, if they also refused to obey, 'we be not forced to make some example or reformation of you according to your deserts' (Doc. 33). In this instance the queen in effect reverted to the type of supremacy she had known and exercised in the first year of her reign: she was content to work through her bishops only so long as they carried out her orders to the full. If her archbishop did not in every respect comply with her intentions, she disregarded him completely. Despite their personal respect for Grindal and for his principles, which many of them shared, the bishops of the southern province very significantly obeyed the queen's command.

When need arose the queen felt no diffidence over intervening directly in the matter of faith and doctrine, the sphere in particular where Grindal thought she had most need first to consult with her divines (Doc. 25). Normally the queen made her incursions into matters of faith to prevent the imposition of precise formularies and so to avoid controversy within the church: nevertheless, this was an exercise of royal power at which ecclesiastics were the most likely to cavil. It seems that ambiguities remained in the 1559 settlement because the queen wished them to be there. The Marian exiles and the radical Protestant minority in the House of Commons in 1559 wanted the country to adopt the 1552 Prayer Book of Edward VI or a more Protestant version of it. The queen probably only consented to the 1559 Book when sentences from the 1549 Book had been included which would allow of belief in the real presence at the eucharist, the black rubric had been dropped which denied transubstantiation, and hostile references to the bishop of Rome excised. She continued to refuse to permit a very precise definition of doctrine throughout her reign.

In 1563 Convocation attempted to provide a doctrinal formulary for the established church, and Parker went to great pains to prepare for discussions based on the Edwardian articles of religion. These articles were revised and emerged as the Thirty-nine Articles with the full approval of Convocation. The article on the eucharist, however, specifically denied the real presence and would have been offensive not only to Catholics but also to Lutherans. Since any definition of doctrine at this time would have been politically inconvenient the queen ordered the article on the eucharist to be omitted when the other articles of religion were published. In 1566 she would not allow the articles of religion to be confirmed by act of Parliament in spite of the petition from the archbishop of Canterbury and thirteen other bishops that they should be given parliamentary authorization (Doc. 13). By 1571 political conditions had changed considerably: the excommunication of the queen made any particular consideration of Catholic sensibilities futile, and she then permitted the Thirty-nine Articles to be published in full and to be confirmed by Parliament. The queen had been forced to recognize the opinion that not only the jurisdiction within the church, but also the doctrine of the church, should be formally allowed by Parliament.

Until her death Elizabeth continued to supervise any form of theological speculation which might lead to unrest within the church. She did not hesitate to intervene in Cambridge in 1595 and over-rule the agreement which her archbishop had just achieved.[1] Baro, a Frenchman who had once studied under Calvin, had for some time in Cambridge been questioning the high Calvinist teaching on pre-destination, and to the dismay of the Puritan heads of houses he seemed in the 1590s to be recruiting support among some of the younger members of the university. The heads complained to Whit-gift about the outrageous behaviour of Barrett, a particularly rash adherent of Baro, and to define their position and also what they considered to be that of the established church, they drew up a sum-mary of the orthodox Calvinist doctrine of predestination. Whitgift modified their definitions somewhat and then gave the articles his full personal approval (Doc. 38). No sooner had he done so than the queen repudiated his action and forbade the promulgation of the articles in the university (Doc. 39). Whitgift could do nothing except comply with the royal directive (Doc. 40). While acknowledging that the articles were 'undoubtedly true and not be denied of any sound divine', and maintaining, almost certainly wrongly, that the queen her-self was 'persuaded of the truth of the propositions', he somewhat lamely passed on the royal command to the dons to refrain from controversy. Elizabeth may well have acted in the interests of the peace of the church: that she felt no reserve about publicly humiliating Whitgift, the archbishop with whom she appeared to be in most sym-pathy, provides yet another instance of her insensitivity towards her clergy.

Just as the queen without apology overrode the pronouncements of her leading ecclesiastics even on matters of doctrine so she never at any time in her reign showed any particular respect for the estate of the church in general, even though she must have realized that the church provided the most loyal defenders of the monarchy she

[1] H. C. Porter, *Reformation and Reaction in Tudor Cambridge*, Cambridge, 1958, pp. 364-375.

possessed. When she interfered in doctrinal matters her supporters could with some justification argue that she had the greater good of the church at heart, but in her treatment of ecclesiastical revenues not even her most devoted admirers could maintain that she acted as a nursing mother to the church. Already by 1558 a massive amount of church land had been transferred from the clergy to the laity: between 1536 and 1540 the crown had acquired all the monastic property and with this the right of presenting to about two-fifths of all benefices in England; under Edward VI the government confiscated the properties of all chantries and also made some inroads into episcopal lands. The first fruits which all except the poorest clergy paid on their institution, and the tenths they paid annually on the assessed value of their benefices, brought in over £40,000 a year to the crown. At her accession Elizabeth seemed determined to continue this economic exploitation. Her poverty probably made some reliance upon ecclesiastical income inevitable, but the degree to which she subjected the church to spoliation both by herself and by her servants indicates again her lack of real concern for the church's welfare.[1]

The act of 1559 relating to bishops' lands set the precedent for the royal treatment of ecclesiastical revenues for the whole of the reign. By this act Parliament empowered Elizabeth when any bishopric fell vacant to exchange episcopal lands for royal property of nominally the same value: in practice the queen intended to exchange impropriate tithes, difficult to collect and unlikely to appreciate much in value, for under rated episcopal manors. Churchmen had no illusions about the disadvantageous implications of these exchanges, and, weak as their position was, in October 1559 Parker and other bishops elect addressed a petition to the queen (Doc. 29). First they attempted to persuade her to forgo the exchanges all together, and offered in compensation an annual pension of 1,000 marks. If she determined upon the exchanges despite this proposed gift they asked that there should be some safeguard of the rights of the incumbents of impropriate rectories, and that the exchanges should prejudice the church as little as possible. In 1559 the church was in an exceptionally vulnerable state: as one by one the surviving Marian bishops resigned their sees all the bishoprics came into royal possession, and the queen made agreement to an unfavourable exchange of lands the condition of the next bishop's appointment. James Pilkington could not overcome his scruples concerning the exchange of lands belonging to the see of Winchester, so the queen passed him over for this bishopric and chose a more amenable candidate. The bishops elect had no weapon they could use against the crown. Cox in despair appealed to the queen's better nature and to the verdict of

[1] C. Hill, *The Economic Problems of the Church*, Oxford, 1956, ch. I.

history; in a private letter he besought Elizabeth 'that it might stand with your highness' pleasure to command your officers not to proceed any further in the exchange appertaining to your grace's bishoprics, which will be as noble and as famous an act as the like hath seldom been seen'. Bishops had a particular objection to receiving impropriate tithes in compensation for their confiscated lands: 'it will be unto us a grievous burden to take benefices impropered because we are persuaded in conscience that the parishes ought to enjoy them in such sort, and for such godly end, as they were appointed for at the beginning'.[1] All the protests availed nothing. The queen determined to exercise her rights and appointed commissioners to survey vacant bishoprics: in the meantime episcopal revenues continued to be diverted to the Exchequer.[2] Whenever later in the reign a bishopric became vacant the incoming bishop could expect to be faced with a demand for an exchange of lands either by the queen or, by her express permission, by one of her servants. Normally these exchanges imposed a severe and permanent financial loss upon the bishopric, although very occasionally an exchange could bring incidental and unintentional advantages. Dr Owen in his study of the diocese of London showed that largely through the amount of patronage which came to the bishop in connection with impropriate rectories, which the crown had exchanged for episcopal lands, Bishop Aylmer succeeded in imposing a surprising degree of conformity on the parish clergy of the city of London.[3]

The exploitation of ecclesiastical property begun in 1559 continued with scarcely any remission, or any consideration for the political position of the church, until the queen's death. Dr Hill has demonstrated in considerable detail that Elizabeth regarded episcopal lands as her father had regarded monastic lands, as a source from which pensions could be paid to her servants and from which other favours could be bestowed.[4] Richard Cox of Ely suffered in a particularly spectacular way: already of venerable age in the 1570s he endured little short of persecution at the hands of Roger Lord North and Sir Christopher Hatton. Hatton began the harrying in 1575: he wanted a long lease on advantageous terms of the bishop's house in Holborn, but Cox refused to grant one, so Hatton obtained a letter from the queen ordering him to alienate the house. The bishop replied that his conscience would not permit him to grant away the property of the see. In a similar way North tried to get possession of Somer-

[1] Strype, *Annals*, I, 1725, pp. 98–99.

[2] *Zurich Letters*, I, no. XXIV.

[3] H. G. Owen, 'London Parish Clergy in the Reign of Elizabeth I', Unpublished London Ph. D. thesis, 1957.

[4] Hill, *Economic Problems*, ch. II.

sham, one of the best manors of the bishopric, and, because Cox would not yield it to him, promptly tried to stir up the queen against him. Cox did not flinch from suggesting that the queen came near to committing the sin of sacrilege by permitting such plundering of the church. 'For Christ Jesus sake', he implored, 'be ye a most pious nurse, favourer and defender of your clergy, in this wicked and atheistical age.' He drew up a paper of reasons against alienating the goods of the church: North retaliated with a list of malpractices he alleged Cox had fallen into as a landlord, and a long lawsuit ensued. The troubles started all over again in 1579, and Cox petitioned to be allowed to resign, but, like Grindal, he died before the elaborate machinery involved in a bishop's resignation had been completed. All his sufferings, Strype maintained, had been caused because of his zeal to preserve his episcopal property entire for his successor. The crown had its revenge after his death: from 1581 until 1599 Elizabeth kept the see of Ely vacant and its revenues went into the Exchequer.[1]

Considerably before 1581 proposals had been made that certain bishoprics should be kept permanently vacant for the benefit of the crown's finances. When Parker died in 1575 a scheme was devised, though not carried through, for translating all the bishops in England and so obtaining a windfall of first fruits for the Treasury. The author of the scheme entitled it 'a note how the bishoprics in England may be transferred without any just cause of much offence to the bishops, November 1575'. He considered that more than £20,000 could be raised for the crown, and proposed that the sees of Chester, worth £420 a year, and Rochester, £360 a year, should never again be filled and their revenues be diverted to the queen.[2] Other royal servants, while making a token acknowledgement of royal needs, put their own penury before the crown's. Leicester, having failed to get property belonging to the church of Southwell, tried in 1587 to persuade the queen to confiscate lands from the vacant sees of Durham, Ely, Oxford and Bristol to the value of £2,000 a year, giving impropriations in return. He then asked the queen to grant him half of these underrated episcopal estates in exchange for lands of his own nominally also worth £1,000. His death, however, in the following year put an end to the plan. As Archbishop Sandys remarked, when an attempt was made in 1588 to get him to lease York House in London, 'These be marvellous times. The patrimony of the church is laid open, as a prey, unto all the world.'[3] Perhaps Sir John Puckering in about 1594

[1] Strype, *Annals*, II, 1725, pp. 359–370, 579–584.
[2] Strype, *Annals*, II, pp. 387–388.
[3] Strype, *Annals*, III, pp. 461–469, 550–551.

thought out the most ingenious scheme of all for exploiting ecclesiastical revenues. He wanted a lease of lands from the see of Ely which could not be made while there was no bishop, so he suggested that the queen should at last end the vacancy and appoint one of the 'eldest bishops'; he considered the bishop of Norwich who was already eighty-eight years old would be especially suitable. 'It may perchance be objected that your majesty, having now the revenue of the bishopric, doth forgo the same by making of a bishop. Answer, your majesty by giving the bishopric shall have the first fruits, which is one year's profits, and the tenths and subsidies besides, which you cannot have while the bishopric remains in your majesty's hands.' In addition, with a new bishop of such great age the lands of the see would be certain to revert to the crown within a very short time.[1]

These are mere isolated examples of attempts to obtain ecclesiastical revenues in which all ranks of the laity, from the queen downwards, indulged given a favourable opportunity. Dr Hill has also calculated that the clergy paid proportionately far more to the crown in direct taxation than did the laity.[2] On top of the first fruits and tenths they also paid subsidies, their benefices being rated at 6s in the pound on the valuation given in the *Valor Ecclesiasticus*. Whitgift did succeed in preventing a revaluation of clerical incomes which had been proposed in 1585 to take account of the price rise, but this gave the clergy only a little relief.[3] They still remained liable to contribute to benevolences and forced loans. Bishop Cooper in 1589 summed up the situation when he said that the bishops and other clergy of England did not 'grudge or murmur to have their lands and livings to be tributary to the prince, and subject to all taxes and services, that by the laws of this realm may be, either to the maintenance of her person, or to the defence of our country' (Doc. 14). With rather less resignation five years later Bishop Wickham told the queen that if the temporalities of the bishops continued to be exploited in the next thirty years to the extent to which they had been exploited in the past thirty, then hardly any see would have sufficient revenues to keep its cathedral in repair. Still Elizabeth paid little heed to the warnings that by weakening the church she indirectly weakened the state. James I, however, realized where the support for the monarchy lay and in the first year of his reign gave assent to an act which forbade archbishops and bishops to alienate the lands of their sees even to the crown.

Elizabeth's failure to curb the plunder of the church by the laity,

---

[1] Strype, *Annals*, IV, pp. 246–248.
[2] Hill, *Economic Problems*, pp. 188–195.
[3] Strype, *Whitgift*, 1718, pp. 232–233.

indeed her very encouragement of the practice by her own example, enormously increased the influence of the laity over the church, an achievement in the political field she always strove to prevent. Merely by allowing the sale of impropriations to her subjects to continue at an ever accelerating rate, by the end of her reign she had permitted the laity to gain possession of an amount of patronage which far exceeded that remaining to the clergy. In 1604 a committee of bishops asserted that the laity, including the crown, controlled five-sixths of the benefices in England, but by this date the crown had only a minor share in this patronage: Elizabeth had granted away the impropriate tithes, which frequently included the right of presentation, of over 2,200 parishes.[1] Because of her necessity in the economic sphere, she never pretended that the revenues of the church should be confined to ecclesiastics alone. But having unintentionally encouraged the laity to encroach upon the clergy's rights in one area, she found she could not exclude their influence in another. Even in the matter of ecclesiastical jurisdiction, where if anywhere the queen might have hoped to govern her church exclusively through her ecclesiastics, Elizabeth had been forced, by the end of her life, tacitly to recognize, and to a limited extent submit to, the growing power of lay interests.

The repudiation of the authority of the pope by the act of supremacy placed the crown again at the apex of the series of ecclesiastical courts just as it had always been at the apex of the secular courts, and in theory very considerably enhanced the royal prerogative. The old medieval courts which had grown up to supervise the clergy, adjudicate between the clergy and the laity, and to judge the laity in certain aspects of religion and morals, survived the changes of the Reformation in England unscathed apart from the important substitution of the monarch for the pope as the final overlord. The law of these courts remained the medieval canon law, when applicable, adapted by parliamentary statute. Since, however, the only penalties these courts could impose were the various degrees of excommunication, their general effectiveness seems to have been declining in the second half of the sixteenth century, and the queen and the laity in consequence seem to have been content to allow this ancient form of jurisdiction to continue with remarkably little interference. Conscientious Protestants, admittedly, frequently objected to the abuse of excommunication by these courts, and a considerable number of the laity wanted the archdeacon's and bishop's courts to be transformed into a more efficient method of disciplining the lower orders, but on the

[1] Hill, *Economic Troubles*, pp. 141, 145.

whole ecclesiastical lawyers continued to hold these courts with little disturbance, if not with great success.[1]

Far more controversial, because far more powerful, were the series of prerogative ecclesiastical courts which developed in England during Elizabeth's reign. The act of supremacy for the first time expressly allowed the monarch to delegate to commissioners the ecclesiastical jurisdiction inherent in the prerogative of the crown (Doc. 6). It enjoined upon these commissioners the punishment of crimes within the ecclesiastical law, the settlement of ecclesiastical disputes and the enforcement of uniformity. In 1559 the queen issued the first ecclesiastical commission of the reign to Matthew Parker, archbishop of Canterbury elect, Edmund Grindal, nominated bishop of London, Sir Francis Knollys, Sir Ambrose Cave, Sir Anthony Cooke, Sir Thomas Smith, William Bill (the royal almoner and an ecclesiastic), Walter Haddon and Thomas Sackford, masters of requests, four lay serjeants at law, three doctors of law and five other gentlemen: the laymen enjoyed a clear numerical majority over the clergy. The commission gave them powers to fine and imprison and assigned them a registrar to keep a record of all 'acts, decrees and proceedings' and to certify all fines taken into the Exchequer. From this type of commission the Court of High Commission grew.[2]

R. G. Usher's somewhat tentative thesis that the court of High Commission for the southern province gradually evolved during the first two decades of Elizabeth's reign until it had become a fully effective permanent court by about 1580 probably now stands in need of modification. The rediscovery of the act books for the northern High Commission makes it quite certain that the High Commission sat as a formal court in York from very soon after Elizabeth's accession. The first entry in the first surviving act book is dated February 27, 1562, but since it refers back to cases begun in previous years there must have been at least one earlier book. If, therefore, a formal prerogative ecclesiastical court existed at York by 1562 it seems reasonable to suggest that a similar development had taken place at approximately the same time in the southern province, but because of the destruction of the High Commision records in the south this can be no more than a supposition. Nevertheless, Usher may still be correct in associating a further development in the authority of the southern High Commission court with the coming to power of Whitgift, Aylmer and Bancroft towards the end of Grindal's archiepiscop-

---

[1] Elton, *Tudor Constitution*, pp. 214–216. F. D. Price, 'The Abuses of Excommunication and the Decline of Ecclesiastical Discipline under Queen Elizabeth', *English Historical Review*, LVII, 1942, pp. 106–115.

[2] Elton, *Tudor Constitution*, pp. 221–225.

ate: in their attempts to suppress Puritanism these clerics extended to the full the potentialities of the court.[1]

The northern High Commission court, in comparison, never seems to have been used as a weapon against Puritans, whatever may have been the queen's intention. With the exception of the two prebendaries deprived in Durham about 1567 the northern High Commission displaced no minister willing to work within the settlement until the Laudian Archbishop Neile succeeded Toby Matthew in 1628. During the Elizabethan period Catholic recusancy occupied the court almost to the entire exclusion of Puritanism. Until the 1581 act made conversion to Rome a treasonable offence and also provided for the fining of recusants in common law courts, the courts of High Commission were the only courts which could fine and imprison recusants. In the north, particularly after the rebellion of 1569, the court concentrated on hearing cases of recusancy. The summary of one particular sitting in July 1580 illustrates the formal procedure of the court and incidentally reveals the interchangeability of membership between the northern High Commission, and the Council in the North, though invariably when the court of High Commission was in session the archbishop or his deputy presided, whereas when the Council in the North sat the lord president had charge of the proceedings (Doc. 34). Throughout Elizabeth's reign the majority of High Commissioners in the north were laymen: Dr Tyler had estimated that in 1561 just over half the members of the commission were laymen; by 1585 the majority had risen to almost two-thirds, but by 1596 the lay majority had fallen again to rather more than half. Lay participation markedly declined as the reign progressed: except for rare occasions the lord president did not attend sessions after 1581, although he had been a fairly diligent attender before then, and the cause of this must partly be attributed to the fact that major Catholic offenders could now be tried in the common law courts, while preliminary examinations of priests were held in the Council in the North itself.[2] By Elizabeth's death the northern court of High Commission had become little more than a routine ecclesiastical court, dominated by the clergy, an ancilliary court to the Council in the North.

The decline of the northern court of High Commission in comparison with the Council in the North was brought about at least partly by the lack of interest of the laity. Whether the fortunes of the

[1] R. G. Usher, *The Rise and Fall of High Commission*, Oxford, 1968 reprint, pp. xxvi–xxxiv, 64–90. P. Tyler, 'The Significance of the Ecclesiastical Commission at York', *Northern History*, II, 1967, pp. 27–44. P. Tyler, 'The Ecclesiastical Commission for the Province of York, 1561–1641', Unpublished Oxford D. Phil. thesis, 1965.

[2] C. Cross, *The Puritan Earl: the Life of Henry Hastings, Third Earl of Huntingdon, 1536–1595*, 1966, pp. 227–236.

southern court followed a similar pattern seems doubtful; rather, the southern High Commission court appears to have been at the height of its influence under the direction of Whitgift, yet even in connection with the premier ecclesiastical prerogative court in England the laity succeeded in curbing clerical ambitions. Whitgift used the southern court of High Commission as his main instrument to combat Puritanism and compel conformity. He certainly did not pioneer the use of the *ex officio* oath (at least from 1562 it had been regularly employed in the north), but he did employ it in a novel way in order to try to extract information from Puritan ministers which the ecclesiastical authorities could not otherwise obtain.[1] The Twenty-four Articles he drew up early in 1584 and submitted to a minister suspected of nonconformity only after he had taken the *ex officio* oath, if answered fully, would have caused the prisoner not only to incriminate himself but also his fellow suspects (Doc. 35). Burghley's protest against this mode of proceeding 'too much savouring of the Romish inquisition' typified the hostile reaction of the lay ruling class. He had already received representations from the nonconforming clergy, and Knollys and Beale, the Puritan lawyer, probably persuaded him to write the letter (Doc. 36). Lay councillors stood their ground in resisting any resurgence of clerical power. Burghley advised Whitgift on the need for 'the spirit of gentleness' rather than this 'canonical sifting of poor ministers', and however much Whitgift might defend his use of the oath, and compare the procedure of the court of High Commission with that of the prerogative civil courts (Doc. 37), since Hatton alone of the lay councillors supported him he eventually had little choice but to moderate his policy. After 1584 he took action only against the most radical of the nonconformists and left the moderate Puritans undisturbed.

The attack on the *ex officio* oath by no means ended in 1584. The Separatist Barrow absolutely refused to take the oath when brought before the High Commission in 1587, and his behaviour provided a precedent for Cartwright and the other Presbyterian ministers when they came to trial in 1591.[2] Cartwright and the other imprisoned ministers not only refused to take the oath, but gave reasoned objections why they did so:

'The oath offered in generally to answer to whatsoever shall be demanded we dare not yield unto, for fear of taking the name of God in vain, which we cannot avoid if we should take it, first because an oath should (as all other duties of the worship of God) be taken in faith, wherein the party is assured that his service is acceptable to

---

[1] Collinson, *Puritan Movement,* pp. 266–267, 270.

[2] Pearson, *Thomas Cartwright,* pp. 315–336.

God, being according to his will. But in this oath faith can have no
such assurance to please God, seeing we are denied to know the
matters before we swear, in the which the conscience can have no
stay whereon to rest, contrary to all the examples and precepts of
swearing in the scripture.'[1]

The anonymous author of a contemporary treatise on the *ex officio*
oath went on to elaborate in considerable detail the popish ante-
cedents of the oath and, taking his illustrations from Foxe, demonstrated how the godly from the time of Wyclif had been tormented
by their persecutors imposing upon them this antichristian oath.[2]
Cartwright's refusal of the oath blocked his trial, for the High
Commissioners would not hear his unsworn answers. They could have
kept him in prison until he consented to swear, or they could have
fined him for contempt, but they were effectively prevented from
securing a conviction. In fact Whitgift took the signal step of acknowledging the weakness of the clerical commissioners, when acting without the open support of the laity, and transferred the case entire from
the court of High Commission to the secular prerogative court of Star
Chamber. This one action by itself shows the limited success the queen
achieved in her formal policy of ruling the church independently
through her ecclesiastics alone. Without the co-operation of the laity
the government of the church could not continue.

II. LAY INTERVENTION IN THE CHURCH IN PARLIAMENT

At Westminster throughout the second part of the sixteenth century
the relationship between the supreme governor of the church and the
laity remained in the balance; neither side won the mastery over the
other. While on the one hand laymen managed to limit the freedom of
action of High Commissioners to whom the queen had assigned her
judicial powers over the church, so on the other hand the queen
almost invariably contrived after 1559 to restrain laymen whenever
they attempted to obtain a further reform of the church through Parliament. It may be because of the concessions Elizabeth had had to make
in 1559 in allowing the adoption of the second more radical Prayer
Book of Edward VI that she felt extremely sensitive to any further
move which could be construed as an encroachment upon her
ecclesiastical prerogative for the remainder of her reign. She never
subsequently officially authorized discussion of church affairs in
Parliament and unwaveringly maintained that the government of the
church was exclusively a matter for her and her clergy represented

[1] *Cartwrightiana*, p. 29.
[2] *Cartwrightiana*, pp. 30–46.

in Convocation. The godly gentlemen who formed a definable group in all Elizabeth's Parliaments, and until late in the 1590s included privy councillors among their number, could not or would not understand the queen's attitude. Because of the major part played by Parliament in establishing the church settlement in 1559 they continued to assume that inevitably further reform would also come through Parliament. Having tasted power they refused to surrender it and persisted in debating ecclesiastical affairs in Parliament after Parliament despite the prohibitions of the queen. They believed that since the English church included the English commonwealth its government concerned the whole nation, not merely the clerical estate. Erastianism and Protestant fervour combined to prevent the laity from conceding a new superiority to the clergy. The queen in practice failed to prevent religious matters being discussed in the Commons, but she succeeded in stopping any parliamentary legislation for a greater Protestant reformation of the church. The members of the Commons, in spite of continuous lobbying, gained no further formal control over religion, though they did achieve some minor concessions from Convocation.

The demand for the reformation of abuses within the established church became a constant theme running through all the Elizabethan Parliaments. Had the queen allowed Convocation to develop into an actively reforming body, as it showed signs of doing in 1563 when the lower house favourably received numerous petitions against popish ceremonies and an insufficiently Protestant Prayer Book, there is just a chance that the lay zealots might have been willing to relinquish the formal direction of the church to the clergy. As it was, the curbing of the active reformers in Convocation, symbolized by the defeat of the moderate reform proposals in the lower house in 1563, merely served to turn the attention of all the godly both lay and clerical more and more firmly to Parliament. The Parliament which sat from September 1566 until the beginning of January 1567 saw the first concerted attempt to secure moderate parliamentary reform of the church. A whole series of bills touching religion, the so-called alphabetical bills, were introduced into the Commons. Bill A asked that statutory confirmation be given to the Articles of Religion approved in the Convocation of 1563. It received two readings in the Commons, and in the Lords the bishops thoroughly approved of it, but the queen commanded that the measure should go no further. In spite of her hostility the bishops went on to petition her to allow the articles to be confirmed by Parliament (Doc. 13), thus further illustrating the community of interest between the Protestant laity and the higher clergy which was only gradually dissipated as the reign progressed. The other alphabetical bills, B, C, D, E, and F dealt with proposals for the improvement of the educational standards of the

clergy and with measures to prevent non-residence, corrupt presenta-
tions to benefices, simony and the payment of pensions from livings
to the disadvantage of the present incumbent. Although the Commons
tried holding up government measures until redress was granted they
made absolutely no progress with these bills.[1]

The conspicuous lack of success in 1567 in no way inhibited the
new Parliament of 1571 from continuing the agitation the previous
Parliament had begun. Sandys's sermon, delivered at the opening of
Parliament, in which he called for the purging of the church of 'all
false doctrine . . . all idolatry and superstition', only further stimulated
the zeal of the Protestant laymen already raised to a new intensity
by the recent papal excommunication of the queen. The government
stood in a weak position for it needed greater powers to deal with
Catholics but did not want, or at least the queen did not want,
Protestant reform. Sir Nicholas Bacon grasped the difficulty: he bade
the Commons 'consider first whether the ecclesiastical laws concerning the discipline of the church be sufficient or not; and if any want
shall be found, to supply the same', but at the same time reminded
his auditors, 'thereof the greatest care ought to depend of my lords
the bishops, to whom the execution thereof especially pertains, and
to whom the imperfections of the same is best known'. The members
immediately disregarded this warning and resumed consideration of
the alphabetical bills brought in in the previous Parliament, demanding that a committee be set up to confer with the bishops for reform
of the church. The bill which Walter Strickland exhibited for the alteration of the Prayer Book would have taken away the use of vestments
and the surplice, the cross at baptism, the ring at marriage, kneeling at communion, indeed all that the protagonists in the Vestiarian
Controversy had found most offensive. In spite of his personal sympathies Knollys had to remind the House that in discussing
ceremonies they infringed upon the royal prerogative. Tristram Pistor's
reaction, lamenting the fact that matters which touched all their souls
could not be freely spoken of, shows how the zealots totally failed to
understand the queen's view of her supremacy (Doc. 41). The even
more audacious attempt by Thomas Norton to get the Commons to
promote the Edwardian proposal for the reform of the antiquated canon
law, the *Reformatio legum*, encroached much more significantly on
the prerogative and again got nowhere. At the end of the session the
queen rebuked those who 'have showed themselves audacious, arrogant and presumptuous, calling her majesty's grants, and prerogatives also, into question, contrary to their duty'. She condemned them
'for their audacious, arrogant and presumptuous folly, thus by
frivolous and superfluous speech, spending the time and meddling

[1] Neale, *Elizabeth and her Parliaments*, I, pp. 129–176.

with matters neither pertaining unto them nor within the capacity of their understanding', and ordered that in future religious bills 'should first have been debated in the Convocation and by the bishops and not by them . . .'.[1] This Parliament gave confirmation to the Thirty-nine Articles, something of a concession by the crown, but scarcely a victory for the more radical members who had tried to achieve the enforcement of the doctrinal articles only, and so to secure protection for ministers with scruples over ceremonies. Already a break had come about between the more extreme radical members and the bishops: Wentworth did not refrain from telling Parker to his face that the Commons would not accept without discussion matters decided for them by the clergy, but no attack came on the theory of episcopacy. Had the reforms been allowed, the English church would have been thoroughly Protestant in its doctrine, discipline and form of worship, but it would have remained an episcopal church.[2]

In ecclesiastical matters the fourth Parliament of Elizabeth displayed no more circumspection than the third. In 1572 the bill concerning 'rites and ceremonies' which asked that the act of uniformity be enforced only against those suspected of indulging in popish practices and that preaching ministers, with the consent of their bishop, be permitted to omit parts of the Prayer Book and to use instead the form of service of the Dutch or French reformed church got as far as its third reading before Burghley demanded particulars of the bill and the queen sent word that no bills were to be accepted unless they had first been approved by the bishops. After this attempt to gain toleration for limited Protestant nonconformity came to nothing, the Presbyterian ministers, led by Field, appealed to the public at large with their *Admonition to the Parliament*. Perhaps frightened by the intemperance of this manifesto, the next session of this Parliament in 1576, though still as eager for the reform of abuses, acted in a way more likely to conciliate the queen and presented a petition to her, bringing to her notice the unlearnedness of the clergy, the abuse of the penalty of excommunication, and the problem of non-residence. The queen responded much more favourably to a petition rather than to a bill, and 'alloweth well that her subjects, being aggrieved therewith, have in such sort and discreet manner both opened their griefs and remitted them to be reformed by her majesty'. She promised that the clergy would take action (Doc. 42). Since this way of proceeding had proved acceptable to the crown, this same Parliament at its next session in 1581 employed it again and petitioned for further

---

[1] Neale, *Parliaments*, I, pp. 177–240.
[2] Collinson, *Puritan Movement*, pp. 116–118.

reforms over the admission of insufficient men to benefices, excommunication and the conduct of ecclesiastical courts in general, and the issue of dispensations for non-residence, pluralism, and marriage without bans. Again the queen promised redress, condemning her clergy for slackness in no uncertain terms (Doc. 43). Some members of Parliament wanted the parish to have the right to protest against an uncongenial incumbent within twenty days of his institution; for ordinations to be public; for the bishop to act with the advice of his dean and chapter or of six learned preachers of the diocese. The gentry were striving for further influence over the church to modify episcopacy but not to destroy it altogether.[1]

Through the ostensibly more revolutionary Parliaments of the 1580s and the more submissive Parliaments of the last decade of the reign, members proposed the same measures for the reform of the church with an almost monotonous regularity. On the suggestion of Mildmay, the Commons in 1584 set up a committee to consider ecclesiastical grievances and then sent a petition to the Lords asking for the removal of unlearned ministers, that no proceedings be taken against ministers for omitting part of the Prayer Book, that no *ex officio* oath be tendered to them, and that exercises be permitted to encourage the learning of the clergy. Whitgift replied curtly to the petition and greatly offended the members by his 'cardinal and metropolitical answer'. His attempt to impose his articles upon the clergy by means of the extended use of the court of High Commission and his renewed enthusiasm for uniformity seemed to threaten the laity with a fresh growth of clerical power: the Commons reacted by bringing in a bill to compel the bishops to swear allegiance to the queen and forbidding them to swear canonical obedience to their metropolitan. Together with another bill nominally against the taking of excessive fees in ecclesiastical courts which would have required bishops to make visitations in person and to investigate only 'just causes complained of', this aimed at controlling the church by the common and statute law. Another Commons bill for the reformation of the statute made 13 Elizabeth for the reformation of ministers of the church provided for a body of twelve laymen to test the efficiency of a minister. When he spoke in support of this bill Fleetwood reminded the House what laymen had been permitted to do on the royal visitation of 1559: then indeed they had sat in judgement on the clergy. At the end of the session members brought in yet another bill on behalf of the godly deprived ministers who would subscribe to the doctrinal articles of religion. The pronounced anticlerical tone of the House caused Whitgift to plead with the queen

---

[1] Neale, *Parliaments*, I, pp. 241–312. Collinson, *Puritan Movement*, pp. 118–120, 162, 187.

not to hand over the church to the laity. She responded with another personal pronouncement at the end of the session that she would not tolerate the invasion by Parliament of her royal prerogative.[1]

In spite of Cope's attempt in 1587 to get a hearing for the radical bill and book, the great majority of members do not seem to have sympathized with the scheme to establish Presbyterianism: instead they still called for the earlier, relatively moderate plans for church reform and dared to set up a committee to consider the use of the *ex officio* oath and to confer on the provision of a better-educated clergy. Only the closing of Parliament could end this agitation.[2] In an effort to circumscribe parliamentary discussion in the next Parliament of 1589, the queen informed the Commons through Hatton that she was 'most fully and firmly settled in her conscience, by the word of God, that the estate and government of the church of England, as it now standeth in this reformation, may justly be compared to any church which hath been established in any Christian kingdom since the apostles' times; that both in form and doctrine it is agreeable with the scriptures, with the most ancient general councils, with the practice of the primitive church, and with the judgements of all the old learned fathers'.[3] The House, notwithstanding, again considered a bill against clerical non-residence and pluralism, another for encouraging a learned ministry and a third, for the confirmation of Magna Carta, which would have prevented the imprisonment of Protestant ministers without a common law warrant.

The deepening alliance between an autocratic monarch and an autocratic ecclesiastic (an alliance, however, in which the monarch never lost the initiative), together with the deaths between 1588 and 1598 of Leicester, Mildmay, Warwick, Walsingham and lastly Knollys, which deprived the gentry in Parliament of their main leadership among the crown servants, tended to curb the demand for ecclesiastical reform in Elizabeth's last three Parliaments. Nevertheless, there is no reason to suppose that the desire for moderate reform had abated. James Morice in 1593 gained much support for his attack on the proceedings of High Commission, and many members sympathized with his argument that the bishops were acting against the common law. Again in 1597 the ninth Parliament of the reign set up a committee to receive grievances touching ecclesiastical causes and produced a bill against the taking of excessive fees in ecclesiastical courts; some members even spoke of modifying the act of uniformity and the act of 1571 confirming the Thirty-nine Articles in favour of scrupulous

---

[1] Neale, *Elizabeth and her Parliaments*, II, pp. 13–101.

[2] Neale, *Parliaments*, II, pp. 103–191, 193, 239. Collinson, *Puritan Movement*, pp. 303–316.

[3] Quoted in Neale, *Parliaments*, II, p. 198.

ministers. The last Parliament of the reign considered bills brought
in by members against pluralism, for putting down commissaries'
courts and for the better keeping of the Sabbath, and although the
latter bill, divided to become a bill against Sunday fairs and a bill
against wilful absence from church on Sundays, failed by a narrow
margin to pass the House, yet the desire for further reform of the
church, and reform moreover partially supervised by the laity, still
persisted.[1] The continuing bills and petitions on behalf of the
deprived ministers, and against abuses remaining in the church
presented in the earlier Parliaments of James I prove that the
campaign of Whitgift and Bancroft to prohibit parliamentary discussion of religious matters had no lasting success.

The ultimately abortive attempt by members of Parliament to
obtain a further Protestant reformation of the English church has
been described as a largely unchanging movement, waxing in intensity in the 1580s, waning somewhat in the 1590s, but emerging essentially unaltered in the first decade of James' reign. This disregards
entirely the scheme which failed, first in 1584 and then in 1587, to
set up by parliamentary means a Presbyterian form of church government.[2] A group of Elizabethan ministers, inspired by Cartwright, led
by John Field from at least the time of Whitgift's elevation to Canterbury campaigned tirelessly for the establishment of Presbyterianism
first through Parliament, and then, parliamentary support falling
away, through local action until Field's death in 1588 and Bancroft's
exposure of the movement, resulting in the High Commission case,
broke the organization. Whether this clerical movement ever
received much informed lay support seems unlikely. As long as the
Presbyterians confined themselves to attacking abuses in the church
they carried those gentlemen with them who wanted a further purge
of popish ceremonies, who sympathized with their ministers deprived
by an episcopate obsessed by the idea of uniformity, or who merely
resented growing clerical pretensions. When, however, the Presbyterian platform could be demonstrated to be the substitution for one
form of clerical domination of another even more unqualified because
less subject to the royal supremacy then, at any rate in Parliament,
most of the gentry seem to have drawn back. Peter Turner, the son
of the radical dean of Wells, who first brought the bill and the
book before the Commons on December 14, 1584, received very
little support. Knollys, the ardent enthusiast for church reform and
the unceasing critic of clerical ambitions, seems to have taken the
initiative on this occasion and to have spoken against the House even

[1] Neale, *Parliaments*, II, pp. 241–323, 325–367, 369–432.
[2] Collinson, *Puritan Movement*, pp. 277–288, 303–316.

considering the measure. Turner probably only represented the extreme wing of the Puritan laity. The situation had altered somewhat in 1586. The Parliament which met then did indeed contain a nucleus of committed Presbyterian members, Anthony Cope, Job Throckmorton, Robert Bainbridge, Edward Lewknor, Ranulf Hurleston, who worked in closest collaboration with the Presbyterian ministers. The book which Cope at last got leave to introduce to the Commons on February 27, 1587, was the Geneva service book which he advocated substituting for the Book of Common Prayer: his bill called for the immediate revocation of all existing laws, statutes and ordinances defining the worship and government of the English church. The House never had a chance of hearing details of either measure from their sponsors, for the following day the queen confiscated both Cope's book and papers, and Turner's proposal from the previous Parliament. Not until May 4th did the House hear details of the contents of the bill and book from the royal servants Hatton, Egerton and Mildmay who enlightened members concerning the Presbyterian threat which they emphasized would destroy not only the royal prerogative in ecclesiastical matters but also lay rights to church patronage and impropriations. Their exposure of Presbyterianism does not appear to have deterred the lay advocates of moderate reform who, while remaining loyal to the dispossessed ministers and continuing to attack abuses, do not seem to have wished to abandon a modified form of episcopacy. Part of the antagonism felt towards ecclesiastics like Bancroft and Whitgift, and Hatton and his supporters at court, was caused by their unscrupulousness in branding all reformers, however mild, as Presbyterians.

Although for the understanding of Elizabethan history it is vital to distinguish between the apparently small group of lay Presbyterians and the far larger, more amorphous body of zealous Protestants who never abandoned the idea of a modified episcopal government, to the queen all laymen irrespective of motive who called so insistently in Parliament for the further reformation of the church potentially undermined her royal supremacy: as such she refused to tolerate them. She never relented from her belief that the 'fault finders with the order of the clergy' offered 'a slander to myself and the church, whose overruler God hath made me' (Doc. 44). After 1559, despite the virtually continuous lobbying, she never gave her consent to a Commons bill for the reformation of the church in a more Protestant direction. Nevertheless, because of the parliamentary agitation the queen did ultimately allow some reforms, but only through what she considered to be the proper constitutional channels, the bishops and Convocation. Until the death of Grindal, Convocation, though by its very nature conservative, does seem to have acted as an agency for the correction of glaring ecclesiastical abuses.[1] Grindal appears to have had every intention of reforming the church through Convocation, and in 1576 made a beginning when he secured the consent of Convocation to his proposals for the stricter examination of ordination candidates, for a fixed minimum age for deacons and priests and for ordinations to be performed in public. Convocation also approved the scheme of study for all ministers under the degree of M.A. which Grindal had earlier tried out in York. During his sequestration this reforming activity ceased, and this may have been partly responsible for the petition of members of Parliament for the correction of abuses which they addressed to the queen in 1581. The queen's threat to recalcitrant bishops (Doc. 43) seems to have been meant as more than a sop to the unruly laity. After Parliament had ended Elizabeth passed on the Commons' articles to Sandys who consulted with five other bishops, and they decided upon some reforms which they could grant with a good conscience. The queen herself refused to countenance any alteration of ecclesiastical law, but did approve of certain rather minor reforms that the bishops had agreed upon, and instructed them to enforce them.[2]

As archbishop of York, Sandys was nominally in control of the 1581 Convocation, but already Whitgift dominated the scene. When he succeeded Grindal at Canterbury two years later the mood of Convocation seems subtly to have changed. Under Grindal it had shown a genuine if moderate desire for reform: under Whitgift it represented rather the embattled clerical estate on the alert against the hostile laity. It gave the impression of granting reforms chiefly in order to circumvent the demands of the House of Commons. In 1584 Whitgift promised a Commons deputation complaining of ill-educated ministers, 'for the better enforcing of such unlearned ministers to study etc. we were purposed to devise some kind of exercise for them, not like unto that which they call prophecies . . . but some other more private, such as shall seem best to ourselves, both for the peace of the church, and their better instruction.'[3] Convocation then passed decrees providing for a closer scrutiny of men admitted to holy orders, regulating the commuting of penance, moderating the granting of marriage licences and restraining excessive excommunication and pluralism. It also requested bishops to send in surveys of ministers in their respective dioceses, almost certainly to counteract the earlier, hostile Puritan surveys. The next Convocation made new regulations to promote the education of the clergy. These presupposed

---

[1] Strype, *Grindal*, 1710, pp. 193–196, 257–259.

[2] F. Peck, *Desiderata Curiosa*, I, 1779, p. 102.

[3] Strype, *Whitgift*, 1718, p. 180.

that all clerics would be familiar with the Prayer Book, and enjoined them to study weekly one chapter of the Old Testament and one of the New, and exhibit their notes to their clerical supervisors: in addition once a quarter they expected the bishop to set them an exercise in divinity which they should answer in Latin, if they were able, or in English. For laymen eager for a preaching ministry these constituted very minor changes.[1] In 1589 Whitgift anticipated further complaints the Commons were likely to make regarding the state of the clergy, and before Parliament assembled he instructed his bishops to put in force canons made in 1584 and 1587. He now asked for a yearly episcopal return on admissions to benefices. Faced with the Commons demand for the abolition of pluralism he retorted: 'It requireth an impossibility. For of 8,800 and odd benefices with cure, there are not 600 sufficient for learned men. . . . This bill restraineth not laymen to have divers impropriate benefices, and to serve them by silly curates; and denieth it to learned divines who personally discharge their duty, and in their absence have sufficient substitutes etc.' Yet, despite his blustering, Whitgift made some concessions. In future Convocation ordered single-beneficed men to reside on their cures and double-beneficed men to spend six months on each living. It instructed men who absented themselves from their benefices for more than a hundred and twenty days to keep curates.[2]

Before Parliament met in 1593 the queen took the initiative by asking to see the certificates concerning the state of the clergy in order to check whether the bishops had observed the regulations for the admitting of properly qualified candidates. In reply to the attack in the Commons on the *ex officio* oath, and abuses in ecclesiastical courts in general, after the dissolution of Parliament, she ordered Whitgift to make a survey of all ecclesiastical courts. This, Strype reported, served 'to stop the mouths of such as clamoured so much against the bishops for their commissaries, officials etc'.[3] Whitgift answered fresh attacks on ecclesiastical courts in 1598 by producing a table of fees permitted to ecclesiastical officers. Convocation also made constitutions again restricting abuses of pluralism and excommunication and providing for more preaching in cathedrals, and the queen confirmed these by letters patent.[4] Still, however, in 1601 the Commons could find fault with the church for allowing pluralism, non-residence and abuses in commissaries' courts to continue: Whitgift reacted by exhorting Convocation to enforce earlier canons, and

[1] Strype, *Whitgift*, pp. 211–212.
[2] Strype, *Whitgift*, pp. 278–282.
[3] Strype, *Whitgift*, pp. 386, 418–419.
[4] Strype, *Whitgift*, pp. 508–514.

sent out a special letter requiring bishops' officials to hold less frequent courts in order to avoid vexing the inhabitants of the diocese, to cut down on the numbers of their apparitors and sumners, to lessen the commutation of penance and forbidding archdeacons from issuing marriage licences.[1] It is difficult to avoid the conclusion that he consistently offered the most minor reforms possible, which then as often as not were not executed, when the laity demanded, and the ecclesiastical system needed, wholesale reform. Nevertheless, however insignificant these concessions, the parliamentary agitation did gain with royal permission some practical reforms from Convocation, whereas in Parliament the queen blocked any reforming bills.

III.   LAY INTERVENTION IN THE CHURCH IN THE LOCALITIES

At a national level the gentry had to be content with these very limited reforms sponsored by Convocation: in theory the queen kept her ecclesiastical prerogative intact and made good her claim for legislation in church affairs to be effected not by Parliament but by Convocation. Yet, debarred as they were in Westminster from carrying forward a further reformation of the church on a national scale, in the localities laymen triumphed. The local magistrates knew the religious needs of their own areas; the queen did not. From the beginning of the reign they began spontaneously to reform their churches, and except in the most flagrant cases of disobedience, the queen had not the power to curb her subjects' zeal. The Protestant changes of the reign of Edward VI, although rapid, had affected parts of England more than some historians have thought and some areas had developed an enthusiasm for Protestantism which the counterchanges of Mary had not been able to destroy. Only a surviving tradition of Protestantism can account for the behaviour of a town like Coventry just after Elizabeth's accession. Thomas Lever, who on his return from exile undertook a preaching tour throughout the country, described to Bullinger in 1560 how he came to settle there.

'There is a city in the middle of England, called Coventry, in which there have always been, since the revival of the gospel, great numbers zealous for evangelical truth; so that in that last persecution under Mary, some were burnt, others went into banishment together with myself; the remainder, long tossed about in great difficulty and distress, have at last, in the restoration of pure religion, invited other preachers and myself in particular, to proclaim the gospel to them at Coventry. After I had discovered by the experience of some weeks that vast numbers in this place were in the habit of frequenting the

[1] Strype, *Whitgift*, pp. 546–555.

public preaching of the gospel, I consented to their request that I should settle my wife and family among them; and thus now for nearly a whole year, I have preached to them without any hindrance, and they have liberally maintained me and my family in this city. For we are not bound to each other, neither I to the townsmen, nor they to me, by any law or engagement, but only by free kindness and love.'[1]

Subsequently Lever held the office of archdeacon of Coventry but the fact that he had been called to the town by the inhabitants themselves weighed with him far more than any formal episcopal institution.

No two towns were alike and some, from the Protestant standpoint, remained backward throughout the Elizabethan period. Yet a significant number seem to have acted very early, as Coventry did, in providing for themselves a supply of evangelical preaching. Colchester, Ipswich, Leicester all established civic lectureships relatively soon after Elizabeth came to the throne. By 1562 weekday lectures in addition to the Sunday sermons were being delivered regularly in Leicester and the corporation ordered one member of every household in the town to attend the lectures given on Wednesday and Friday mornings in St Martin's church on pain of a fine. Lincoln, apparently a rather more conservative town, appointed a city preacher in 1572: by 1584 it had a scheme of Wednesday and Sunday preaching and a similar regulation enjoining the attendance of one member of every family. Often the minister whom the local magistrates somewhat impetuously engaged to preach either temporarily or permanently had to rely on voluntary contributions. At first in Leicester the corporation seems to have made random gifts to preachers as it did in 1565 when it sanctioned a collection being taken to support one Thorne, 'a preacher of God's word': later, however, the stipend of a lecturer became as regular a charge upon the corporation's revenues as that of any other civic official.[2] Dr Collinson estimates that by 1580 the two preachers which Ipswich retained may have cost the town £100 a year. The corporation of Yarmouth granted its preacher the generous stipend of £50 a year.[3] Towns willing to contribute as

[1] *Zurich Letters*, I, no. XXXV.

[2] See my articles in the *Historical Journal*, III, 1960, pp. 1–16, and *Transactions of the Leicestershire Archaeological and Historical Society*, XXXVI, 1960, pp. 6–21. J. W. F. Hill, *Tudor and Stuart Lincoln*, Cambridge, 1956, p. 99. J. W. F. Hill, 'The Beginnings of Puritanism in a Country Town', *Transactions of the Congregational Historical Society*, XVIII, 1957, pp. 40–49. R. B. Walker, 'The Growth of Puritanism in the County of Lincoln in the reign of Queen Elizabeth I', *Journal of Religious History*, I, 1961, pp. 148–159.

[3] Collinson, *Puritan Movement*, pp. 50, 229.

much as this could command the services of some of the leading Elizabethan preachers, and the corporation of Leicester was not being unreasonably ambitious when it asked its patron to try to secure for the town Walter Travers whose preaching (until he had been silenced that very year) had been drawing crowds to the Temple (Doc. 47). As Travers had no inclination to leave London, Huntingdon brought William Pelsant to Leicester. The corporation respected Pelsant, a bachelor of divinity who had conscientious scruples over wearing the surplice, but they found his successor, Thomas Sacheverall, less acceptable and showed their disapprobation by falling into arrears with his stipend.[1]

Town livings being on the average so poor (in many towns and cities like York, Bristol, Norwich and London which all contained an abundance of small parishes most livings were officially valued at less than £10 a year) they could not be expected to attract educated ministers, and consequently if the townspeople wanted regular preaching they had to turn to self help. Elizabethan London was famed for its preaching and in this the citizens could take a proper pride for the quality of preaching had been brought about largely through their own efforts, though in London individual parishes had taken the initiative, whereas in provincial towns the corporation had usually led the way. In the vestry of St Christopher-le-Stocks 'request was made that there might be some learned man appointed to read a lecture in this parish twice a week, and for the maintenance thereof a collection should be made of the benevolence of the parishioners'. Candidates for the lectureship at St Botolph's Aldgate delivered trial sermons, and only after hearing these did the vestry choose between the candidates. The vestry of St Margaret, New Fish Street, actually voted for its lecturer in 1582. Dr Owen calculated that one out of every two parishes in London had, or had had, a lecturer by 1603 and noted that parishes where the minister did not reside were particularly likely to employ a lecturer.[2] Quite often, where a living was too poor to attract an educated man a parish would appoint their vicar as their lecturer, thereby indirectly supplementing the living and at the same time attaining some control over the type of man chosen. An unpopular vicar could find that the parish did not renew his lectureship and it might well then prove financially impossible for him to remain in the parish.

Some towns in practice achieved, or came near to achieving, the direct appointment of their incumbents. All the seven churches of Ipswich were impropriate, and in five out of the seven parishes the

[1] Cross, *Puritan Earl*, pp. 140–141.

[2] H. G. Owen, 'Lectures and Lectureships in Tudor London', *Church Quarterly Review*, CLXII, 1961, pp. 63–76.

parish itself obtained the right to nominate its stipendiary curate. At Bury St Edmunds the townspeople claimed the right to appoint to both the livings in the town. The congregation of St Andrew's, Norwich, being a donative cure, chose its own ministers.[1] Although the right of presentation to the parish church of All Saints, North-ampton belonged to the crown, from 1566 onwards the corporation had virtually gained control of it, and early in the seventeenth century it legalized the position by acquiring the rectorial rights.[2] The eagerness with which leading parishioners desired a voice in the appointment of their own minister can be seen particularly clearly at Leeds. In 1588 there was still only one parish in this expanding town, compared with twenty-three parishes in neighbouring York. Its leading parishioners subscribed £130 to buy the advowson of St Peter's from the patron, Oliver Darnley. As soon as they owned the advowson they persuaded the aged and inactive clergyman to retire and in his place brought in a zealous Protestant.[3]

In addition to appointing their own lecturers, and occasionally even appointing incumbents to town livings, many Elizabethan towns encouraged the establishing of exercises designed partly to stimulate preaching among the less well-educated clergy, partly to teach the laity the fundamental tenets of their faith. Under the influence of John More who ministered at St Andrews for more than twenty years, and with the approval of Bishop Parkhurst, prophesyings began early in the reign at Norwich, 'continually supported by worthy and sincere preachers, and graced by the presence of so many grave and religious magistrates'. Very reluctantly Parkhurst on the instructions of Parker stopped these gatherings in 1574, but they began again after his death in the following year until Bishop Freke after four years struggle finally succeeded in dispersing the Presbyterian brethren. Norwich, indeed, provides positive evidence to substantiate the queen's belief that the prophesyings led to the establishment of Presbyter-ianism, though it could equally well be used to show that persistent persecution encourages radicalism. After their first silencing the Norwich ministers in 1575 restricted the membership of their assembly to the godly and excluded the uneducated for whom the exercises had primarily been designed.[4] Presbyterian, or near Presby-terian assemblies existed elsewhere in England. Percival Wiburn con-sciously devised the orders for the church in Northampton in imitation of Calvin's Geneva (Doc. 45). He laid down a scheme for the clergy

[1] Collinson, *Puritan Movement*, pp. 340–341.

[2] J. C. Cox, *Records of the Borough of Northampton*, II, Northampton, 1898, p. 397.

[3] Cross, *Puritan Earl*, pp. 256–257.

[4] Collinson, *Puritan Movement*, pp. 176, 186, 213–214.

of the town and the immediate neighbourhood to assemble in a prophesying once a week, and the ministers of the whole county to meet once a quarter. He intended that there should be a constant cycle of sermons for the local inhabitants and communions four times a year at which attendance was compulsory. At last enthusiasts in Northampton had a chance of setting up discipline, enforced partly by the minister and church wardens, partly by the mayor and bailiffs. Although it is doubtful whether the scheme was ever fully realized, for Wiburn was silenced and deprived in 1572, the willingness of ministers and magistrates together to work for the further reformation of the church in the town indicates the zeal of some of the inhabitants.[1]

Even at Northampton Wiburn contemplated working with the permission of the bishop of Peterborough: his church order could have been contained in a modified episcopal system. Elsewhere exercises grew up which never threatened episcopacy. In the north, where the queen's ban did not extend, bishops actively promoted exercises as a means of combating popery and by the 1590s towns like Northallerton and Richmond, with some encouragement from the lord president of the Council in the North, could support exercises, though by this date these may have become mainly clerical gatherings. In the south, when the queen had prohibited prophesyings the lay zealots found an acceptable substitute in regular fasts. James Gosnell made elaborate preparations with Anthony Gilby in 1579 for preaching at a fast to be held in Leicestershire designed almost exclusively for the laity.[2] From his cell in Wisbech Castle in the 1590s the Jesuit, William Weston, watched the godly from all over the Fens as they read in their Bibles, made notes on the sermons, and sang psalms at a day-long fast.[3] Whatever regulations the queen might issue, it proved impossible to keep lay enthusiasts from their devotions.

Historians have only just begun to attempt to define who these laymen were who demanded the further reform of the church. To speak of a strictly popular element in Puritanism is misleading; the Protestant zealots among the Elizabethan populace probably favoured Anabaptism or similar radical sects. The godly who frequented exercises and called for an educated ministry came from a higher rank in society and seem to have been, in the main, independent householders, their families and some of their more towardly servants: the emphasis on Bible reading demanded a high degree of literacy. These people could both dominate their parish congregations and also exert

[1] Collinson, *Puritan Movement*, pp. 141–143.

[2] Cross, *Puritan Earl*, p. 139.

[3] P. Caraman, ed. *William Weston: Autobiography of an Elizabethan*, 1955, p. 164.

considerable control over their minister. Dr Collinson has stressed the extent to which Protestant ministers were constrained to accommodate themselves to the prejudices of their forward congregations.[1] Troubled by the demands of their bishop on the one hand and of their parishioners on the other, they rarely lacked critics. At the time of the controversy over the surplice ministers seem to have been far more ready than their congregations to consider vestments a matter indifferent. A godly parishioner all too often might ask his minister, 'Why therefore wear ye not a cap like unto an honest citizen or preacher of Germany, rather than like unto a mass-monger?'[2] Cecil on a royal progress in Norfolk and Suffolk in 1561 saw how far some congregations there had already gone in their independence. 'The bishop of Norwich is blamed even of the best sort for his remissness in ordering his clergy,' he reported to Parker. 'He winketh at schismatics and Anabaptists, as I am informed. Surely, I see great variety in ministration. A surplice may not be borne here. And the ministers follow the folly of the people, calling it charity to feed their fond humour.'[3] In some areas of Essex and Kent, to take only these counties in the south-east of England, Lollard traditions may have remained. Several parishes in Essex had outdoor preaching places and clandestine sermons: at Hornchurch a Protestant conventicle kept its children from baptism. The preachers had the difficult task of trying to impose Calvinist order on this spiritual anarchy, and their hold over their congregations could be endangered by a sudden demand from a bishop to wear the surplice. Grindal, when bishop of London, realized the tribulations of some of his fellow workers and licensed an Essex minister for the time being not to wear the hated garment because of the prejudice of his congregation. Forced by Parker and the queen to impose uniformity in clerical dress upon the London clergy, the unfortunate bishop found himself besieged by a crowd of women vehemently objecting to the suspension of their lecturer, John Bartlett. As late as 1590 when the Protestant ministers of south east Lancashire were asked to wear the surplice Dr John Reynolds could still remind them that 'the godly would mislike thereof, and would depart, divers of them, from their public ministration'.[4] A minister, however zealous, could never feel completely confident he had full authority over his godly parishioners: he always had to lead them, he could not command them. Consequently even if the queen had secured the unquestioning obedience of the lower clergy she still would not have

[1] Collinson, 'The Godly: Aspects of Popular Protestantism . . .', *Past and Present* Conference Papers, July, 1966.

[2] Quoted in Collinson, *Puritan Movement*, p. 95.

[3] *Parker Correspondence*, no. CVII.

[4] Collinson, 'The Godly . . .', *Past and Present* Conference Papers, 1966.

obtained the automatic quiescence of her lay subjects in matters of religion.

Right until the end of the reign the godly, much to the queen's abhorrence, preserved their freedom of choice concerning religious observance. They boycotted 'dumb' ministers; in spite of all the directions to attend their parish church on a Sunday, they flocked to a neighbouring parish which had a sermon when none was provided in their own. In parts of Northamptonshire in 1573 nonconformity had almost got out of hand. The bishop of Peterborough reported to Burghley how

'. . . in the town of Overton where Mr Carleton dwelleth there is no divine service upon most Sundays and holidays according to the Book of Common Prayer, but instead thereof two sermons. . . . When they are determined to receive the communion, they repair to Whiston where it is their joy to have many out of divers parishes, principally out of Northampton town and Overton . . . with other towns thereabout, there to receive the sacraments with preachers and ministers to their own liking, and contrary to form prescribed by the public order of the realm. . . . To their purposes they have drawn divers young ministers to whom it is plausible to have absolute authority in their parishes. In their ways they be very bold and stout, like men that seem not to be without great friends.[1]

By depriving ministers who refused to observe the Book of Common Prayer Whitgift seems on the whole to have checked the attempt in some parishes to substitute the Genevan form of prayer for the Prayer Book but he could not restrain the zeal of some lay Protestants for additional meetings for worship. Even in the 1590s prayer meetings persisted, which the authorities called unlicensed conventicles. Lay enthusiasts could not be prevented from assembling with their minister for religious edification. At Aythorp Roding, in Essex, for example, the godly met in the house of one Davies 'to the number of ten persons or thereabouts of his kindred and neighbours, being invited thither to supper'. At supper they conferred of 'such profitable lessons as they had learnt that day at public catechizing', and after the meal some 'attended to one that read in the Book of Martyrs', the rest to their vicar, John Huckle, who 'was reading by the fireside a piece of a catechism'. After they had prayed and sung a psalm they departed at ten o'clock.[2]

To be in command of the church in practice as well as in theory the royal governor required the active co-operation of the laity in the

---

[1] W. H. Frere and C. E. Douglas, eds *Puritan Manifestoes*, 1954, pp. xxi–xxii.

[2] Quoted in Collinson, 'The Godly . . .', *Past and Present* Conference Papers, pp. 13–14.

localities, and this is what she so noticeably failed to get. Indeed the godly layman seems to have felt more free to censure royal lapses in religious matters than did the godly cleric who was usually more aware of his dependence upon the crown. William White, a London baker and also a remarkably articulate layman, had no qualms at all about proceeding straight ahead with reform in his own part of London. Since his parish church had not been sufficiently purged of popery, he had gone to worship with the godly at Plumbers Hall. Imprisoned several times for his nonconformity he rebuked Grindal himself for his hard dealing, and told him that bishops should labour that

'. . . all remnants, badges and marks of antichrist, with all plants which our heavenly father hath not planted may at once be plucked up by the roots, that God's holy word may be the only rule and line to measure his religion by, and that all man's wisdom, policy and good intents may be so trodden under the obedience of God's word.'

When still in 1574 the discipline he longed for had not been imposed White openly taught that, because of the negligence of the state and church, the people should lead the way:

'. . . our common error at this day is that sith by our godly prince (whom God preserve) and bishops much good hath been done to Christ's church in England, for which all true Christians are and ought to be thankful, therefore we must allow and receive in the service of God whatsoever they command.'[1]

White may have exercised considerable influence upon Field and Wilcox, the organizers of the attempt to introduce a Presbyterian church in England.[2] The significance of zealous Protestants like White is that they did not favour sectarian Protestantism: White himself was a most hostile opponent of the Anabaptists. By calling for a modified form of episcopacy, or sometimes for Presbyterianism, nothing separated them theologically from the godly among the gentry and the nobility with whom they made common cause.

In the final analysis the queen failed to impose her idea of religious uniformity upon the localities because of this Protestant enthusiasm, so foreign to her way of thinking, which penetrated all sections of society from the devout citizenry to royal courtiers. The Protestant lay zealots may not have been numerically very many but their influence pervaded the whole community largely because they met little organized lay Protestant opposition in defence of the middle

[1] A. Peel, 'William White: an Elizabethan Puritan', *Transactions of the Congregational Historical Society*, VI, 1913–15, pp. 4–19.

[2] Collinson, *Puritan Movement*, p. 116.

way. Their opponents among the laity were Catholics inflamed by the new Counter Reformation ardour: enthusiastic lay 'Anglicans' seem to have been virtually non-existent. Even the most highly educated laymen conceived of religion in the clearest of terms: Christ or antichrist, Protestantism or Catholicism. Once they had become convinced of the truths of Protestantism they pursued their beliefs with little heed for the consequences. The desire to win converts which inspired White had its parallels far higher in lay society. Francis Hastings, a younger son of the second earl of Huntingdon, could write in 1574 in exactly the same spirit to instruct his cousin in the 'understanding of true religion' and to forearm her against the insidious arguments of Catholic friends:

'I know, Cousin Anne, there be many worldly persuasions ready to be laid before you, which with flesh and blood may carry a great stroke: and I know also you shall meet with such as can and will lay them before you very dangerously if you will look no further than to the words uttered, but if you will weigh mightily from what they would draw you, and to what they would allure you, I trust their practices shall be to little purpose, and that you shall continue free from their popish poison: but herein you are to call for assistance from the Highest, who is always ready to deliver his from danger and without whom no danger can be avoided; and for me I will not fail to pray to him for you. . . .'[1]

Hastings had studied for several years at Magdalen College, the great centre of evangelical zeal in Oxford, soon after Lawrence Humphrey had been made president. The passionate interest in theology he developed there remained with him throughout his long life. As a young man from his home at Market Bosworth he did all in his power to further the growth of Protestantism in Leicestershire: moving to Somerset about 1583, he immediately turned his attention to the state of religion there.[2] His rebuke to a local incumbent for neglecting his ministerial duties is remarkable for the freedom with which a layman felt competent to instruct a cleric (Doc. 48). Yet the tone of Hastings's letter is altogether different from the censures the queen gave to her bishops: Hastings thought of himself and Price, whatever his backslidings, as fellow labourers in the task of propagating the gospel; the queen appears to have seen the bishops primarily as royal servants and as pastors of the people of God only so far as this did not conflict with their secular obligations. In Somerset Hastings gathered together a small group of enthusiastic clergy with whom he

[1] Huntington Library, California. H. A. 5079.

[2] See my forthcoming edition of the letters of Sir Francis Hastings to be published by the Somerset Record Society in 1969.

and his equally godly wife discussed religion: on her death bed his wife grieved that the common people paid such little heed to their spiritual advisers. The advanced ministers, for their part, welcomed this gentry support: Philip Bisse, the archdeacon of Taunton, likened Hastings's circle to a meeting of Christian philosophers.[1]

Throughout England the zealots among the gentry and nobility spurred on the clergy to win the country for Protestantism and not infrequently seized the initiative while the clergy somewhat hesitantly followed in their wake. When William Chaderton became bishop of Chester in 1579, the third earl of Huntingdon, then president of the Council in the North, bombarded him with letters in an attempt to get him to take vigorous missionary action in a notoriously Catholic diocese. Like his brother Francis Hastings, Huntingdon did not hesitate to lecture a cleric on specifically pastoral problems. From his experience of the town of Leicester he suggested a scheme of intensive Protestant teaching in the Manchester area:

'. . . the well planting of the gospel in Manchester and the parishes near to it, shall, in time, effect much good in other places; if in Manchester there were an hour spent every morning from six to seven, or from seven to eight, in prayer and a lecture, as *a short prayer*, then as it is said, *reaches the heavens*, so short lessons often taught [it] is like no doubt but that the grace of God will pierce many hearts. The prayer and lecture might begin and end with the clock. The work is so good, and for it that place is so fit, as I am bold thus to put you in mind of it.'[2]

Noblemen and gentlemen of this degree of enthusiasm possessed very extensive powers to influence the religion of their own localities in all practical respects independent of the central government. By establishing Anthony Gilby as lecturer at Ashby de la Zouch, where he remained unmolested from his return from the Marian exile until his death in 1585, Huntingdon profoundly affected religion in Leicestershire. In addition he took considerable pains over the type of incumbents he presented to the livings he owned in the county. Whitgift rightly saw lay impropriation as the great obstacle to attracting educated men to enter the church but some impropriators at least, provided they had and retained the right of presenting candidates they considered godly, did go on to implement the revenues of livings they possessed. Huntingdon was willing to pay for the succession of godly preachers at Ashby de la Zouch which spanned the reign, and continued into the 1630s: Gilby came to Ashby straight from Geneva,

[1] Huntington Library. H. A. 2380.
[2] F. Peck, *Desiderata Curiosa*, 1779, pp. 109–110.

and Thomas Widdows, who actually held the living, joined him there and carried on Gilby's work after his death. When Widdows himself died in 1593 Huntingdon called Hildersham to be vicar of Ashby (Doc. 49), and he perpetuated the tradition of moderate nonconformity until his death in 1632.

In county after county comparable examples of active Protestant lay patronage have been discovered. Already by 1558 the nobility and the gentry owned a substantial portion of patronage of parochial livings and Elizabeth added to it by her continuing sale of former monastic lands. Dr Collinson has shown how in West Suffolk the radical Puritan Sir Robert Jermyn held the presentation to ten livings, and his fellow zealot, Sir John Higham, to four. Puritan gentry and noblemen, including Lord North and Sir Nicholas Bacon, controlled at least thirty more Suffolk parishes around 1580. These patrons deliberately chose zealous Protestants to be their incumbents; they occasionally went so far as to consider the requests of the godly members of the congregations the ministers were appointed to serve. The leading parishioners of Warham All Saints wrote to Nathaniel Bacon concerning a candidate they considered suitable for their living when it was about to fall vacant, and he passed on their recommendation to the lord chancellor who held the presentation to lesser crown livings.[1] This type of indirect intervention can never be measured, but it is quite clear that lay zealots influenced the presentation of candidates to far more livings than those they actually owned. The earl of Huntingdon, to cite but one patron, did not possess a single advowson in the north of England, and yet he succeeded in getting the living of Halifax for his chaplain, John Favour, he brought John Udall briefly to lecture at Newcastle on Tyne, and, when the government summoned him south, replaced him there with another chaplain, Richard Holdsworth; he obtained a living at Thorp Arch for another cleric who later dedicated a religious treatise to him, and invariably supervised the choice of civic preachers at York. These are only isolated instances when evidence of his intervention happens to have survived.[2]

The bishops had the power to deprive nonconformist incumbents, and with Whitgift's insistence that lecturers should actively participate in Prayer Book services, as well as preach, they gained far greater control over parish clergy, but, given the conventions of Elizabethan society, the chaplains kept by noblemen and gentlemen always remained outside episcopal reach. In Northamptonshire the godly alliance of George Carleton, who may well have introduced Percival

---

[1] Collinson, *Puritan Movement*, pp. 337–338.
[2] Cross, *Puritan Earl*, pp. 255–256.

Wiburn to Northampton, his stepson Anthony Cope, Peter and Paul Wentworth, Sir Richard Knightley and his sons may well have paralysed the bishop of Peterborough. At Gorhambury Lady Ann Bacon acted as a notable patroness 'of God's saints and faithful servants' and in the 1590s took into her household Wiburn, Humphrey Wilblud and William Dyke when Whitgift's campaign made it impossible for them any longer to hold a benefice.[1] Contemporaries noticed that the ecclesiastical authorities did not trouble Thomas Cartwright in his wardenship of Leicester's hospital at Warwick until after his patron's death.

These gentlemen and noblemen succeeded in exercising so much control over the church in their localities largely because of the sympathy which government servants at Westminster showed to their aspirations. Francis Hastings's outpourings over the international Catholic conspiracy found a ready listener in Sir Francis Walsingham.[2] Laurence Tomson who had been a fellow of Magdalen when Hastings studied there and who then went to the universities of Heidelberg and Geneva where he made an English version of Beza's translation of the New Testament, eventually became Walsingham's secretary. Sir Walter Mildmay, the chancellor of the Exchequer and founder of Emmanuel College expressly designed to produce zealous Protestants, voiced in Parliament his criticisms of episcopal negligence. Knollys, a Privy Councillor, never failed to sound the alarm at what he considered a resurgence of clericalism. While still clerk of the Council, Robert Beale dared to conduct his attack on the *ex officio* oath. Even Burghley himself, less enthusiastic though married to a godly wife, patiently heard the complaints of the dispossessed ministers, and remonstrated with Whitgift over his severity. Probably Sir Christopher Hatton alone among the royal servants of comparable stature whole heartedly supported Whitgift and Bancroft in their attempt to realize the queen's idea of uniformity.

The connection between Thomas Wood and the earl of Leicester most vividly reveals the interaction between the godly laymen in the localities and the queen's leading ministers. Thomas Wood was another layman with a passion for theology who, like Laurence Tomson, in a different age might have entered the church but instead worked for the state and ended his life a minor country gentleman. Considerably older than Tomson, he may have been at Cambridge about 1530. He went into exile in Mary's reign and was involved in the troubles at Frankfort: he later claimed he taught William Whittingham to hate the vestments prescribed in the 1552 Prayer Book.

---

[1] Collinson, *Puritan Movement*, pp. 439–440.
[2] Huntington Library. H. A. 5086.

He seceded with Knox to Geneva and there rose to be one of the elders of the congregation. After Elizabeth's accession he attached himself to the Dudley family and went with Warwick to Le Havre in 1562 where he acted as clerk to his council of war. Later in the decade he settled in Leicestershire and seems to have been in close contact with the Hastings family, for he lent money to the earl of Huntingdon and acted as an overseer of a will with Francis Hastings. Wood, however, was by no means a social equal of the Hastings or the Dudleys, yet in a matter of religion he could address Leicester as if he were already a Presbyterian elder, and Leicester a mere member of the laity (Doc. 46). Wood later acknowledged that he had wronged Leicester in attributing the banning of the Southam exercise to him; yet he never relaxed his demand that his patron should join boldly in the 'perfect building up of Sion'. He believed Leicester had the power, if he chose to use it, to correct the abuses in the established church, curb the prelates and set up the discipline.[1] Within five days of Leicester's death Francis Hastings wrote to Essex urging him to take on his stepfather's responsibilities as protector of the godly.[2]

The evidence which has survived goes far to confirm the importance which Wood placed on the part played by Leicester (and with him of a small group among the nobility) in planting Protestantism in England, at least in the first half of Elizabeth's reign.[3] It is noticeable how little Elizabeth's first ecclesiastics, with the partial exception of Parker, understood her idea of a middle-way church. The first bishops were not conservative Protestants, and the difference between their outlook and the queen's may have been caused partly by Elizabeth's negligence. At her accession she all too readily delegated her ecclesiastical patronage to her servants, a lack of foresight which she corrected in her later years. Dr Collinson considers that Leicester followed a consistent policy of promoting convinced, but not radical, Protestants to high office in the church. He helped Thomas Young to become archbishop of York, Edmund Grindal to the see of London, Edwin Sandys to the see of Worcester. Robert Horne, Edmund Scambler, James Pilkington all owed their bishoprics at least partly to him. It may have been the influence of Leicester more than that of any one other man that brought Grindal eventually to Canterbury and took Sandys to York. Thomas Cooper of Lincoln, William Chaderton of Chester and William Overton of Coventry and Lichfield all at one time served as Leicester's chaplains. He it seems was

[1] P. Collinson, ed. *Letters of Thomas Wood, Puritan, 1566–1577*, Bulletin of the Institute of Historical Research, Special Supplement, no. 5, 1960, pp. iv–xi, xv–xxi.

[2] Huntington Library. H. A. 5090.

[3] Collinson, *Puritan Movement*, pp. 61–64.

behind the promotion of Thomas Sampson to be dean of Christ Church, of William Whittingham to be dean of Durham; on Whittingham's death he supported Toby Matthew to succeed him as dean, and advanced Matthew Hutton to become dean of York. Apart from Young, these men were all convinced Calvinists, and most had gone into exile under Mary. At the time of the Vestiarian Controversy, Leicester intervened on behalf of Humphrey and Sampson and partly through his influence, partly through that of his brother-in-law, Huntingdon, Sampson after his deprivation was offered a comfortable refuge in Leicester.[1] The favour which the Privy Council almost invariably showed to nonconforming ministers in the 1570s and 1580s seems largely attributable to Leicester's ascendancy. The Protestant gentry always looked to him to further their cause. Sir Richard Knightley told Leicester of the gentry's respect for him 'for that they espy in your lordship a zeal and care for the helping and relieving of the poor church which hath so many and mighty enemies that few, such as your lordship is, are friends to it'.[2]

With Leicester worked a small and closely interrelated group of Protestant noblemen: his brother, Warwick, the patron of Whittingham and from 1565 married to Bedford's pious daughter, their brother-in-law Huntingdon, who after his appointment as president of the Council in the North in 1572 had extensive patronage throughout the north of England, and Bedford himself who exercised great power in the west country and may have been largely responsible for finding seats for radical Protestants in the crucial Parliament of 1559. None of these noblemen consciously supported Presbyterianism though they may have protected individual Presbyterians; at their most spiritual they aimed at purifying English Protestantism, at their most material at lay exploitation of the church. They wished to lessen (but not destroy) the monarchical authority of bishops. They approved of schemes to breathe new life into the ancient office of rural deans, or for bishops in some other way to share their powers with a body of learned ministers in their dioceses. They commended the exercises, another way in which ecclesiastics and gentlemen together could work for the reformation of a locality. Huntingdon or Bedford could equally well have delivered this censure of Leicester to the bishop of Peterborough in 1578:

'Remember, my lord, how before you were bishop you would find fault with negligence of bishops, how much you cried out to have preachers and good ministers to be increased and carefully placed. And so did you all almost that be now bishops. But let me now look

---

[1] Collinson, ed. *Wood's Letters*, pp. xx–xxxv.
[2] Quoted in Collinson, ed. *Wood's Letters*, p. xxviii.

into your deeds, and behold in every diocese the want of preachers, nay the great discouragement that preachers find at your hands.'[1]

Some years before his death Leicester's influence within the church was beginning to weaken. He made his gravest mistake, although he did not immediately recognize it, in not preventing Whitgift from becoming archbishop of Canterbury. Hatton, in deliberate rivalry with Leicester, supported the queen's policy of church government and first among the government servants attacked both Papists and Puritans for their contempt of the established church. While Leicester campaigned in the Netherlands, Hatton's followers, Buckhurst and Cobham, as well as Whitgift himself, all became members of the Privy Council. In the decade between 1585 and 1595 these noble protectors of Puritans died. No longer could the Protestant nonconformists expect Privy Councillors almost automatically to shield them from the wrath of the queen and the bishops. Essex, although he may have tried to build up a Puritan following, never attained Leicester's former preeminence among the godly. Yet while at the centre the great patrons had disappeared, in the localities still the gentry stood behind their Puritan ministers. The patronage of some of the nobility and their allies had allowed a church far more Protestant than the queen had intended to take root and it was to prove impossible to eradicate it. At the time of his attack on the *ex officio* oath Beale spread the rumour that once Whitgift had brought all the clergy to conformity he would turn his attention to the laity and require all lawyers and justices to subscribe articles which, among other things, asserted that episcopal government was lawful by the word of God, and that the English church in its present state was a true member of the church of Christ.[2] Merely to broadcast the idea of a subscription for Protestant laymen ensured that such an opposition would have been forthcoming as could have defeated the plan overwhelmingly. Whitgift was wise enough never to attempt it. By 1603 some measure of outward Protestant conformity may have been achieved (though new evidence suggests that the extent of this conformity has been exaggerated): in practice in the localities religious uniformity scarcely existed.

It would be misleading to imply that zealous lay patrons directed their energies exclusively to the spreading of Protestantism; indeed, all the evidence indicates that Catholic laymen through the patronage they extended to priests played a decisive part in the survival of Catholicism in England. In the first years of the reign, when the papacy made no provision for spiritual ministration to English Catholics, gentlemen gave deprived Marian priests refuge in their

[1] Collinson, ed. *Wood's Letters*, p. xxxv.
[2] Collinson, *Puritan Movement*, p. 408.

households and enabled them to say Mass there to small congregations of the faithful. With the coming of the seminary priests and, later, of the Jesuits these gentry households became natural staging posts for the priests on the English mission. Robert Parsons, with his customary efficiency, organized circuits which would take a priest from his first landing in England from Catholic family to Catholic family right across the country, and Nicholas Owen, a Jesuit lay brother, specialized in constructing hiding places in these houses for the priests. Although significant pockets of popular Catholicism have been discovered in towns like Winchester and York, and in the area around Scarborough, where the Catholics seem to have been largely independent of gentry influence, time and again recusant historians have found that Catholicism persisted in a particular locality because of the protection given by a gentry household. In Hampshire a string of Catholic gentry families near the coast provided shelter for priests immediately on their arrival from the continent: in the North Riding of Yorkshire almost without exception Catholicism centred upon gentry households. The Lancashire recusant gentry were mainly responsible for the pattern of Catholic survival there while in Cambridgeshire and Essex, both Protestant counties, gentry like the Huddlestones, the Wisemans and the Petres alone made the continuance of Catholicism possible. These Catholic families tended to intermarry, to choose Catholic servants for reasons of security, even to appoint only Catholic tenants with the result that some isolated areas became small enclaves of Catholicism which local officials despite periodic harassment never succeeded in destroying. By 1603 committed Catholics only accounted for a very small proportion of the population but their numbers were almost certainly increasing.[1]

Although much has been written about the contribution of the recusant gentry in the preservation of Catholicism no historians have yet studied systematically the influence these lay Catholics must have exerted on the development of English Catholicism.[2] It seems scarcely probable that those laymen who on occasion risked their lives and their estates for the sake of the priests formed the docile, malleable congre-

---

[1] J. E. Paul, 'Hampshire Recusants in the time of Elizabeth I, with special reference to Winchester', *Proceedings of the Hampshire Field Club*, XXI, 1959, pp. 61–81. H. Aveling, *Northern Catholics: the Catholic Recusants of the North Riding of Yorkshire 1558–1790*, 1966, pp. 11–198. J. S. Leatherbarrow, *The Lancashire Elizabethan Recusants*, Chetham Society, New Series, 110, Manchester, 1947. P. Caraman, ed. *John Gerard: the Autobiography of an Elizabethan*, 1951. P. Caraman, ed. *William Weston: the Autobiography of an Elizabethan*, 1955. For a dispassionate discussion of the numbers of Catholics, and Puritans, in 1603 see McGrath, *Papists and Puritans*, pp. 374–378.

[2] W. R. Trimble, *The Catholic Laity in Elizabethan England 1558–1603*, Cambridge, Mass. 1964 does not consider this question.

gations described by Gerard and Weston. The households which regularly maintained a priest can hardly have failed, albeit unconsciously, to have placed some restraint upon his freedom of action and expression. John Gerard's hosts may have treated him as a visiting gentleman, but Edward Norris of Speke in Lancashire who kept two priests in 1599 used one of them to wait at table in a 'livery coat and cognizance'.[1] Dr Alban Langdale's declaration in 1580, immediately after Parsons had published *A Brief Discourse containing certain reasons why Catholics refuse to go to Church*, that English Catholics did not refuse to attend the state church can hardly have displeased his highly patriotic patron, Lord Montague, whose hospitality he had enjoyed for the previous eighteen years.[2] It may partly be because of the constricting influence of lay patrons that most seminary priests and Jesuits deliberately chose not to reside permanently in one household: at least in Yorkshire they succeeded in setting up and maintaining out of their own resources a circuit based on houses they hired for themselves. Yet even in Yorkshire Mr Aveling has shown that the priests failed to prevent the heads of Catholic households from practising occasional conformity. Perhaps the worldly wisdom of these laymen achieved more for their fellow Catholics than the unbending nonconformity enjoined by the seminary priests and carried out by some lay people would ever have done. Their willingness to appear from time to time in their parish church brought them and their families a *de facto* toleration from local justices who had the power to persecute them to extinction.[3]

In spite of this example of the North Riding gentlemen refusing to obey the papal prohibition of attending the English church, the Elizabethan Catholic laity do not seem to have thought or acted as one monolithic block. They did not, as might have expected, unanimously support the Appellant priests, who were working for some sort of accommodation with the Elizabethan government, in their quarrels with the Jesuits. Both clerical parties in the disputes of the 1590s made overtures to the laity: some gentlemen, like the Wisemans, replied by giving their verdict in favour of the Jesuits while others intervened to rebuke the seculars for their vehemence against their brother priests.[4] Nevertheless, Dr Bossy's thesis seems generally to be borne out that the form of Catholicism which many Catholic gentlemen approved, an inward looking Catholicism almost entirely

[1] Leatherbarrow, *Lancashire Elizabethan Recusants*, p. 139.

[2] L. Hicks, ed. *Letters and Memorials of Father Robert Persons, S. J.*, Catholic Record Society XXXIX, 1942, p. xxxiii.

[3] Aveling, *Northern Catholics*, pp. 112–198.

[4] P. Renold, ed. *The Wisbech Stirs 1595–1598*, Catholic Record Society, LI, 1958, no. iii.

disassociated from politics, eventually overcame the militant Catholicism of many of the missionary priests who could contemplate an invasion of England by a foreign power in order to restore the kingdom to Rome.[1] Catholic patrons could no more control the opinions of this type of priest than Protestant patrons could restrain determined Presbyterian ministers but Catholic gentlemen still in their own way presented a similar potential threat to the independence of the clergy, and in the long run their dislike of political action against the English government brought about the failure of clerical plans.

In other respects and at other times Catholic laymen came near to exercising a freedom of action comparable to that of Protestants. In the absence of priests, and in the first half of the reign many Catholics must have been without priests for the greater part of the year, if not for years on end, lay Catholics had to fend for themselves or lose their Catholicism entirely. When there was no priest available some laymen took it upon themselves to teach their Catholic neighbours, like John Hodgson of Egton in the North Riding who, when his sister-in-law was in danger of death after the birth of her child, 'did read unto her exhorting her . . . after the popish manner'. Catholic laymen, again like enthusiastic Protestants, acted as lay evangelists: one Parkinson, a recusant layman of Thirsk, lent Thomas Bell a book which convinced him in 1570 'that the religion now established in this realm is not the Catholic religion and the true doctrine of Christ . . .'[2] The vigorous proselytizing of the physician Thomas Vavasour and his devout wife must have been partly responsible for the continuance of Catholicism in York. Much research remains to be done on the activities of the Catholic laity in the localities who have hitherto usually been regarded as passive congregations: it may well confirm this impression of lay initiative which Catholic lay people probably exercised as freely as Protestants.

In the last resort the state failed to compel the laity into uniformity because the zealots, both Catholic and Protestant, disregarding the parochial system, made their own households into centres of evangelism.[3] There the Elizabethan state had not the power to intrude, except for rare occasions. At Hackness Lady Margaret Hoby who had been educated as a young girl in the household of the earl of Huntingdon, converted her smaller family into a centre of Protestant piety for the

[1] J. Bossy, 'Character of Elizabethan Catholicism', *Past and Present*, XXI, 1962, pp. 39–59.

[2] Aveling, *Northern Catholics*, pp. 192, 28.

[3] McGrath, *Papists and Puritans*, pp. 373–398. Collinson, 'The Role of Women in the English Reformation, illustrated by the life and friendships of Anne Locke,' G. J. Cumings, ed. *Studies in Church History*, II, 1965, pp. 258–272.

surrounding area. She eventually secured the village living for her chaplain, whose direct sermons she preferred to the 'unprofitable' preaching of the York Minster dignitaries. Her servants attended with her the round of Sunday services, and with her on the Sabbath evenings repeated the main points of the sermon (Doc. 50). In Somerset in the same decade Lady Magdalen Hastings made her household into a similar model of Protestantism.[1] Catholic and Protestant zealots approached very near to each other in their enthusiasm and practice. The large household of the earl of Huntingdon for which Anthony Gilby composed a special set of devotional exercises cannot have been very different from that of the Catholic Lady Montague, whose confessor described how at Battle,

'... she maintained a great family, which consisted of eighty persons, and sometimes more, and almost all Catholics, and these she maintained not only for her honour ... but also to support them in the Catholic religion. And to these she allowed not only plentiful food and competent wages, but (which is much more to be admired) afforded them the same benefit of the word of God and the sacraments that she herself enjoyed ... she maintained three priests in her house, and gave entertainment to all that repaired to her....

She built a chapel in her house (which in such a persecution was to be admired).... Here almost every week was a sermon made, and on solemn feasts the sacrifice of the mass was celebrated with singing and musical instruments and sometimes also with deacon and sub-deacon.'[2]

What the nobility and gentry did on a large scale the religious zealots lower in society imitated, much to the queen's disapproval. Margaret Clitherow, a convert to Catholicism and the wife of a York butcher, took upon herself to organize her own religious life in blithe disregard of the laws of the state.

'When she had leisure,' John Mush, her spiritual director, recorded soon after her martyrdom, 'she most delighted to read the New Testament of Rheims Translation, Kempis "Of the following of Christ", Perin's "Exercise", and such like spiritual books. I have heard her say, if that it pleased God so to dispose, and set her at liberty from the world, she would with all her heart take upon her some religious habit, whereby she might ever serve God under obedience. And to this end (not knowing what God would do with her) she learned our Lady's Matins in Latin.'[3]

[1] Huntington Library. H. A. 5099.

[2] A. C. Southern, ed. *An Elizabethan Recusant House*, [1954], pp. 39, 43.

[3] J. Morris, ed. *The Troubles of our Catholic Forefathers*, Third Series, 1877, pp. 393–394.

H

The Reformation had accustomed the laity to think for themselves in a new way, and to a certain extent offered them a choice in religion. Having emancipated themselves from clerical control they would not willingly accept state direction. Elizabeth might upbraid her bishops over the religious licence in the city of London 'where every merchant must have his schoolmaster and nightly conventicles, expounding scriptures and catechizing their servants and maids: insomuch, that I have heard how some of their maids have not sticked to control learned preachers and say that "such a man taught otherwise in our house".' Yet she knew she did not have the force or influence to contain lay enthusiasm throughout England.[1]

As the supreme governor over the English church Elizabeth achieved only a partial success. Clerical apologists constructed an impressive theoretical defence of the royal supremacy but neither Catholic nor Protestant thinkers ever fully accepted their case and throughout her reign some loyal churchmen remained uneasy over the precise extent of royal powers in ecclesiastical affairs. The laity for their part had been forced to acknowledge that the queen's own intentions for the church could not be altered and that in Parliament they had not the strength to bring her against her will to consent to legislation controlling the church. Elizabeth retained her nominal ascendancy. Yet in practice in the localities she could not curb the laity. In limited areas all over England laymen allied with priests to preserve Catholicism: on a much greater scale laymen joined forces with zealous ministers to set up the very type of Protestantism the queen herself most opposed. By 1662 the experience of the Civil War and the Interregnum had taught numbers of gentlemen to appreciate the positive virtues of the church of England, but during her own life time the supreme governor of the English church signally failed to communicate to her lay, and indeed to many of her clerical subjects, her belief in 'mediocrity'.

[1] Quoted in Neale, *Parliaments*, II, pp. 70–71.

DOCUMENTS

I. The Royal Supremacy in Theory

(i) Prologue. Protestant and Catholic Attitudes to a Lay Head of the Church

1. FROM J. KNOX, *The First Blast of the Trumpet against the Monstrous Regiment of Women*, Geneva, 1558, pp. 9, 10v–11, 22v.

To promote a woman to bear rule, superiority, dominion or empire above any realm, nation or city is repugnant to nature, contumely to God, a thing most contrarious to his revealed will and approved ordinance, and finally it is the subversion of good order, of all equity and justice.

What would this writer [Aristotle] (I pray you) have said to that realm or nation where a woman sitteth crowned in Parliament amongst the midst of men? O, fearful and terrible are thy judgements, O Lord, which thus hast abased man for his iniquity. I am assuredly persuaded that if any of those men, which illuminated only by the light of nature, did see and pronounce causes sufficient why women ought not to bear rule nor authority should this day live and see a woman sitting in judgement, or riding from Parliament in the midst of men, having the royal crown upon her head, the sword and sceptre borne before her, in sign that the administration of justice was in her power: I am assuredly persuaded, I say, that such a sight should so astonish them that they should judge the whole world to be transformed into Amazons, and that such a metamorphosis and change was made of all the men of that country, as poets do feign was made of the companions of Ulysses, or at least that albeit the outward form of men remained yet should they judge that their hearts were changed from the wisdom, understanding and courage of men to the foolish fondness and cowardice of women. Yea, they further should pronounce that where women reign or be in authority that there must needs vanity be preferred to virtue, ambition and pride to temperancy and modesty, and finally that avarice, the mother of all mischief, must needs devour equity and justice.

... It is plain that the administration of the grace of God is denied to all women. By the administration of God's grace is understood not only the preaching of the word and administration of the sacraments, by which the grace of God is presented and ordinarily distributed unto man, but also the administration of civil justice, by the which virtue ought to be maintained and vices punished. The execution whereof is no less denied to women than is the preaching of the Evangel or administration of the sacraments. . . .

2. FROM A. GILBY, 'An Admonition to England and Scotland to call them to repentance' in J. Knox, *The Appellation*, Geneva, 1558, pp. 69–71.

In the time of King Henry the Eighth, when by Tyndale, Frith, Bilney and other his faithful servants God called England to dress his vineyard, many promised full fair, whom I could name. But what fruit followed? Nothing but bitter grapes, yea briars and brambles, the wormwood of avarice, the gall of cruelty, the poison of filthy fornication, flowing from head to foot, the contempt of God and open defence of the cake idol by open proclamation to be read in the churches instead of God's scriptures. Thus was there no reformation but a deformation in the time of that tyrant and lecherous monster. The boar I grant was busy rooting and digging in the earth, and all his pigs that followed him. But they sought only for the pleasant fruits that they winded with their long snouts. And for their own bellies sake they rooted up many weeds, but they turned the ground so, mingling good and bad together, sweet and sour, medicine and poison; they made, I say, such confusion of religion and laws, that no good thing could grow, but by great miracle, under such gardeners. And no marvel, if it be rightly considered: for this boar raged against God, against Devil, against Christ and against Antichrist, as the sum[1] that he cast out against Luther, the racing forth of the name of the pope, and yet allowing his laws, and his murder of many Christian soldiers and of many Papists do clearly and evidently testify unto us. Especially the burning of Barnes, Jerome and Garrat, three faithful preachers of the truth, and hanging the same day for maintenance of the Pope Paul Abel and Fetherstone doth clearly paint his beastliness that he cared for no manner of religion. This monstrous boar for all this must needs be called the head of the church in pain of treason, displacing Christ our only head who ought alone to have this title. Wherefore, in this point, O England, ye were no better than the Romish Antichrist, who by the same title maketh himself a god, sitteth in men's consciences, banisheth the word of God, as did your King Henry whom ye so magnify. For in his best time nothing was heard but the king's book and the king's proceedings, the king's homelies in the churches where

[1] Summa, summary treatise.

God's word should only have been preached. So made you your king
a god, believing nothing but that he allowed. . . . I desire you to call to
remembrance your best state under King Edward when all men with
general consent promised to work in the vineyard, and ye shall have
cause, I doubt not, to lament your wickedness, that so contemned the
voice of God for your own lusts, for your cruelty, for your covetous-
ness that the name of God was by your vanities evil spoken of in
other nations. I will name no particular things, because I reverence
those times, save only the killing of both the king's uncles, and the
imprisonment of Hooper for popish garments. . . . But to speak of the
best, whereof ye used to boast, your religion was but an English
matins, patched forth of the pope's portesse[1]; many things were in
your great book superstitious and foolish, all were driven to a prescript service like the Papist's, that they should think their duties
discharged if the number were said of psalms and chapters. Finally,
there could no discipline be brought into the church, nor correction
of manners. . . .

To what contempt was God's word and the admonition of his
prophets come in all estates, before God did strike, some men are not
ignorant. The preachers themselves for the most part could find
no fault in religion, but that the church was poor and lacked living.
Truth it is that the abbey lands and other such revenues, as afore
appertained to the papistical church, were most wickedly and ungodly spent, but yet many things would have been reformed before
that the kitchen[2] had been better provided for to our prelates in
England. It was most evident that many of you under the cloak of
religion served your own bellies: some were so busy to heap benefice
upon benefice, some to labour in Parliament for purchasing of lands,
that the time was small which could be found for the reformation of
abuses, and very little which was spent upon the feeding of your
flocks. I need not now to examine particular crimes of preachers. Only
I say, that the gospel was so lightly esteemed, that most part of men
thought rather that God should bow and obey to their appetites than
that they should be subject to his holy commandments. For the
commons did continue in malice and rebellion, in craft and subtlety,
notwithstanding all laws that could be devised for reformation of
abuses. The merchants had their own souls to sell for gains, the
gentlemen were become Nimrods and giants, and the nobility and
council would suffer no rebukes of God's messengers though their
offences were never so manifest. Let those that preached in the court
that Lent before King Edward deceased speak their conscience and

[1] Portable breviary.
[2] Kitchen meat.

accuse me if I lie; yea, let a writing written by that miserable man, the duke of Northumberland to Master Harlow[1] for that time bishop of Hereford be brought to light and it shall testify that he ashamed not to say that the liberty of the preachers' tongues would cause the council and nobility to rise up against them: for they could not suffer so to be intreated. These were the fruits even in the time of harvest a little before the winter came.

3. FROM J. AYLMER. *At Harborow for faithful and true Subjects against the late blown blast concerning the Government of Women*, Strassburg, 1559, sig. B 4 v, D 4 v, I 4, O 4.

Seeing then that in all ages God hath wrought his most wonderful works by most base means, and showed his strength by weakness, his wisdom by foolishness, and his exceeding greatness by a man's exceeding feebleness, what doubt we of his power, when we lack policy, or mistrust his help which hath wrought such wonders? Who is placed above him, saith Job, to teach him what he should do? Or who can say to him: thou hast not done justly? He sendeth a woman by birth; we may not refuse her by violence. He stablisheth her by law, we may not remove her by wrong. He maketh her a head; we may not make her a hand or foot.

... Christ knowing the bounds of his office would not meddle with extern policies, translating of realms and depriving of true inheritors. No, when he was desired to be arbiter betwixt two brethren he asked not how the plea stood but who made him an officer. Divines, me think, should by this example not give themselves too much the bridle and too large a scope to meddle too far with matters of policy as this is, whereupon dependeth either the welfare or the ill-fare of the whole realm. If those two offices, I mean ecclesiastical and civil, be so jumbled together as it may be lawful for both parties to meddle in both functions there can be no quiet nor any well ordered commonwealth.

If you reason in this place of St Paul ... I suffer not a woman to speak in the congregation: ergo, not to rule, thinking it is a formal ... from the less to the more, your logic and divinity both do fail you. For it is not to be taken thus: Paul forbiddeth her the less for her unaptness; ergo, he debarreth her of the greater. But indeed it is contrary wise; he forbiddeth her the greater and more chargeable function which is the spiritual ministry and preaching: therefore, it followeth not that he shutteth her from the less, which is

---

[1] John Harlow, or Harley, bishop of Hereford, March 1553–March, 1554, deprived.

extern policy. No man I think doubteth but that the ecclesiastical
function is greater and more chargeable than the other, for the
one concerneth the body, and the other the soul. The one reacheth
no further than outward acts, but the other pierceth to the heart and
thoughts. That bindeth in earth the body, this fettereth both in
heaven and earth the soul. The one, as St Augustine saith, threateneth
prisons, the other eternal damnation. The one may be executed by
deputies; the other must execute himself *by your hand* etc. To the
one is required justice and no great learning; the other can not be
without great learning and knowledge. . . .

Thus we see that St Paul thrusting that sex from the greater function and office doth not also disable it to execute the other which is
less. But you will say in England she must have both. How can she
discharge both if you make the one so hard? I answer that indeed both
belong to her, but not in one manner. For in the one (as policy) she
hath a function; that is she must be a doer: in the other she hath
the oversight but not the function and practice as we see in the
commonwealth of the Jews, first betwixt Aaron and Moses. Moses
controlled Aaron, but yet he executed not Aaron's office; he offered
no incense nor sacrifice ordinarily; he meddled not with the ark, nor
any such thing as belonged to the priesthood; he wore not the
garments; he ministered not the sacraments, and yet had he authority to redress his faults, as it appeareth in the matter about the calf,
and by the commission which he received at God's hand . . . 'Thou
shalt be his God, and he thy speechman'.

Come off you bishops; away with your superfluities; yield up
your thousands; be content with hundreds as they be in other
reformed churches where be as great learned men as you are. Let
your portion be priestlike not princelike. Let the queen have the rest
of your temporalities and other lands to maintain these wars which
you procured and your mistress left her, and with the rest to build
and found schools throughout the realm: that every parish church
may have his preacher, every city his superintendent to live honestly
and not pompously which will never be unless your lands be dispersed and bestowed upon many which now feedeth and fatteth but
one. Remember that Abimelech when David in his banishment would
have dined with him kept such hospitality that he had no bread in
his house to give him but the shewbread. Where was all his super-
fluity to keep your pretended hospitality? For that is the cause that
you allege why you must have thousands as though you were
commanded to keep hospitality rather with a thousand than with a
hundred. I would our countryman Wyclif's book which he wrote *Of
the Church* were in print, and there should you see that your wrinches

and cavillations be nothing worth. It was my chance to happen of it in one's hand that brought it out of Bohemia.

4. B. M. Cot. Ms. Vesp. D. XVIII, 112, 113, 120v, 123. Printed, but inaccurately, in H. Gee, *The Elizabethan Prayer Book and Ornaments*, 1920, pp. 236–252.

FROM a speech made by Bishop Scot of Chester against the Supremacy Bill, March 1559.

This bill that hath been here read now the third time doth appear unto me such one as it is much to be lamented that it should be suffered either to be read, or any ear to be given unto it of Christian men so honourably assembled as this is; for it doth not only call into question and doubt those things which we ought to reverence without any doubt moving, but maketh further earnest request for alteration, the rather for the clear abolishing of the same. And if that our religion, as it was here of late discreetly, godly and learnedly declared, doth consist partly in inward things, in faith, hope and charity; and partly in outward things, as in common prayer and the holy sacraments universally ministered.

Now, as concerning those outward things, this bill doth clearly in very deed extinguish them, setting in their places I cannot tell what. And the inward it doth also shake, that it leaveth them very bare and feeble.

And as for the certainty of our faith, whereof the story of the church doth speak, a thing of all other most necessary; if it shall hang upon an act of Parliament, we have but a weak staff to lean unto. And that I shall desire you to take me here [not] as to speak in derogation of the authority of the Parliament, which I knowledge to be of great strength in matters whereto it extendeth. But for matters of religion, I do not think it ought to meddle withal, partly for the certainty which ought to be in our faith and religion, and the uncertainty of the statutes and acts of Parliament. For we see that often times that which is established by Parliament one year is abrogated the next year following, and the contrary allowed. And we see also that one king disalloweth the statutes made under another. But our faith and religion ought to be most certain, and one in all times, and in no condition wavering: for, as St James saith, 'He that doubts or staggereth in his faith is like the waves of the sea, and shall obtain nothing at the hands of God'. And partly for that the Parliament consisteth for the most part of the noblemen of the realm, and certain of the commons, being lay and temporal men; which, although they be of good wisdom and learning, yet not so studied nor exercised in the scriptures, the holy doctors and practice of the church, as to be accounted judges in such matters. . . .

Now, my lords, consider, I beseech you, the matter here in variance; whether your lordships be able to discuss them according to learning, so as the truth may appear, or not: that is, whether the body of Christ be by this new book consecrated, offered, adored, truly communicated or no; and whether these things be regarded necessarily by the institution of our Saviour Christ, or no; and whether the book goeth near the truth. These matters, my lords, be, as I have said, weighty and dark, and not easy to be discussed. And likewise your lordships may think of the rest of the sacraments, which be either clearly taken away or else mangled after the same sort by this new book.

The third thing here to be considered is the great danger and peril that doth hang over your heads if you do take upon you to be judges in these matters and judge wrong; bringing both yourselves and other from the truth unto untruth, from the highways to bypaths. It is dangerous enough, our Lord knoweth, for a man himself to err, but it is more dangerous not only to err himself, but also to lead all other men into error. It is said in scripture of the King Jeroboam to aggravate his offences, that. . . . 'He did sin himself, and caused Israel to sin'. My lords, take heed that the like be not said by you; if you pass this bill, you shall not only, in my judgement, err yourselves, but you shall also be the authors and causers that the whole realm shall err after you. For the which you shall make an account before God.

But now, because I have been long, I will make an end of this matter with the sayings of two noble men in the like affairs. The first is Theodosius, which said thus. . . . 'It is not lawful,' saith he, 'for him that is not of the order of the holy bishops to intermeddle with the intreating of ecclesiastical matters.' Likewise said Valentinian the emperor, being desired to assemble certain bishops for the examining of a matter of doctrine, in this wise. . . . 'It is not lawful for me', said the emperor, 'being one of the lay people, to search out such curious matters, but let the priests, unto whom the charge of these things do belong, meet together in what place soever they will'. He meaneth, for the discussing thereof. But and if these emperors had nothing to do with such matters, how should your lordships have to do withal?

5. FROM M. A. S. HUME, ed. *Calendar of State Papers, Spanish,*
1558–1567, 1892, pp. 59–61.

24 April, 1559. Philip II to Count de Feria, Spanish ambassador
in London.

By your letter of the 11th. instant, I have learnt the discussions you
have had with the queen and council about the peace and other affairs
you had in hand, and I cannot refrain from highly praising the
prudence and dexterity you have displayed. I thank you also for the
note you sent me of the points which have to be borne in mind and
provided for in my interest to obviate what may happen in England,
which I can assure you is one of the things that is giving me just now
most anxiety. I have ordered it to be well considered and discussed at
once, and after due deliberation it appears that at present the most
advantageous course will be for you to endeavour to confirm the queen
and her friends in the fear you say they feel of the peril and danger
in which they stand, so that they may understand thoroughly that
they are ruined unless I succour and defend them. We have no doubt
they will easily grasp this if they think it over, as it is so very clear.
The duke of Alba, Ruy Gomez, and the bishop of Arras tell me that
in the conversations they had with the queen's commissioners at
Chateau Cambresi the latter confessed that this was so, and it is to
be supposed that they will have reported to the same effect and this
together with what you have told her (the queen) will have set her
thinking in a matter that so deeply concerns her. When you have
frightened the queen about this, in the manner you find most suitable
to open her eyes to her interests and to convince her of the zeal which
leads me to advise her, you will assure her from me that I will never
fail to help her in all I can to preserve her realm and settle her affairs
exactly the same as if they were my own, both on account of the
great love and affection I bear her, from which neither the peace nor
my alliance with France will ever estrange me; rather will I try to
bind us closer by all the kindness and good offices I can show, and
also for my own interests, which would be greatly injured if her kingdom were to fall into other hands than hers, which God forbid. This
might easily happen if she do not provide against it, and at once adopt
the only true remedy, which is to forbid any innovations in religion
which usually cause risings and turbulence in countries and in the
hearts of subjects. If she do this and take one of the archdukes, my
cousins, for a husband, respecting which I have already written to
you, she will smooth down and settle all her affairs and enjoy more
tranquility and contentment than can be described, and I will remain
a good brother to her as she will see by my acts. You will enlarge
in this sense according as you see her disposition and the conversa-

tion permits with all the tact and suavity you know how to employ as you have done in other matters. This course has seemed the best to follow with the queen, because under this head what is proposed is so absolutely true that you can bring as much pressure to bear as may be needed, and that you may be provided at all points, I have thought well to send you enclosed the letter for her written with my own hand, the tenor of which you will see by the copy. Amongst other points you may tell her not to wonder if in these matters I press her more than is customary between princes, but as they are so important and necessary to the welfare of her realm, whose rehabilitation and preservation depend entirely upon them, and concern me inasmuch as they concern her as well as touching my own interests, I cannot and ought not to fail to do it as a good brother.

I have been very glad to learn what you say about the queen refusing the title offered to her of supreme head of the church, and delaying her sanction to what had been done in Parliament, because it looks as if there were still some hopes of salvation. Seeing this and how damaging it would be if the pope were to declare her a bastard, which he might decide to do since I am not to marry her, I thought it time to approach his holiness, and I sent a despatch on the subject to Rome advising his holiness of the state of things there and of the hopes still entertained of an amendment, which I was trying my best to bring about, and asking him not to make any change until the result of my efforts were seen, of which result I would inform his holiness. This step was thought very desirable in order to keep his holiness in hand and delay the matter as was in all respects to be desired. You will advise me of all that happens, so that we may act accordingly. . . .

Postscript. After writing this I have received your last letter of 23rd (18th?) instant, and have been glad of your news, although in the matter of religion what you say about the Parliament having agreed that the queen should take the title of governess of the church fills me with new anxiety, as it is so dangerous and troublesome on all accounts. Advise me if it has passed the Upper House and whether the queen has accepted it, and take the steps which may be advisable in accordance with what I have said. The other points in your letter shall be answered later so as not to detain this post.

Brussels, 24 April, 1559.

(ii) The Acts of Supremacy and Uniformity and the Comments of Protestant Ministers

---

6. FROM *Statutes of the Realm,* IV, pt. I, pp. 350–55.
The Act of Supremacy, 1559. I Eliz. I c. I.

An act restoring to the crown the ancient jurisdiction over the state ecclesiastical and spiritual, and abolishing all foreign power repugnant to the same.

I   Most humbly beseech your most excellent majesty your faithful and obedient subjects, the Lords spiritual and temporal and the Commons in this your present Parliament assembled: that where in time of the reign of your most dear father of worthy memory, King Henry the Eighth, divers good laws and statutes were made and established as well for the utter extinguishment and putting away of all usurped and foreign powers and authorities out of this your realm and other your highness's dominions and countries, as also for the restoring and uniting to the imperial crown of this realm the ancient jurisdictions, authorities, superiorities and preeminences to the same of right belonging and appertaining; by reason whereof we your most humble and obedient subjects, from the five and twentieth year of the reign of your said dear father, were continually kept in good order, and were disburdened of divers great and intolerable charges and exactions before that time unlawfully taken and exacted by such foreign power and authority as before that was usurped, until such time as all the said good laws and statutes by one act of Parliament made in the first and second years of the reigns of the said late King Philip and Queen Mary, your highness' sister, entitled an act repealing all statutes, articles and provisions made against the see apostolic of Rome since the twentieth year of King Henry the Eighth, and also for the establishment of all spiritual and ecclesiastical possessions and hereditaments conveyed to the laity, were all clearly repealed and made void, as by the same act of repeal more at large doth and may appear. By reason of which act of repeal your said humble subjects were eftsoons brought under an usurped foreign power and authority, and yet do remain in that bondage, to the intolerable charges of your loving subjects, if some redress by the authority of this your high court of Parliament with the assent of your highness, be not had and provided. May it therefore please your highness, for the repressing of the said usurped foreign power, and the restoring of the rights, jurisdiction and preeminences appertaining to the imperial crown of this your realm that it may be enacted by the authority of this present Parliament, that the said act made in the said first and second years of the reigns of the said late King Philip and Queen Mary and all and every branch, clauses and articles therein contained (other than such branches, clauses and sentences as hereafter shall be excepted) may from the last day of this session of Parliament, by authority of this present Parliament, be repealed, and shall from thenceforth be utterly void and of none effect.

II [And that the statutes made 23 Henry VIII c. 9 prohibiting citation of persons outside their own diocese; 24 Henry VIII c. 12 against appeals to Rome; 23 Henry VIII c. 20 against payment of Annates to Rome; 25 Henry VIII c. 19 for submission of the clergy; 25 Henry VIII c. 20 for consecration of bishops; 25 Henry VIII c. 21 against paying exactions to Rome; 26 Henry VIII c. 14 for consecration of suffragens; and 28 Henry VIII c. 16 against obtaining dispensations from Rome may extend to Elizabeth and her heirs as fully as they did to Henry VIII.]

V And that it may also please your highness that it may be enacted by authority aforesaid, that one act and statute made in the first year of the reign of the late King Edward the Sixth, your majesty's most dear brother, entitled an act against such persons as shall unreverently speak against the sacrament of the body and blood of Christ, commonly called the sacrament of the altar, and for the receiving thereof under both kinds, and all and every branches, clauses, and sentences therein contained, shall and may likewise from the last day of this session of Parliament be revived and from thenceforth shall and may stand, remain and be in full force, strength and effect to all intents, constructions and purposes, in such like manner and form as the same was at any time in the first year of the reign of the said late King Edward the Sixth; any law, statute or other matter to the contrary in any wise notwithstanding.

VI [Repeals heresy laws revived by Mary.]

VII And to the intent that all usurped and foreign power and authority, spiritual and temporal, may for ever be clearly extinguished, and never to be used nor obeyed within this realm or any other of your majesty's dominions or countries; may it please your highness that it may be further enacted by the authority aforesaid, that no foreign prince, person, prelate, state or potentate, spiritual or temporal, shall at any time after the last day of this session of Parliament, use, enjoy or exercise any manner of power, jurisdiction, superiority, authority, preeminence of privilege, spiritual or ecclesiastical, within this realm or within any other your majesty's dominions or countries that now be or hereafter shall be, but from henceforth the same shall be clearly abolished out of this realm and all other your highness' dominions for ever: any statute, ordinance, custom, constitutions or any other matter or cause whatsoever to the contrary in anywise notwithstanding.

VIII   And that also it may likewise please your highness that it may be established and enacted by the authority aforesaid, that such jurisdictions, privileges, superiorities and preeminences, spiritual and ecclesiastical, as by any spiritual or ecclesiastical power or authority hath heretofore been or may lawfully be exercised or used for the visitation of the ecclesiastical state and persons, and for reformation, order and correction of the same and of all manner of errors, heresies, schisms, abuses, offences, contempts and enormities, shall forever, by authority of this present Parliament, be united and annexed to the imperial crown of this realm; and that your highness, your heirs and successors, kings or queens of this realm, shall have full power and authority by virtue of this act, by letters patents under the great seal of England, to assign, name and authorize, when and as often as your highness, your heirs or successors shall think meet and convenient, and for such and so long time as shall please your highness, your heirs or successors, such person or persons, being natural born subjects to your highness, your heirs or successors, as your majesty, your heirs or successors shall think meet, to exercise, use, occupy and execute under your highness, your heirs and successors, all manner of jurisdictions, privileges and preeminences in any wise touching or concerning any spiritual or ecclesiastical jurisdiction within these your realms of England and Ireland or any other your highness' dominions or countries; and to visit, reform, redress, order, correct and amend all such errors, heresies, schisms, abuses, offences, contempts and enormities whatsoever, which by any manner spiritual or ecclesiastical power, authority or jurisdiction can or may lawfully be reformed, ordered, redressed, corrected, restrained or amended to the pleasure of Almighty God, the increase of virtue and the conservation of the peace and unity of this realm: and that such person or persons so to be named, assigned, authorized and appointed by your highness, your heirs or successors, after the said letters patents to him or them made and delivered as is aforesaid, shall have full power and authority by virtue of this act and of the said letters patents, under your highness, your heirs or successors, to exercise, use and execute all the premises according to the tenor and effect of the said letters patents: any matter or cause to the contrary in any wise notwithstanding.

IX And for the better observation and maintenance of this act, may it please your highness that it may be further enacted by the authority aforesaid, that all and every archbishop, bishop and all and every other ecclesiastical person, and other ecclesiastical officer and minister, of what estate, dignity, preeminence or degree soever he or they be or shall be, and all and every temporal judge, justicer, mayor and other lay or temporal officer and minister, and every other person having your highness' fee or wages within this realm, or any your highness' dominions, shall make, take and receive a corporal oath upon the Evangelist, before such person or persons as shall please your highness, your heirs or successors, under the great seal of England, to assign and name, to accept and take the same according to the tenor and effect hereafter following, that is to say: I, A. B. do utterly testify and declare in my conscience, that the queen's highness is the only supreme governor of this realm and of all other her highness' dominions and countries, as well in all spiritual or ecclesiastical things or causes as temporal, and that no foreign prince, person, prelate, state or potentate hath or ought to have any jurisdiction, power, superiority, preeminence or authority, ecclesiastical or spiritual, within this realm; and therefore I do utterly renounce and forsake all foreign jurisdictions, powers, superiorities and authorities, and do promise that from henceforth I shall bear faith and true allegiance to the queen's highness, her heirs and lawful successors, and to my power shall assist and defend all jurisdictions, preeminences, privileges and authorities granted or belonging to the queen's highness, her heirs and successors, or united or annexed to the imperial crown of this realm: so help me God, and by the contents of this book.

X [Penalty for any ecclesiastical or lay officer refusing the oath is loss of office: any man prefered to any ecclesiastical or lay office in the future shall take the oath before he can be admitted to that office.]

I

XI   [Persons suing livery or doing homage shall take the oath, as also shall persons taking holy orders or degrees at the universities.]

XIV   And for the more sure observation of this act, and the utter extinguishment of all foreign and usurped power and authority, may it please your highness that it may be further enacted by the authority aforesaid, that if any person or persons dwelling or inhabiting within this your realm, or in any other your highness' realms or dominions, of what estate, dignity or degree soever he or they be, after the end of thirty days next after the determination of this session of this present Parliament, shall by writing, printing, teaching, preaching, express words, deed or act, advisedly, maliciously, and directly affirm, hold, stand with, set forth, maintain or defend the authority, preeminence, power or jurisdiction, spiritual or ecclesiastical, of any foreign prince, prelate, person, state or potentate whatsoever, heretofore claimed, used or usurped within this realm or any dominion or country being within or under the power, dominion or obeisance of your highness, or shall advisedly, maliciously and directly put in ure or execute anything for the extolling, advancement, setting forth, maintenance or defence of any such pretended or usurped jurisdiction, power, preeminence, or authority, or any part thereof, that then every such person and persons so doing and offending, their abettors, aiders, procurers and councellors, being thereof lawfully convicted and attainted according to the due order and course of the common laws of this realm, for his or their first offence shall forfeit and lose unto your highness, your heirs and successors, all his and their goods and chattels, as well real as personal; [or be imprisoned for one year, if not worth £20 in goods: the benefices and promotions of ecclesiastics shall be void. The second offence shall merit the penalties of *Praemunire*. The third offence shall be adjudged high treason.]

XIX   Provided always, and be it enacted as is aforesaid, that no manner of order, act or determination for any matter of religion or cause ecclesiastical, had or made by the authority of this present Parliament, shall be accepted, deemed, interpretate or adjudged at any time hereafter to be any error, heresy, schism, or schismatical opinion: any order, decree, sentence, constitution or law, whatsoever the same be, to the contrary notwithstanding.

XX Provided always, and be it enacted by the authority aforesaid, that such person or persons to whom your highness,
your heirs or successors, shall hereafter by letters patents under
the great seal of England give authority to have or execute any
jurisdiction, power or authority spiritual, or to visit, reform,
order or correct any errors, heresies, schisms, abuses or enormities by virtue of this act, shall not in any wise have authority
or power to order, determine or adjudge any matter or cause
to be heresy, but only such as heretofore have been determined, ordered or adjudged to be heresy by the authority of
the canonical scriptures, or by the first four general councils,
or any of them, or by any other general council wherein the
same was declared heresy by the express and plain words of
the said canonical scriptures, or such as hereafter shall be
ordered, judged or determined to be heresy by the high court
of Parliament of this realm, with the assent of the clergy in
their Convocation; anything in this act contained to the
contrary notwithstanding.

XXI [Offences under this act shall be proved by two witnesses
confronted with the accused.]

7. FROM *Statutes of the Realm*, IV, pt. 1, pp. 355–58.
The Act of Uniformity, 1559. 1 Eliz. I c. 2.

An act for the uniformity of common prayer and divine service in
the church, and the administration of the sacraments.

I Where at the death of our late sovereign lord, King Edward
the Sixth, there remained one uniform order of common service and prayer and of the administration of sacraments, rites
and ceremonies in the church of England, which was set forth
in one book entitled the Book of Common Prayer and administration of sacraments and other rites and ceremonies in the
church of England, authorized by act of Parliament holden in
the fifth and sixth years of our said late sovereign lord King
Edward the Sixth, entitled an act for the uniformity of
common prayer and administration of the sacraments; the
which was repealed and taken away by act of Parliament in
the first year of the reign of our late sovereign lady, Queen
Mary, to the great decay of the due honour of God and discomfort to the professors of the truth of Christ's religion:
Be it therefore enacted by the authority of this present Parliament that the said statute of repeal and everything therein
contained only concerning the said book and the service,
administration of sacraments, rites and ceremonies contained

or appointed in or by the said book shall be void and of none effect from and after the feast of the nativity of St John Baptist next coming; and that the said book with the order of service, and of the administration of sacraments, rites and ceremonies with the alteration and additions therein added and appointed by this statute shall stand and be from and after the said feast of the nativity of St John Baptist in full force and effect according to the tenor and effect of this statute, anything in the aforesaid statute of repeal to the contrary notwithstanding.

II   And further be it enacted by the queen's highness, with the assent of the Lords and Commons in this present Parliament assembled, and by authority of the same, that all and singular ministers in any cathedral or parish church or other place within this realm of England, Wales and the marches of the same, or other the queen's dominions shall from and after the feast of the nativity of St John Baptist next coming be bounded to say and use the matins, evensong, celebration of the Lord's Supper and administration of each of the sacraments and all their common and open prayer in such order and form as is mentioned in the said book so authorized by Parliament in the said fifth and sixth years of the reign of King Edward the Sixth, with one alteration or addition of certain lessons to be used on every Sunday in the year, and the form of the litany altered and corrected, and two sentences only added in the delivery of the sacrament to the communicants, and none other or otherwise. And that if any manner of person, vicar or other whatsoever minister that ought or should sing or say common prayer mentioned in the said book, or minister the sacraments, from and after the feast of the nativity of St John Baptist next coming refuse to use the said common prayers or to minister the sacraments in such cathedral or parish church or other places as he should use to minister the same in such order and form as they be mentioned and set forth in the said book, or shall wilfully or obstinately (standing in the same) use any other rite, ceremony, order, form or manner of celebrating of the Lord's Supper, openly or privily, or matins, evensong, administration of the sacraments or other open prayers than is mentioned and set forth in the said book, (open prayer in and throughout this act is meant that prayer which is for other to come unto or hear, either in common churches or private chapels or oratories, commonly called the service of the church) or shall preach, declare or speak anything in the derogation or depraving of the said book or anything therein contained or any part thereof, and shall be thereof lawfully

convicted according to the laws of this realm by verdict of
twelve men, or by his own confession, or by the notorious
evidence of the fact, shall lose and forfeit to the queen's highness, her heirs and successors, for his first offence the profit
of all his spiritual benefices or promotions coming or arising
in one whole year next after his conviction; and also that the
person so convicted shall for the same offence suffer imprisonment by the space of six months without bail or mainprize.
[For second offence he shall be imprisoned for one year, and
be deprived of all his spiritual offices; for third offence deprivation and imprisonment for life. If a man is not beneficed, for
the first offence he shall be imprisoned for a year, for the
second imprisoned for life.]

III   And it is ordered and enacted by the authority abovesaid that
if any person or persons whatsoever after the said feast of the
nativity of St John Baptist next coming shall in any interludes,
plays, songs, rhymes, or by other open words declare or speak
anything in the derogation, depraving or despising of the same
book, or of anything therein contained, or any part thereof, or
shall by open fact, deed or by open threatenings compel or
cause or otherwise procure or maintain any person, vicar or
other minister in any cathedral or parish church or in chapel
or in any other place to sing or say any common or open prayer,
or to minister any sacrament, otherwise or in any other manner
and form than is mentioned in the said book, or that by any of
the said means shall unlawfully interrupt or let any person,
vicar, or other minister in any cathedral or parish church,
chapel or any other place to sing or say common and open
prayer, or to minister the sacraments or any of them, in such
manner and form as is mentioned in the said book, that then
every such person being thereof lawfully convicted in
form abovesaid shall forfeit to the queen, our sovereign lady,
her heirs and successors, for the first offence a hundred marks.
[For second offence, 400 marks; for third offence forfeiture of
goods and imprisonment for life: on non-payment of fines
for first and second offences imprisonment for six and
twelve months respectively.] And that from and after the said
feast of the nativity of St John Baptist next coming all and
every person and persons inhabiting within this realm or any
other the queen's majesty's dominions shall diligently and
faithfully, having no lawful or reasonable excuse to be absent,
endeavour themselves to resort to their parish church or chapel
accustomed, or upon reasonable let thereof to some usual place
where common prayer and such service of God shall be used in

such time of let, upon every Sunday and other days ordained and used to be kept as holy days, and then and there to abide orderly and soberly during the time of the common prayer, preachings or other service of God there to be used and ministered; upon pain of punishment by the censures of the church, and also upon pain that every person so offending shall forfeit for every such offence twelve pence, to be levied by the churchwardens of the parish where such offence shall be done, to the use of the poor of the same parish, of the goods, lands and tenements of such offender by way of distress.

IV   And for due execution hereof the queen's most excellent majesty, the Lords temporal and all the Commons in this present Parliament assembled doth in God's name earnestly require and charge all the archbishops, bishops and other ordinaries that they shall endeavour themselves to the uttermost of their knowledges that the due and true execution hereof may be had throughout their dioceses and charges, as they will answer before God for such evils and plagues wherewith Almighty God may justly punish his people for neglecting this good and wholesome law. And for their authority in this behalf, be it further enacted by the authority aforesaid, that all and singular the same archbishops, bishops and all other their officers exercising ecclesiastical jurisdiction, as well in places exempt as not exempt within their dioceses, shall have full power and authority by this act to reform, correct and punish by censures of the church all and singular persons which shall offend within any their jurisdictions or dioceses after the said feast of the nativity of St John Baptist next coming, against this act and statute; any other law, statute, privilege, liberty or provision heretofore made, had or suffered to the contrary notwithstanding.

V   And it is ordained and enacted by the authority aforesaid, that all and every Justices of Oyer and Determiner or Justices of Assize shall have full power and authority in every of their open and general sessions to enquire, hear and determine all and all manner of offences that shall be committed or done contrary to any article contained in this present act within the limits of the commission to them directed, and to make process for the execution of the same, as they may do against any person being indicted before them of trespass or lawfully convicted thereof.

VI   [Provided always that all archbishops and bishops may at pleasure associate themselves with the above Justices of Oyer and Determiner and Assize at sessions held within their dioceses.]

VII   [Prayer books shall be provided for every parish church and cathedral by the feast of the nativity of St John Baptist at the charge of the parishioners.]

XIII Provided always and be it enacted that such ornaments of the church and of the ministers thereof shall be retained and be in use, as was in the church of England by authority of Parliament in the second year of the reign of King Edward the Sixth, until other order shall be therein taken by the authority of the queen's majesty, with the advice of her commissioners appointed and authorized under the great seal of England for ecclesiastical causes, or of the metropolitan of this realm. And also that, if there shall happen any contempt or irreverence to be used in the ceremonies or rites of the church by the misusing of the orders appointed in this book, the queen's majesty may by the like advice of the said commissioners or metropolitan ordain and publish such further ceremonies or rites as may be most for the advancement of God's glory, the edifying of his church and the due reverence of Christ's holy mysteries and sacraments.

XIV   And be it further enacted by the authority aforesaid that all laws, statutes and ordinances wherein or whereby any other service, administration of sacraments or common prayer is limited, established or set forth to be used within this realm or any other the queen's dominions or countries shall from henceforth be utterly void and of none effect.

8. Lambeth. Ms. 959 no. 40. Printed in J. Bruce and T. T. Perowne, eds. *Correspondence of Matthew Parker*, Parker Society, Cambridge, 1853, no. XLIX.

30 April, 1559. Edmund Sandys to Matthew Parker.

Greetings in Christ. Ye have rightly considered that these times are given to taking and not to giving, for ye have stretched forth your hands further than all the rest. They never ask us in what state we stand, neither consider that we want; and yet in the time of our exile were we not so bare as we are now brought. But I trust we shall not linger here long, for the Parliament draweth towards an end. The last book of service is gone through with a proviso to retain the ornaments which were used in the first and second year of King Edward, until it please the queen to take other order for them. Our gloss upon this text is that we shall not be forced to use them, but that others in the meantime shall not convey them away, but that they may remain for the queen.

After this book was passed, Boxall and others quarrelled with it, that according to the order of the scripture we had not *thanksgiving;* 'for', saith he, '*The Lord took bread and gave thanks,* but in the time of consecration we give no thanks'. This he put into the treasurer's head, and into Count de Feria's head, and he laboured to alienate the queen's majesty from confirming of the act, but I trust they cannot prevail. Mr Secretary is earnest with the book, and we have ministered reasons to maintain that part.

The bill of supreme government of both the temporalty and clergy passeth with a proviso that nothing shall be judged heresy which is not condemned by the canonical scriptures and four general councils. Mr Lever, wisely, put such a scruple in the queen's head that she would not take the title of supreme head. The bishops, as it is said, will not swear unto it as it is, but rather lose their livings. The bill is in hand to restore men to their livings; how it will speed I know not. The Parliament is like to end shortly, and then we shall understand how they mind to use us. We are forced, through the vain bruits of the lying Papists, to give up a confession of our own faith, to show forth the sum of that doctrine which we profess, and to declare that we dissent not amongst ourselves. The labour we have now in hand and purpose to publish it so soon as the Parliament is ended. I wish that we had your hand unto it.

Ye are happy that ye are so far from these tossings and griefs, alterations and mutations; for we are made weary with them. But ye cannot long rest in your cell.[1] Ye must be removed to a more large abbey, and therefore in the meantime take your pleasure, for after ye will find but a little.

Nothing has been enacted about the marriage of the clergy but so far left in the air. Lever was married now of late. The queen's majesty will wink at it but not establish it by law, which is nothing else but to bastard our children. Others things another time. Thus praying you to commend me to your abbesses I take my leave of you for the present. Hastily at London. *Last of* April, 1559.

Your E. Sandys.

9. FROM H. ROBINSON, ed. *The Zurich Letters,* I, Parker Society, Cambridge, 1842, no. XII.

21 May, 1559. John Parkhurst to Henry Bullinger.

Jewel and I received your very courteous letter at the beginning of April, by which I perceived your intention of sending your son

---

[1] Parker was master of Corpus Christi College, Cambridge, at this time. None of the other preferments, of which he had been deprived in Mary's reign, had yet been restored to him.

Rodolph, at some appointed time, to improve his education at the university of Oxford. This, however, as things now are, I would not advise your to do; for it is as yet a den of thieves, and of those that hate the light. There are but few gospellers there, and many Papists. But when it shall have been reformed, which we both hope and desire may ere long be the case, let your Rodolph at length come over. I will not now tell you how much I shall be gratified by his arrival in England; for I would express my regard towards him by deeds rather than words.

The Book of Common Prayer, set forth in the time of King Edward, is now again in general use throughout England, and will be every-where, in spite of the struggles and opposition of the pseudo bishops. The queen is not willing to be called the head of the church of England, although this title has been offered her; but she willingly accepts the title of governor which amounts to the same thing. The pope is again driven from England to the great regret of the bishops and the whole tribe of shavelings. The mass is abolished. The Parliament broke up on the eighth of May. The earl of Bedford has made a present of three crowns to our friend Wolfgang who in this respect is more fortunate than many others.

The bishops are in future to have no palaces, estates or country seats. The present owners are to enjoy for life those they are now in possession of. They are worthy of being suspended not only from their office but from a halter; for they are as so many Davuses[1] throwing everything in confusion. The monasteries will be dissolved in a short time.

I cannot now write more for within four days I have to contend in my native place[2] both from the pulpit and in mutual conference with those horrid monsters of Arianism; for which end I have read with much attention your very learned treatise on both natures of Christ. I hope to come sufficiently prepared to the contest and so to over-come the enemies of Christ. Christ lives, he reigns, and will reign in spite of Arians, Anabaptists and Papists.

Farewell, most excellent and very dear sir. . . .

 10. FROM H. ROBINSON, ed. *The Zurich Letters*, I, Parker Society, Cambridge, 1842, no. XIV.

 22 May, 1559. John Jewel to Henry Bullinger.

Much health. Your letter, most accomplished sir, was most gratify-ing to my friend Parkhurst and myself, both as coming from one to whom we can never forget how greatly we are indebted, and also, as retaining the deepest traces of that courtesy and kindness of yours

---

[1] Dervishes.   [2] Guildford.

towards us, which we so largely experienced during the whole time of our exile. And I wish we may be able, some time or other, in some measure to requite your kindness: but howsoever this may be the inclination, at least, shall not be wanting. Your exhortation that we should act with firmness and resolution was a stimulus so far from being unacceptable to us that it was almost necessary. For we have at this time not only to contend with our adversaries, but even with those of our friends who, of late years, have fallen away from us and gone over to the opposite party; and who are now opposing us with a bitterness and obstinacy far exceeding that of any common enemy; and, what is most vexacious, we have to struggle with what has been left us by the Spaniards, that is, with the foulest vices, pride, luxury, and licentiousness. We are doing, however, and have done all that is in our power: may God prosper our exertions, and give them a happy issue! But at present we are so living as scarcely to seem like persons returned from exile: for to say nothing else, not one of us has yet had even his own property restored to him. Yet, although this long waiting is very tiresome to us, we doubt not but that in a short time all will be well. For we have a wise and religious queen, and one too who is favourably and propitiously disposed towards us. Religion is again placed on the same footing on which it stood in King Edward's time: to which event, I doubt not, but that your own letters and exhortations, and those of your republic, have powerfully contributed. The queen is unwilling to be addressed, either by word of mouth, or in writing, as the head of the church of England. For she seriously maintains that this honour is due to Christ alone, and cannot belong to any human being soever; besides which, these titles have been so foully contaminated by antichrist that they can no longer be adopted by anyone without impiety. . . .

(iii) The Erastian View of the Royal Supremacy

---

11. FROM J. JEWEL, *An Apology or Answer in defence of the Church of England*, 1564, sig. C I–C II, [N VII]–O I, Q I–Q II. J. Ayre, ed. *Works of John Jewel*, III, Parker Society, Cambridge, 1850, pp. 59, 98–9, 105–6.

We believe that there is one church of God, and that the same is not shut up (as in times past among the Jews) into some one corner or kingdom, but that it is catholic and universal, and dispersed throughout the whole world. So that there is now no nation which can truly complain that they be shut forth, and may not be one of the church and people of God. And that this church is the kingdom, the body and the spouse of Christ: and that Christ alone is the prince of this kingdom; that Christ alone is the head of this body, and that Christ alone is the bridegroom of this spouse.

Furthermore that there be divers degrees of ministers in the church; whereof some be deacons, some priests, some bishops; to whom is committed the office to instruct the people, and the whole charge and setting forth of religion. Yet notwithstanding we say that there neither is nor can be any man which may have the whole superiority in this universal state; for that Christ is ever present to assist his church, and needeth not any man to supply his room, as his only heir to all his substance; and that there can be no one mortal creature which is able to comprehend or conceive in his mind the universal church, that is to wit, all the parts of the world, much less able to put them in order and to govern them rightly and duly.

... I say besides all these things we see by histories and by examples of the best times that good princes ever took the administration of ecclesiastical matters to pertain to their duty.

Moses, a civil magistrate and chief guide to the people, both received from God and delivered to the people, all the order for religion and sacrifices, and gave Aaron the bishop a vehement and sore rebuke for making the golden calf and for suffering the corruption of religion. Joshua also, though he were no other than a civil magistrate, yet as soon as he was chosen by God, and set as a ruler over the people, he received commandments especially touching religion and the service of God.... And to rehearse no more examples out of the old law, let us rather consider since the birth of Christ how the church hath been governed in the gospel's time. The

Christian emperors in old time appointed the councils of the bishops. Constantine called the council at Nice, Theodosius the First called the council at Constantinople; Theodosius the Second the council at Ephesus, Martian the council at Chalcedon. . . . Continually for the space of five hundred years the emperor alone appointed the ecclesiastical assemblies, and called the councils of the bishops together.

We now, therefore, marvel the more at the unreasonable dealing of the bishop of Rome, who knowing what was the emperor's right when the church was well ordered, knowing also that it is now a common right to all princes, for so much as kings are now fully possessed in the several parts of the whole empire, doth so without consideration assign that office alone to himself, and taketh it sufficient in summoning a general council to make a man that is prince of the whole world no otherwise partaker thereof than he would make his own servant. And although the modesty and mildness of the Emperor Ferdinando be so great that he can bear this wrong, because peradventure he understandeth not well the pope's packing, yet ought not the pope of his holiness to offer him that wrong, nor to claim as his own another man's right.

And as for us, we of all others most justly have left him. For our kings, yea, even they which with greatest reverence did follow and obey the authority and faith of the bishops of Rome have long since found and felt well enough the yoke and the tyranny of the pope's kingdom. For the bishops of Rome took the crown off from the head of our King Henry the Second, and compelled him to put aside all majesty, and like a mere private man to come unto their legate with great submission and humility, so as all his subjects might laugh him to scorn. More than this, they caused bishops and monks and some part of the nobility to be in the field against our King John, and set all the people at liberty from their oath whereby they ought allegiance to their king: and at last, wickedly and most abominably they bereaved the king not only of his kingdom but also of his life. Besides this they excommunicated and cursed King Henry the Eighth, the most famous prince, and stirred up against him sometime the emperor, sometime the French king, and, as much as in them was, put in adventure our realm to have been a very prey and spoil. Yet were they but fools and mad to think that either so mighty a prince could be scared with bugs and rattles; or else that so noble and great a kingdom might so easily, even at one morsel, be devoured and swallowed up.

And yet, as though all this were too little, they would needs make all the realm tributary to them, and exacted thence yearly most unjust and wrongful taxes. So dear cost us the friendship of the city of Rome.

Wherefore if they have gotten these things of us by extortion through their fraud and subtle sleights, we see no reason why we may not pluck away the same from them again by lawful ways and just means. And if our kings in that darkness and blindness of former times gave them these things of their own accord and liberality for religion's sake, being moved with a certain opinion of their feigned holiness, now, when ignorance and error is spied out, may the kings their successors take them away again, seeing they have the same authority the kings their ancestors had before. For the gift is void except it be allowed by the will of the giver: and that cannot seem a perfect will which is dimmed and hindered by error.

12. FROM *The Works of the very learned and reverend Father in God, John Jewel*, 1611, 'The Defence of the Apology', pp. 12–13.

The Apology, chap. 2, division 3.

That we renew, and as it were, fetch again from hell the old and many a day condemned heresies: that we sow abroad new sects, and such broils as never erst were heard of; also that we are already divided into contrary parts and opinions, and could yet by no means agree well among ourselves.

M. Harding.

Sith that ye raise up again the heresy of Arius in denying prayer for the dead, who was for the same accounted an heretic eleven hundred years past; sith that ye raise up the heresy of Manichaeus that lived before him in taking away free will; sith that ye raise up the heresy of Vigilantius in refusing to pray to saints, and to honour their holy relics and to keep lights in churches to the honour of God, and many other heresies beside of old time condemned; sith that ye raise up the heresies of Berengarius in denying the presence of Christ's very body in the blessed sacrament of the altar; and sith that ye add to those more heresies of your own, as the appointing of the supreme pastorship or regiment of the church in all things and causes spiritual to a lay magistrate ... all these things besides sundry other of like enormity being true, as they be most true, this other cry made upon you is true.

The bishop of Sarisbury.

This heap is great in show and light in substance. Touching Berengarius, gentle reader, for shortness' sake I must refer thee to my former reply to M. Harding. Arius the Arian heretic, the breach of vows, the dissension of judgements in religion shall be answered, God willing, hereafter, each matter severally in his place. We flatter not our prince with any new imagined extraordinary power, but only give him that prerogative and chiefty that evermore hath been due unto him by the ordinance and word of God: that is to say, to be the nurse of God's religion; to make laws for the church; to hear and take up cases, and questions of the faith, if he be able; or otherwise to commit them over by his authority unto the learned; to command the bishops and priests to do their duties, and to punish such as be offenders. Thus the godly Emperor Constantinus sat in judgement in a cause ecclesiastical between Cicilianus and Donatus *a Casis Nigris,* and in the end himself pronounced sentence. Greater authority than Constantinus the emperor had and used our princes require none. This, I trust, hitherto is no great heresy.

13. P.R.O. S P 12/41/43. Printed in J. Bruce and T. T. Perowne, eds. *Correspondence of Matthew Parker,* Parker Society, 1853, no. CCXXV.

14 December, 1566. The bishops' petition to the queen to allow a bill to enforce subscription to the Thirty-nine Articles.

To the queen's most excellent majesty.

Most humbly beseecheth your most excellent majesty your faithful, loving and obedient subjects, the archbishops and bishops of both the provinces within this your majesty's realm, whose names are hereunder written, that it would please your highness, according to your accustomed benignity, to have gracious consideration of their humble suit ensuing.

Whereas a bill hath lately passed in your majesty's Lower House of Parliament concerning uniformity in doctrine, and confirmation of certain articles agreed upon by the whole clergy of this your majesty's realm in the late Convocation called together by commandment of your majesty's writ accustomed, and thereby holden in the fifth year of your majesty's most happy reign: which bill was lately exhibited to your highness' Upper House of Parliament, with special recommendation as well at the first delivery thereof, as again of late by recommendation renewed from the said Lower House, and thereupon was once read in the said Upper House. So it is that we understand that the further reading of the said bill in your Upper House is stayed by your majesty's special commandment. Whereupon we your highness' humble and faithful subjects think ourselves bound in conscience as well to the sacred majesty of Almighty God, as in respect of our ecclesiastical office and charge toward your highness and loving subjects of your realm, to make our several and most humble suit unto your majesty, that it may please the same to grant that the said bill, by order from your majesty may be read, examined and judged by your highness' said Upper House, with all expedition; and that if it be allowed of and do pass by order there, it would please your majesty to give your royal assent thereunto. The reasons that enforce us to make this humble petition are these. First the matter itself toucheth the glory of God, the advancement of true religion, and the salvation of Christian souls, and therefore ought principally, chiefly, and before all other things, to be sought. Secondly in the book which is now desired to be confirmed are contained the principal articles of Christian religion most agreeable to God's word publicly sithens the beginning of your majesty's reign professed, and by your highness' authority set forth and maintained. Thirdly, divers and sundry errors, and namely such as have been in this realm wickedly and obstinately by the adversaries of the gospel defended, are by the same articles condemned. Fourthly, the approbation of these articles by your majesty shall be a very good mean to establish and confirm all your highness' subjects in one consent and unity of true doctrine, to the great quiet and safety of your majesty and this your realm: whereas now, for want of a plain certainty of articles of doctrine by law to be declared, great distraction and dissension of minds is at this present among your subjects, and daily is like more and more to increase, and that with very great danger in policy, the circumstances considered, if the said book of articles be now stayed in your majesty's hands, or (as God forbid) rejected. Fifthly, considering that this matter so narrowly toucheth the glory of God, the sincerity of religion, the health of Christian souls, the godly unity of your realm, with the utility thereof, and the dangers on the contrary, we thought it our most bounden duties, being placed by God and your highness as pastors and chief ministers in this church, and such as are to give a reckoning before God of our pastoral office, with all humble and earnest suit to beseech your majesty to have due consideration of this matter, as the governor and nurse of this church, having also an account to render unto Almighty God, the King of kings, for your charge and office. Thus, most gracious sovereign lady, your said humble subjects, moved with the causes above rehearsed, besides divers others here for brevity sake omitted, beseech your most excellent majesty, that this our petition may take good effect, as the weightiness of the cause requireth, and that before the end of this present session of Parliament. And we, according to our most bounden duties, shall daily pray to God for the preservation of your majesty in honour, health and prosperity long to reign.

Matthew [Parker.] Archbishop of Canterbury.

Thomas [Young.] Archbishop of *York*.

Edmund [Grindal. Bishop of] London.

James [Pilkington. Bishop of] Durham.

Robert [Horne. Bishop of] *Winchester.*
William [Barlow. Bishop of] *Chichester.*
John [Scory. Bishop of] Hereford.
Richard [Cox. Bishop of] Ely.
Edwin [Sandys. Bishop of] *Worcester.*
Nicholas [Bullingham. Bishop of] Lincoln.
Richard [Davies. Bishop of] *St Davids.*
Thomas [Bentham. Bishop of] Coventry and Lichfield.
William [Downham. Bishop of] *Chester.*
Thomas [Davies. Bishop of] *St Asaph.*
Nicholas [Robinson. Bishop of] Bangor.

14. FROM T. COOPER, *An Admonition to the People of England,*
1589, pp. 209, 212, 214, 215.

It is further alleged out of Christ's doctrine, that when he answered
the Pharisees, Matthew 22, he giveth a plain commandment that
lands and possessions should be at the pleasure of the prince, and that
ministers of the church ought to give them up unto him. For this, he
saith, 'Give to Caesar that which is Caesar's, and to God that is God's'.
But, say they,[1] 'all temporal lands are Caesar's; therefore they ought
to give them unto Caesar: and our Caesar is our gracious prince
and sovereign'.

Truly, it would make any Christian heart to lament in these days
to see God's holy word so miserably drawn, racked and pulled in
sunder from the true meaning thereof. If the bishops and other of
the clergy of England did grudge or murmur to have their lands and
livings to be tributary to the prince, and subject to all taxes and
services, that by the laws of this realm may be, either to the maintenance of her person, or to the defence of our country: or if they
did challenge such an immunity or exemption from the authority
of the prince, as the pope and his clergy did: or if they did find themselves grieved to be punished by the prince for the breach of her
laws, as the Donatists in old time did, and some now in our age do:
if they were such enemies to princes and governors, as they would
exempt them out of the state of true Christianity, and of the church of
God, and make them only to serve their turn in evil affairs: then
indeed did this place make strongly against them. But I trust the
clergy of England are with all good men out of the suspicion of these
points. They are as willing and ready at all times to be contributory,
as any other subjects are: they claim no exemption from her authority: they willingly submit themselves to her correction: they humbly
acknowledge their obedience in all things that any Christian prince

---

[1] Those who were leading the attack on episcopacy.

may require: and this do they principally for conscience sake, because it is the ordinance and commandment of God: but much moved there to also, as men, in consideration of their own state, which next under God dependeth of her majesty. Seeing, therefore, the hand of God hath more straitly bound them unto her, than other common subjects, I doubt not but she willingly hath, and shall have, all duties of obedience at their hands, that any Christian subjects by the word of God are bound unto. Neither are they in any fear that her majesty will press them to anything which shall not stand with the glory of God and furtherance of the gospel. But how these words of Christ before mentioned do command them presently to yield up into her majesty's hands such lands and possessions as by the grant of her goodness and by the law of this realm they now enjoy, indeed I see not. If such a prince shall come (as I trust in my days never to see) that shall put them to this choice either to forgo their lands and livings, or to lose the free course of the gospel: it is before declared what their duty is to do therein. And I doubt not, but in the late time of persecution there were many of them that would have been glad with all the veins in their hearts, by that choice to have enjoyed in this realm the freedom of their consciences, though they had been put to as poor estate as possibly men might have lived in. But how that Christian princes are warranted either by this place of the gospel or by any part of the word of God, so hardly to deal with the state of the ministry, I have not as yet learned, though it be in these days by some boldly affirmed. . . .

The meaning of Christ is in those words to teach his to put a difference between the duty that they owe to the prince and that they owe to God: and to declare that within their due bounds they may both stand together. Therefore, they that will rightly follow Christ in this doctrine must consider in what consisteth the duty towards a prince or magistrate, and wherein resteth our duty towards God. We owe to the prince honour, fear and obedience: obedience, I say, in all those things that are not against the word of God and his commandments. Those things that God commandeth a Christian prince cannot forbid: those things that God forbiddeth no prince hath authority to command. But such things as be external, and by God's word left indifferent, the prince by his authority may so by law dispose either in commanding or forbidding, as in wisdom and discretion he shall think to make most to the glory of God, and to the good and safe state of his people. Among these things external I think lands, goods and possessions to be, and therefore that the same ought to be subject to tax and tribute in such sort as the laws and state of the country requireth: yea, and if there shall happen in any country a magistrate

K

which by violence and extortion shall wrest more unto him of the
lands and substance of the people than law and right requireth; I see
no cause warranted by God's word that the inferior subjects can rebel,
or resist the prince therein, but that they shall evidently show themselves to resist the ordinance of God. For they have not the sword
of correction committed into their hand, and often times God by
evil princes correcteth the sins of the people. Wherefore, if subjects
resist the hard dealings even of evil magistrates they do in that respect
strive against God himself, who will not suffer it unpunished. . . .

We may learn then by this that Christian duty of a subject consisteth in loving, in reverencing, in obeying the prince and magistrate
in all things that lawfully he commandeth: and in those things that
he commandeth unlawfully not by violence to resist him, though the
same touch our goods, our lands, yea and our life also. As touching
our duty toward God, we owe unto him ourselves wholly, both body
and soul, and all things and parts to the same appertaining, according
to that his law requireth: 'Thou shalt love God with all thy heart,
with all thy soul, with all thy mind, and with thy whole power.' For
we are his creatures, and he is our lord and maker. But for as much
as princes, magistrates, rulers, parents, masters and all superiors
have a portion of God's authority over us, as his officers and lieutenants in their callings: therefore God doth permit unto them some
part also of his honour, but so far and in such things, and such manner
as before is declared, retaining unto himself our faith and religion,
with all the parts of his divine worship consisting in spirit and in
truth, the calling upon his blessed name, the confession of his holy
truth, and the obedience of his moral law: which things he doth not
make subject to any prince's authority. And if any prince or magistrate
by violence and cruelty shall break into the bounds of our duty towards God, I say not that private subjects may by violence resist it:
but surely they may not obey it, but rather yield into his hands
goods, lands, country and life too. . . .

This is the true doctrine of the words of Christ before mentioned
by which we are taught to put a difference between our duty towards
God, and that we owe toward the prince, yielding to each that which
is his: a doctrine most profitable and necessary to all Christian
churches and commonweals. But who can gather of this that the
ministers of the church of Christ, living under a Christian prince
favouring and defending the gospel must of necessity give up into
the prince's hands those lands and possessions which by the grant
of the same prince and the law of the land is assigned unto them?
For if the land be Caesar's, and therefore must be delivered to Caesar,

then are all goods Caesar's, and must be also yielded into his hands. God save us from princes that will use like violence and tyranny toward our lands, goods and bodies, as these men use to the word of God.

But the gracious province of Almighty God hath, I trust, put these thorns of contradiction in our sides, lest that should steal upon the church in a slumber, which now, I doubt not, but through his assistance, may be turned away from us, bending thereunto ourselves with constancy, constancy in labour to do all men good, constancy in prayer unto God for all men, her especially, whose sacred power matched with incomparable goodness of nature, hath hitherto been God's most happy instrument, by him miraculously kept for works of so miraculous preservation and safety unto others; that as, 'By the sword of God and Gideon' was some time the cry of the people of Israel, so it might deservedly be at this day the joyful song of innumerable multitudes, yea, the emblem of some estates and dominions in the world, and (which must be eternally confessed, even with tears of thankfulness) the true inscription, style or title of all churches as yet standing within this realm, 'By the goodness of Almighty God, and his servant Elizabeth, we are'.

We hold that seeing there is not any man of the church of England but the same is also a member of the commonwealth; nor any member of the commonwealth, which is not also of the church of England. Therefore, as in a figure triangle the base doth differ from the sides thereof, and yet one and the self same line is both a base and also a side; a side simply, a base if it chance to be the bottom and under lie the rest. So albeit properties and actions of one do cause the name of a commonwealth, qualities and functions of another sort, the name of the church to be given to a multitude; yet one and the self same multitude may in such sort be both. Nay, it is so with us, that no person appertaining to the one, can be denied also to be of the other: contrariwise, unless they against us should hold that the church and the commonwealth are two, both distinct and separate societies; of which two, one comprehendeth always persons not belonging to the other, (that which they do) they could not conclude out of the difference between the church and commonwealth, namely that the bishops may not meddle with the affairs of the commonwealth, because they are governors of another corporation, which is the church; nor kings, with making laws for the church, because they have government not of this corporation, but of another divided from it; the commonwealth and the walls of separation between these two must forever be upheld: they hold the necessity of personal separation which clean excludeth the power of one man's dealing with both; we of natural, but that one and the same person may in both bear principal sway.

When, therefore Christian kings are said to have spiritual dominion or supreme power in ecclesiastical affairs and causes the meaning is, that within their own precincts and territories, they have an authority and power to command even in matters of Christian religion, and that there is no higher nor greater that can in those cases overcommand them, where they are placed to reign as kings. But withal we must likewise note that their power is termed supremacy as being the highest, not simply without exception of anything. For what man is so brain sick as not to except in such speeches God himself, the king of all dominion? Who doubteth but that the king who received it must hold it of, and order the law according to that old axiom, *The king assigns to the law that power which the law has assigned to him.* And again, *The king ought not to be under man but under God and the law.* Thirdly, whereas it is altogether without reason 'That kings are judged to have by virtue of their dominion, although greater power than any, yet not than all the state of those societies conjoined, wherein such sovereign rule is given them': there is not anything hereunto to the contrary by us affirmed, no, not when we grant supreme authority unto kings, because supremacy is not otherwise intended or meant to exclude partly foreign powers and partly the power which belongeth in several unto others, contained as parts in that politic body over which those kings have supremacy: 'where the king hath power of dominion, or supreme power, there no foreign state or potentate, no state or potentate domestical, whether it consisteth of one or many, can possibly have in the same affairs and causes authority higher than the king.' Power of spiritual dominion, therefore, is in causes ecclesiastical that ruling authority which neither any foreign state, nor yet any part of that politic body at home, wherein the same is established, can lawfully over rule. It hath been declared already in general, how 'the best established dominion is where the law doth most rule the king'; the true effect whereof particularly is found as well in ecclesiastical as civil affairs. In these the king, through his supreme power, may do sundry great things himself, both appertaining to peace and war, both at home, and by command and by commerce with states abroad, because the law doth so much permit. Sometimes on the other side, 'The king alone hath no right to do without consent of his Lords and Commons in Parliament: the king himself cannot change the nature of pleas, nor courts, no, not so much as restore blood', because the law is a bar unto him: the positive laws of the realm have a privilege therein, and restrain the king's power; which positive laws, whether by custom or otherwise established without repugnancy to the laws of God, and nature, ought not less to be in force even in supernatural affairs of the church, whether in regard of ecclesiastical laws, we willingly embrace that of Ambrose, *The emperor has authority within the church, not over the church.* 'Kings have dominion to exercise in ecclesiastical causes, but according to the laws of the church.' Whether it be therefore the nature of courts, or the form of pleas, or the kind of governors, or the order of proceeding in whatsoever business, for the received laws and liberty of the church, 'the king hath supreme authority and power, but against them never'. What such positive laws hath appointed to be done by others than the king, or by others with the king, and in what form they have appointed the doing of it, the same of necessity must be kept; neither is the king's sole authority to alter it: yet, as it were a thing unreasonable if in civil affairs the king, albeit the whole universal body did join with him, should do anything by their absolute power for the ordering of their state at home in prejudice of those ancient laws of nations, which are of force throughout all the world, because the necessary commerce of kingdoms dependeth on them. So in principal matters belonging to Christian religion, a thing very scandalous and offensive it must needs be thought, if either kings or laws should dispose of the law of God, without any respect had unto that which of old hath been reverently thought of throughout the world, and wherein there is no law of God which forceth us to swerve from the ways wherein so many and holy ages have gone. . . .

Unto which supreme power in kings, two kinds of adversaries there are which have opposed themselves: one sort defending 'that supreme power in causes ecclesiastical throughout the world appertaineth of divine right to the bishop of Rome'. Another sort, 'that the said power belongeth in every national church unto the clergy thereof assembled'. We which defend as well against the one as against the other, 'that kings within their own precincts may have it' must show by what right it must come unto them. . . .

There are which wonder that we should account any statute a law which the high court of Parliament in England hath established about the matters of church regiment: the prince and court of Parliament having (as they suppose) no more lawful means to give order to the church and clergy in those things than they have to make laws for the hierarchies of angels in heaven: that the Parliament being a mere temporal court, can neither by the law of nature, nor of God, have competent power to define of such matters; that supremacy in this kind cannot belong unto kings as kings, because pagan emperors, whose princely power was true sovereignty, never challenged so much over the church: that power in this kind cannot be the right of any earthly crown, prince or state, in that they be Christians; forasmuch as if they be Christians they all owe subjection to the pastors of their souls: that the prince, therefore, not having it himself cannot communicate it to the Parliament, and consequently cannot make laws here, or determine of the church's regiment by himself, Parliament or any other court subjected unto him.

The Parliament of England, together with the Convocation annexed thereunto, is that whereupon the very essence of all government within this kingdom doth depend; it is even the body of the whole realm; it consisteth of the king, and of all that within the land are subject unto him. The Parliament is a court not so merely temporal, as if it might meddle with nothing but only leather and wool.... The most natural and religious course in making laws is, that the matter of them be taken from the judgement of the wisest in those things which they are to concern. In matters of God, to set down a form of prayer, a solemn confession of the articles of the Christian faith, and ceremonies meet for the exercise of religion, it were unnatural not to think the pastors and bishops of our souls a great deal more fit, than men of secular trades and callings. Howbeit, when all, which the wisdom of all sorts can do, is done for the devising of laws in the church, it is the general consent of all that giveth them the form and vigour of laws, without which they could be no more unto us than the counsel of physicians to the sick. Well might they seem as wholesome admonitions and instructions, but laws could they never be, without consent of the whole church to be guided by them; whereunto both nature and the practice of the church of God set down in scripture is found every way so fully consonant that God himself would not impose, no, not his own laws upon his people by the hand of Moses without their free and open consent. Wherefore, to define and determine even of the church's affairs by way of assent and approbation, as laws are defined in that right of power, which doth give them the force of laws; thus to define of our own church's regiment the Parliament of England hath competent authority.

Now the question is, whether the clergy alone so assembled ought to have the whole power of making ecclesiastical laws, or else consent of the laity may there unto be made necessary, and the king's assent so necessary, that his sole denial may be of force to stay them from being laws....

...It is a thing even undoubtedly natural that all free and independent societies should themselves make their own laws, and that this power should belong to the whole, not to any certain part of a politic body, though haply some one part may have greater sway in that action than the rest; which thing being generally fit and expedient in the making of all laws, we see no cause why to think otherwise in laws concerning the service of God, which in all well ordered states and commonwealths is the first thing that law hath care to provide for. When we speak of the right which naturally belongeth to a commonwealth, we speak of that which must needs belong to the church of God. For if the commonwealth be Christian, if the people which are of it do publicly embrace the true religion, this very thing doth make it the church, as hath been showed. So that unless the verity and purity of religion do take from them which embrace it that power wherewith otherwise they are possessed; look what authority, as touching laws for religion, a commonwealth hath simply, it must of necessity, being of the Christian religion.

It will be therefore perhaps alleged that a part of the verity of Christian religion is to hold the power of making ecclesiastical laws a thing appropriated unto the clergy in their synods; and whatsoever is by their only voices agreed upon, it needeth no further approbation to give unto it the strength of a law, as may plainly appear by the canons of that first most venerable assembly where those things the Apostle and James had concluded were afterwards published and imposed upon the churches of the gentiles abroad as laws, the records thereof remaining still in the book of God for a testimony that the power of making ecclesiastical laws belongeth to the successors of the apostles, the bishops and prelates of the church of God.

To this we answer, that the Council of Jerusalem is no argument for the power of the clergy to make laws. For, first, there hath not been sithence any council of like authority to that in Jerusalem. Secondly, the cause why that was of such authority came by a special accident. Thirdly, the reason why other councils being not like unto that in nature, the clergy in them should have no power to make laws by themselves alone, is in truth so forcible, that, except some commandment of God to the contrary can be showed, it ought, notwithstanding the foresaid example, to prevail....

... Till it be proved that some special law of Christ hath for ever annexed unto the clergy alone the power to make ecclesiastical laws, we are to hold it a thing most consonant with equity and reason that no ecclesiastical laws be made in a Christian commonwealth without consent as well of the laity as of the clergy, but least of all without consent of the highest power.

(*iv*) The Catholic Rejection of a Lay Supremacy

16. FROM W. CAMDEN, *The History of the most renowned and victorious Princess Elizabeth* ... 1688, pp. 146–7. (Original Latin Bull in L. Cherubini, *Magnum Bullarium Romanum*, II, Luxemburg, 1727, pp. 324–5.)

He that reigneth on high, to whom is given all power in heaven and in earth, hath committed his one, holy, Catholic and apostolic church, out of which there is no salvation, to one alone upon earth, namely to Peter, the chief of the apostles, and to Peter's successor, the bishop of Rome, to be by him governed with plenary authority. Him alone hath he made prince over all people and all kingdoms, to pluck up, destroy, scatter, consume, plant and build; that he may preserve his faithful people (knit together with the band of charity) in the unity of the spirit, and present them spotless and unblamable to their Saviour. In discharge of which function, we, who are by God's goodness called to the government of the aforesaid church, do spare no pains, labouring with all earnestness, that unity and the Catholic religion (which the author thereof hath, for the trial of his children's faith and for our amendment, suffered to be tossed with so great afflictions) might be preserved sincere. But the number of the ungodly hath gotten such power, that there is now no place in the whole world left which they have not essayed to corrupt with their most wicked doctrines; and amongst others, Elizabeth, the pretended queen of England, the servant of wickedness, lendeth thereunto her helping hand, with whom, as in a sanctuary, the most pernicious persons have found a refuge. This very woman, having seized on the kingdom, and monstrously usurped the place of supreme head of the church in all England, and the chief authority and jurisdiction thereof, hath again reduced the said kingdom into a miserable and ruinous condition, which was so lately reclaimed to the Catholic faith and a thriving condition.

For having by strong hand prohibited the exercise of the true religion, which Mary, the lawful queen of most famous memory, had by the help of this see restored, after it had been formerly overthrown by Henry the Eighth, a revolter therefrom, and following and embracing the errors of heretics, she hath changed the royal council, consisting of the English nobility, and filled it up with obscure men being heretics; suppressed the embracers of the Catholic faith; constituted lewd preachers and ministers of impiety; abolished the sacrifice of the mass, prayers, fastings, choice of meats, unmarried life, and the Catholic rites and ceremonies; commanded books to be read through the whole realm containing manifest heresy, and appointed impious rites and institutions, by herself entertained and observed according to the prescript of Calvin, to be likewise observed by her subjects; presumed to eject bishops, parsons of churches, and other Catholic priests, out of their churches and benefices, and to bestow them and other church livings upon heretics, and to determine of church causes; prohibited the prelates, clergy and people to acknowledge the church of Rome, or to obey the precepts and canonical sanctions thereof; compelled most of them to condescend to her wicked laws, and to abjure the authority and obedience of the bishop of Rome, and to acknowledge her to be the sole lady in temporal and spiritual matters, and this by oath; imposed penalties and punishments upon those which obeyed not, and exacted them of those which persevered in the unity of the faith and their obedience aforesaid; cast the Catholic prelates and rectors of churches into prison, where many of them, being worn out with long languishing and sorrow, miserably ended their lives. All which things being so manifest and notorious to all nations, and by the serious testimony of very many so substantially proved, that there is no place at all left for excuse, defence or evasion: we seeing that impieties and wicked actions are multiplied one upon another, as also that the persecution of the faithful and affliction of religion growth every day heavier and heavier, through the instigation and by means of the said Elizabeth, and since we understand her heart to be so hardened and obdurate, that she hath not only contemned the godly requests and admonitions of Catholic princes concerning her cure and conversion, but also hath not so much as suffered the nuncios of this see to cross the seas for this purpose into England, are constrained of necessity to betake ourselves to the weapons of justice against her, being heartily grieved and sorry, that we are compelled thus to punish one to whose ancestors the whole state of Christendom hath been so much beholden. Being therefore supported with his authority whose pleasure it was to place us (though unable for so great a burden) in this supreme throne of justice, we do, out of the fulness of our apostolic power, declare the aforesaid Elizabeth, as being an heretic and favourer of heretics, and her adherents in the matters aforesaid, to have incurred the sentence of excommunication, and to be cut off from the unity of the body of Christ. And moreover we do declare her to be deprived of her pretended title to the kingdom aforesaid, and of all dominion, dignity and privilege whatsoever; and also the nobility, subjects and people of the said kingdom, and all others who have in any sort sworn unto her, to be for ever absolved from any such oath, and all manner of duty of dominion, allegiance and obedience: and we also do by authority of these presents absolve them, and do deprive the said Elizabeth of her pretended title to the kingdom, and all other things before named. And we do command and charge all and every the noblemen, subjects, people, and others aforesaid, that they presume not to obey her, or her orders, mandates and laws: and those which shall do the contrary, we do include them in the like sentence of anathema. And because it would be a difficult matter to convey these presents to all places wheresoever it shall be needful; our will is, that the copies thereof under a public notary's hand, and sealed with the seal of an ecclesiastical prelate, or of his court, shall carry altogether the same credit with all men, judicially and extrajudicially, as these presents should do, if they were exhibited or showed. Given at Rome at St Peter's in the year of the incarnation of our Lord one thousand five hundred sixty nine,[1] the fifth of the calends of March, and of our popedom the fifth year.

17. FROM [W. ALLEN] *A True, Sincere and Modest Defence of English Catholics,* 1584, pp. 6–10.

... The queen is commonly of Protestants called, 'supreme head of the church'. So their preachers in pulpit do sound out daily as all men know: and their writers in books dedicated to her (as Mr Bridges against Dr Saunders and Dr Stapleton, and others) do term her expressly. Whereof the wiser sort ... are so ashamed that they would have it given out, (to strangers especially who wonder at the monstrous title) that there is no such thing challenged of her, or given her by the new laws of religion in England.

The truth is that in the first year and Parliament of the queen's reign, when they abolished the pope's authority, and would have yielded the same authority with the title of supreme head to the queen as it was given before to her father and brother, divers specially moved by Minister Calvin's writing (who had condemned in the same princes that calling) liked not the term, and therefore procured that some other equivalent but less offensive might be used. Upon which formality it was enacted that she was 'the chief governor as well in causes ecclesiastical or spiritual, as civil and temporal'. And an oath of the same was conceived accordingly, to be tendered at their pleasures, to all the spiritual and temporal officers in the realm, by which every one must swear that in conscience he taketh and believeth her so to be: and that no priest or other born out of her realm can have or ought to have any manner of power in spiritual matters over her subjects. Which oath is counted the very torment of all English con-

[1] i.e. 1569/70.

sciences, not the Protestants themselves believing it to be true: and of all true Catholics, as before it was deemed in her father a layman, and in her brother a child, very ridiculous; so now in herself, being a woman, it is accounted a thing most monstrous and unnatural, and the very gap to bring any realm to the thralldom of all sects, heresy, paganism, turkism or atheism, that the prince for the time by human frailty may be subject unto: all our religion, faith, worship, service and prayers depending upon his sovereign determination: a thing that all nations have to take heed of by our example, for the redress of which pernicious absurdity so many of our said brethren so willingly have shed their blood.

In the first Parliament of her majesty's reign it was indeed, in a manner, thrust upon her against her will, because otherwise there could have been no colour to make new laws for change of religion; and this title, of chief governess, was thought to be a qualification of the former term of headship. But in truth it is all one with the other, or rather worse: for in some kind of improper speech the king may be called the head or chief of the church of his country, for that he is sovereign lord and ruler of both persons spiritual and temporal: all sorts bound to obey his lawful civil laws and commandments, and so in that sense is he head of the clergy and of all others.

But when in the new form of our statute it is expressly and distinctly added that she is the only supreme governor even in all causes, 'as well spiritual and ecclesiastical as temporal and civil'; and furthermore enacted that all jurisdictions, privileges, superiorities and preeminences ecclesiastical, as by any power spiritual have been or may be exercised, are taken from the pope (to whom Christ gave them in most ample manner) and are united, or rather (as they say) restored by an old decree to the crown of England: this can have no excuse, neither true or likely sense in the world, making indeed a king and a priest all one: no difference betwixt the state of the church and a temporal commonwealth; giving no less right to heathen princes to be governors of the church in causes spiritual, than to a Christian king: it maketh one part of the church in different territories to be independent and several from another, according to the distinction of realms and kingdoms in the world. And finally it maketh every man that is not born in the kingdom to be a foreigner also in respect of the church: these and a thousand absurdities and impossibilities more do ensure, which for brevity we omit. Only this which is in most men's memories we may not overpass, that the very same year that this new preeminence was given by law to the queen, and the oath accordingly ministered to many, some having remorse of the matter, for to avoid danger, pretended for their refusal that it seemed to them by the words of the oath and act, that the queen might minister also the sacraments, whereunto they would not swear by any means.

Whereupon in her next visitation of the clergy a special injunction was printed and published by her commandment declaring that in truth she had no such intent, and that no such thing was implied in her title or claim of spiritual regiment, nor no other thing, nor more than was before granted to her father by term of supreme head; requiring all her loving subjects to receive the oath at least in that sense, and so it should suffice her highness. By which it is now clear by their own authentical declaration, that we speak no untruth . . . nor abuse not the world when we say she is called and taken for the supreme head of the church of England: albeit (the thing itself being far more absurd and of more pernicious sequel than the makers of the law, which were mere laymen and most of them unlearned, could then perceive) their followers now could disavow the same. For this article therefore as the famous bishop of Rochester,[1] Sir Thomas More and a great number more in King Henry the Eight, his days; so did those two last named martyrs,[2] and divers others before them most gladly and constantly yield up their lives, and so consequently died for mere matter of religion only.

[1] John Fisher.
[2] John Slade and John Body executed at Winchester and Andover in 1583.

(v) The Qualified Acceptance of the Royal Supremacy by Presbyterians and Separatists

18. FROM W. H. FRERE and C. E. DOUGLAS, eds. *Puritan Manifestoes*, 1954, pp. 9–13, 19.

An Admonition to the Parliament, 1572.

May it therefore please your wisdoms to understand we in England are so far off from having a church rightly reformed according to the prescript of God's word, that as yet we are not come to the outward face of the same. For to speak of that wherein all consent and whereupon all writers accord. The outward marks whereby a true Christian church is known are preaching of the word purely, ministring the sacraments sincerely, and ecclesiastical discipline which consisteth in admonition and correction of faults severely. Touching the first, namely the ministry of the word, although it must be confessed that the substance of doctrine by many delivered is sound and good, yet herein it faileth, that neither the ministers thereof are according to God's word proved, elected, called or ordained: nor the function in such sort so narrowly looked unto, as of right it ought, and is of necessity required. For whereas in the old church a trial was had both of their ability to instruct, and of their godly conversation also: now, by letters commendatory of some one man, noble or other, tag and rag, learned and unlearned, of the basest sort of the people (to the slander of the gospel in the mouths of the adversaries) are freely received. In those days no idolatrous sacrificers or heathenish priests were appointed to be preachers of the gospel: but we allow and like well of popish massmongers, men for all seasons, King Henry's priests, King Edward's priests, Queen Mary's priests, who of a truth (if God's word were precisely followed) should from the same be utterly removed. Then they taught others, now they must be instructed themselves, and therefore like young children they must learn catechisms. Then election was made by the common consent of the whole church: now everyone picketh out for himself some notable good benefice, he obtaineth the next advowson by money or by favour, and so thinketh himself to be sufficiently chosen. Then the congregation had authority to call ministers: instead thereof now they run, they ride, and by unlawful suit and buying prevent other suitors also. Then no minister placed in any congregation but by consent of the people; now that authority is given into the hands of the bishop alone, who by his sole authority thrusteth upon them such as they many times as well for unhonest life, as also for lack of learning, may and do justly dislike. Then none admitted to the ministry but a place was void before hand, to which he should be called: but now bishops (to whom the right of ordering ministers doth at no hand appertain) do make 60, 80 or a 100 at a clap, and send them abroad into the country like masterless men. Then after just trial and vocation they were admitted to their function, by laying on of the hands of the company of the eldership only: now there is (neither of these being looked unto) required an alb, a surplice, a vestment, a pastoral staff, beside that ridiculous, and (as they use it to their new creatures) blasphemous saying, 'Receive the Holy Ghost'. Then every pastor had his flock, and every flock his shepherd or else shepherds; now they do not only run frisking from place to place (a miserable disorder in God's church) but covetously join living to living, making shipwreck of their consciences, and being but one shepherd (nay, would to God they were shepherds and not wolves) have many flocks. Then the ministers were preachers: now bare readers. And if any be so well disposed to preach in their own charges, they may not without my lord's license. In those days known by voice, learning and doctrine: now they must be discerned from other by popish and antichristian apparel, as cap, gown, tippet etc. Then, as God gave utterance, they preached the word only: now they read homilies, articles, injunctions etc. Then it was painful, now gainful. Then poor and ignominious: now rich and glorious. And therefore titles, livings and offices by antichrist devised are given to them, as metropolitan, archbishop, lord's grace, lord bishop, suffragan, dean, archdeacon, prelate of the garter, earl, county palatine, honour, high commissioners, justice of peace and quorum etc. All which, together with their offices, as they are strange and unheard of in Christ's church, nay, plainly in God's word forbidden, so are they utterly with speed out of the same to be removed. Then ministers were not tied to any form of prayers invented by man, but as the Spirit moved them, so they poured forth hearty supplications to the Lord. Now they are bound of necessity to a prescript order of service, and Book of Common Prayer in which a great number of things contrary to God's word are contained, as baptism by women, private communions, Jewish purifyings, observing of holidays etc. patched (if not altogether, yet the greatest piece) out of the pope's portuise. Then feeding the flock diligently: now teaching quarterly. Then preaching in season and out of season: now once a month is thought sufficient; if twice, it is judged a work of supererogation. Then nothing taught but God's word: now prince's pleasures, men's devices, popish ceremonies and antichristian rites in public pulpits defended. Then they sought them: now they seek theirs.

These, and a great many other abuses are in the ministry remaining, which unless they be removed and the truth brought in, not only

God's justice shall be poured forth, but also God's church in this realm shall never be builded. For if they which seem to be workmen are no workmen in deed, but in name: or else work not so diligently and in such order as the workmaster commandeth, it is not only unlikely that the building shall go forward, but altogether impossible that ever it shall be perfected. The way therefore to avoid these inconveniences, and to reform these deformities is this: your wisdoms have to remove advowsons, patronages, impropriations, and bishops' authority claiming to themselves thereby right to ordain ministers; and to bring in that old and true election, which was accustomed to be made by the congregation. You must displace those ignorant and unable ministers already placed, and in their rooms appoint such as both can and will, by God's assistance, feed the flock. You must pluck down and utterly overthrow without hope of restitution the court of faculties from whence not only licenses to enjoy many benefices are obtained, as pluralities, trialities, totquots[1] etc. but all things for the most part, as in the court of Rome, are set on sale; licenses to marry, to eat flesh in times prohibited, to lie from benefices and charges, and a great number beside of such like abominations. Appoint to every congregation a learned and diligent preacher. Remove homilies, articles, injunctions, a prescript order of service made out of the mass book. Take away the lordship, the loitering, the pomp, the idleness, and livings of bishops, but yet employ them to such ends as they were in the old church appointed for. Let a lawful and godly seigniory look that they preach, not quarterly or monthly, but continually: not for filthy lucre sake, but of a ready mind. So God shall be glorified, your consciences discharged, and the flock of Christ (purchased with his own blood) edified.

Is a reformation good for France? And can it be evil for England? Is discipline meet for Scotland? And is it unprofitable for this realm? Surely God hath set these examples before your eyes to encourage you to go forward to a thorough and a speedy reformation.

19. FROM H. ROBINSON, ed. *The Zurich Letters,* I, Parker Society, Cambridge, 1842, no. XCIV.

15 August, 1573. Edwin Sandys to Henry Bullinger.

On many accounts, most esteemed sir, I am greatly in your debt; both because you have always regarded me with the greatest kindness and affection, and because you have condescended to write to me so diligently and so frequently. For all which things, though I cannot make an equal return, yet I will thank you as much as I can, and shall at all

[1] general dispensations.

times readily acknowledge myself very much indebted to you for your peculiar kindness.

You must not impute it to neglect that I so seldom write to you, but to the unfrequency of the means of communication between us, especially in these most turbulent times, when war and tumults and slaughter are everywhere rife. For there is no one to whom I should write with greater pleasure than to Master Bullinger, whom, as I have always loved him exceedingly for his great courtesy, so have I also much venerated for his singular erudition, and rare piety, and other excellent qualities. For when I call to my remembrance, as I very often do, with how much favour and regard I was entertained by you, how like a brother and a friend you treated me when an exile, and the comfort in which I seemed to myself to live among you, I wish for nothing more than that, relieved from those cases and anxieties with which I am now overwhelmed, I might pass the remainder of my life at Zurich as a sojourner and private person. Thoughts of this kind are continually occurring to me; nor is there anything that I should wish for more. But I perceive that this cannot be. I am not born for myself: our church, which is most sadly tossed about in these evil times, and is in a most wretched state of confusion, vehemently demands all my exertions; I dare not desert the spouse of Christ in her danger; for conscience would cry out against me, and convict me of having betrayed her. New orators are rising up from among us, foolish young men, who, while they despise authority, and admit of no superior, are seeking the complete overthrow and rooting up of our whole ecclesiastical polity, so piously constituted and confirmed, and established by the entire consent of most excellent men; and are striving to shape out for us I know not what new platform of a church. And you would not imagine with what approbation this new face of things is regarded, as well by the people as the nobility. The people are fond of change, and seek after liberty; the nobility [seek for] what is useful. These good folks promise both, and that in abundance. But that you may be better acquainted with the whole matter, accept this summary of the question at issue, reduced under certain heads:

1. The civil magistrate has no authority in ecclesiastical matters. He is only a member of the church, the government of which ought to be committed to the clergy.

2. The church of Christ admits of no other government than that by presbyteries; viz, by minister, elders and deacon.

3. The names and authority of archbishops, archdeacons, deans, chancellors, commissaries, and other titles and dignities of the like kind, should be altogether removed from the church of Christ.

4. Each parish should have its own presbytery.

5. The choice of ministers of necessity belongs to the people.

6. The goods, possessions, lands, revenues, titles, honours, author-ities, and all other things relating either to bishops or cathedrals, and which now of right belong to them, should be taken away forthwith and for ever.

7. No one should be allowed to preach who is not a pastor of some congregation; and he ought to preach to his own flock exclusively, and no where else.

8. The infants of Papists are not to be baptized.

9. The judicial laws of Moses are binding upon Christian princes, and they ought not in the slightest degree to depart from them.

There are many other things of the same kind, not less absurd, and which I shall not mention; none of which, as far as I can judge, will make for the advantage and peace of the church, but for her ruin and confusion. Take away authority, and the people will rush headlong into everything that is bad. Take away the patrimony of the church, and you will by the same means take away not only sound learning, but religion itself. But I seem perhaps to prejudge the matter. I anxiously desire, most learned sir, to hear your opinion, and those of Masters Gualter, Simler, and the rest of the brethren, respecting these things; which for my own part I shall willingly follow, as being sound and agreeable to the word of God. For if the whole matter in controversy were left to your arbitration, it would doubtless much contribute to the peace of our church. These good men are crying out that they have all the reformed churches on their side.

I say nothing of the state of our commonwealth; everything is quiet hitherto, but it is to be feared that these intestine dissensions may tend at length to the ruin of the country.

I send your reverence as much English cloth as will make you a gown. Make use of it, I pray you, and accept it with your wonted kindness. Farewell, most esteemed sir, and commend me, I pray you, to God in your prayers. In haste. London, England. August 15, 1573.

Your brother in Christ,
Edwin Sandys,
bishop of London.

20. FROM [W. TRAVERS] *A Full and Plain Declaration of Ecclesiastical Discipline out of the Word of God and of the Declining of the Church of England from the same,* 1574, pp. 5, 185, 187, 190.

... I thought it my duty, even for the kind affection which I bear to that church in which I have been both born and brought up and there-fore love most dearly for good causes (even as the Apostle saith to

L

live and die together) I thought it, I say, my duty to desire and beseech this church earnestly and carefully to think of this so great a benefit whereby it may be established for ever. And most earnestly to exhort and admonish it to abolish that popish tyranny which yet remaineth in the government thereof and to restore again the most holy policy of ruling the church which our Saviour Christ hath left unto us, and to fear lest that the Lord will punish us and will be revenged of us, if we continue still to despise his discipline.

Neither let magistrates think (although in respect of their civil authority the church be subject to them) that in this behalf they are to be exempted from this precept and commandment of the Apostle, who chargeth everyone to be subject to those who in [the] Lord are set over them; for seeing they ought to be careful as well of the salvation of the magistrate as of others, and that the soul of the magistrate, as well as of the rest, is committed to their charge, they must also as well as the rest submit themselves and be obedient to the just and lawful authority of the officers of the church. For seeing they not only rule by the authority of Jesus Christ, but in a manner do represent his person, seeing they rule not as they themselves list, according to their own will, but only according to this word and commandment, is it not meet that even kings and the highest magistrates should be obedient unto them? For it is meet that all princes and monarchs of the world should give up their sceptres and crowns unto him whom God had made and appointed heir of his kingdom and lord of heaven and earth.

But the magistrates have this proper and peculiar to themselves above the rest of the faithful. To set in order and establish the state of the church by their authority, and to preserve and maintain it according to God's will, being once established. Not that they should rule the ecclesiastical matters by their authority, for this belongeth unto Christ alone and to him he hath committed this charge, but forasmuch as the Apostle teacheth that they are appointed of God to the end that we may live a godly and peaceable life. And that the kings of Israel by the appointment of God had charge to see the execution of all the law, they ought to provide and see that the service of God be established as he hath appointed, and administered by such as ought to minister the same, and afterwards preserved in the same simplicity and sincerity undefiled.

Ordinary and perpetual offices should be appointed in two sorts, whereof the first is such whereas every man hath his several charge. The other, where many have but one and the same charge which they execute by common counsel and authority. Whereof again the first sort consisteth in two kinds: of bishops (which expound and teach religion and the service of God; that is pastors and doctors) and as many deacons (that is to say, deacons and elders) so called figuratively by names which are more general. Of whom some do watch over the life and conversation of all the church, and the other are careful to help the necessities of widows, strangers, sick folk and generally of all the poor: so that both all the house is sufficiently provided for, as well touching the purity of the faith and doctrine, as the honesty and integrity of life and manners, as also the need and necessity of everyone particularly not neglected.

Then, the consistory or the assembly of elders which consisteth of the three first and chief officers of the church, pastors, doctors and elders, have the chief care and charge of this commonwealth; to see that no office want his officer, and how faithfully everyone beareth himself in doing of his office, regarding all with one eye, how offences may be avoided, and how they may be remedied when they do arise. . . .

21. FROM J. AYRE, ed. *Works of John Whitgift*, III, Parker Society, Cambridge, 1853, pp. 189–194.

J. Whitgift, *The Defence of the Answer to the Admonition, against the Reply of Thomas Cartwright.*

T[homas] C[artwright] [*A Reply to an Answer made of M. Doctor Whitgift against the Admonition to the Parliament*], page 144, line 26; and section 1, 2.

It is true that we ought to be obedient unto the civil magistrate which governeth the church of God in that office which is committed unto him, and according to that calling. But it must be remembered that civil magistrates must govern it according to the rules of God prescribed in his word, and that as they are nourises[1] so they be servants unto the church, and as they rule in the church, so they must remember to subject themselves unto the church, to submit their sceptres, to throw down their crowns, before the church, yea, as the prophet speaketh, to lick the dust of the feet of the church. Wherein I mean not that the church doth either wring the sceptres out of princes' hands, or taketh their crowns from their heads, or that it requireth princes to lick the dust of her feet (as the pope under this pretence hath done) but I mean, as the prophet meaneth, that whatsoever magnificence, or excellency, or pomp, is either in them, or in their estates and commonwealths, which doth not agree with the

---

[1] nurses.

simplicity and (in the judgement of the world) poor and contemptible estate of the church, that they will be content to lay down.

And here cometh to my mind that wherewith the world is now deceived, and wherewith M. Doctor [Whitgift] goeth about both to deceive himself and others too, in that he thinketh that the church must be framed according to the commonwealth, and the church government according to the civil government, which is as much to say, as if a man should fashion his house according to his hangings, when as indeed it is clean contrary, that, as the hangings are made fit for the house, so the commonwealth must be made to agree with the church, and the government thereof with her government. . . .

Seeing that good men, that is to say the church, are as it were the foundation of the world, it is meet that the commonwealth which is builded upon that foundation should be framed according to the church, and therefore those voices ought not to be heard, 'This order will not agree with our commonwealth; that law of God is not for our state; this form of government will not match with the policy of this realm'.

John Whitgift.

These words would be well considered, for they contain the overthrow of the prince's authority both in ecclesiastical and civil matters. But I will only give a brief note of them in this place, meaning to set forth this matter more at large elsewhere. When he saith that 'the civil magistrate must govern according to his calling, and according to the rules of God prescribed in his word etc.', although the words be true, yet, if you mark upon what occasion they be spoken, you shall perceive the venom that lieth hid under them; for he doth thereby insinuate that the civil magistrate may not intermeddle with the office of the senior, that is, with ecclesiastical jurisdiction, for he taketh seniors to be the officers appointed by God for that purpose; which is to bereave the civil magistrate of his authority, and to give that to seniors which the pope under the like pretence doth arrogate unto himself. . . .

The second point to be noted is, when he saith that Christian princes 'must subject themselves to the church, submit their sceptres, throw down their crowns before the church etc.' the which kind of speech the pope himself useth, and under the same pretence hath trodden kings under his feet. And, although T.C. seems to mislike this excessive using of authority by the pope, yet would he have the same jurisdiction to remain to his seniors still, whom he understandeth by the name of the church; as appeareth in that which he spake before of these words of Christ, *Tell it to the church*, so that he would have the prince subject herself to the seniors of the church, and throw down her crown before them, that is, to be content to be ruled and governed, to be punished and corrected, to be excommunicated and absolved, by their discretion and at their pleasure. This no doubt is his meaning; neither can it otherwise be; for, if this kind of government be once admitted, the prince must needs be of some peculiar church and congregation, and therefore subject to the seigniory of that church, except it please master pastor (who is the chief), and the rest of his neighbours the parishioners to elect the prince into the seigniory, and make him one of them; and yet must the pastor be his superior, and have authority to call him to consultations, and to direct him in matters of discipline; and, whether he will or no, he must be ordered and ruled by the pastor and most part of the seniors. And yet now I remember myself, the prince cannot be of the seigniory; for T.C. a little after granteth that the seniors be no laymen, but ecclesiastical; so that indeed the prince must be a servant, no master; a subject, no prince; under government, no governor, in matters pertaining to the church. . . .

The third point is in this, that he would have 'the government of the commonwealth and the commonwealth itself framed to the church and the government thereof, as the hangings are made fit for the house;' whereby, as it may seem, he would have all monarchies overthrown, and reduced either to a popular or an aristocratical estate; for these two kinds of government he only alloweth of in the church; as it appeareth by that which he hath thereof oftener than once or twice spoken before.

How the laws of man will bear this, I know not; but I am well assured the law of God will not suffer it. . . .

And surely, howsoever you will dally off these collections upon your manifest words, similitudes and reasons, with some devised interpretation and shift (for it will stand you in hand so to do) yet what occasion you have given thereby to the common people, and other that be contentious, to mislike of this present state and government, wise men can consider. . . .

22. FROM A. PEEL and L. H. CARLSON, eds. *The Writings of Robert Harrison and Robert Browne*, 1953, pp. 152, 153–5, 164.

R. BROWNE, *A Treatise of Reformation without tarrying for any*, 1582.

We say, therefore, and often have taught concerning our sovereign Queen Elizabeth that neither the pope nor other popeling is to have any authority either over her or over the church of God, and that the pope of Rome is antichrist, whose kingdom ought utterly to be taken away. Again we say that her authority is civil, and that power she hath as highest under God within her dominions, and that over all persons and causes. By that she may put to death all that deserve it by law, either of the church or commonwealth, and none may resist her or the magistrates under her by force or wicked speeches, when they execute the laws. Seeing we grant and hold thus much, how do they charge us as evil willers to the queen? Surely for that we hold all those preachers and teachers accursed which will not do the duties of pastors and teachers till the magistrates do force them thereto. They say the time is not yet come to build the Lord's house, they must tarry for the magistrates and for Parliaments to do it. They want the civil sword forsooth, and the magistrates do hinder the Lord's building and kingdom and keep away his government. Are they not ashamed thus to slander the magistrate? They have run their own swords upon the wall and broken them, and now would they snatch unto them the magistrates' sword? Indeed, can the Lord's spiritual government be no way executed but by the civil sword, or is this the judgement that is written, 'such honour shall be to all his saints'?

Except the magistrates will go into the tempest and rain, and be weather beaten with the hail of God's wrath, they must keep under the roof of Christ's government. They must be under a pastoral charge. They must obey to the sceptre of Christ, if they be Christians. How then should the pastor, which hath the oversight of the magistrate, if he be of his flock, be so overseen of the magistrate as to leave his flock when the magistrate shall unjustly and wrongfully discharge him? Yet these preachers and teachers will not only do so, but even holding their charge and keeping with it, will not guide and reform it aright because the magistrates do forbid them, forsooth. But they slander the magistrate, and because they dare not charge them as forbidding them their duties, they have gotten this shift, that they do but tarry for the magistrates' authority, and then they will guide and reform as they ought. Behold, is not all this one thing, seeing they lift up the throne of the magistrates to thrust out the kingdom of Christ? For his government or discipline is wanting (say they) but we keep it not away. And who then? For most of them dare not charge the magistrates but only closely, and with many flatterings, that they might still be exalted by the magistrates. They leave their own burthen, and cry out that it is not carried by fault of the magistrate. So they speak out against them, and lay all the burthen on them: but they themselves will not move it with one of their fingers. Yea, they are bold also some of them, in open places, so to charge the magistrate. So they make them enemies, because they say they withhold the church government. . . .

Now then if the magistrates be enemies unto the Lord's kingdom, why are not these men better warriors to uphold the same? For they give up the weapons of their warfare into the enemies' hands, and then say they cannot do withal. By their weapons I mean those whereof Paul doth speak, that they are not carnal but mighty through God to cast down holds, and so forth. These weapons have they given from them, for they have not the keys of the kingdom of heaven to bind and loose, and to retain or pronounce remitted the sins of men, seeing they grant much open wickedness incurable among them, and also avouch that it must needs be suffered. Yea, they have given up these keys to the magistrates or to the spiritual courts, and therefore have no right to call themselves the church of God, or lawful pastors thereof.

We know that Moses might reform, and the judges and kings which followed him, and so may our magistrates: yea, they may reform the church and command things expedient for the same. Yet may they do nothing concerning the church but only civilly, and as civil magistrates; that is, they have not that authority over the church as to be prophets or priests or spiritual kings, as they are magistrates over the same: but only to rule the commonwealth in all outward justice, to maintain the right, welfare and honour thereof, with outward power, bodily punishment, and civil forcing of men. And therefore also because the church is in a commonwealth, it is of their charge: that is concerning the outward provision and outward justice, they are to look to it; but to compel religion, to plant churches by power, and to force a submission to ecclesiastical government by laws and penalties belongeth not to them, as is proved before, neither yet to the church. Let us not, therefore, tarry for the magistrates. For if they be Christians they give leave and gladly suffer and submit themselves to the church government. For he is a Christian which is redeemed by Christ unto holiness and happiness for ever and professeth the same by submitting himself to his laws and government. And if they be not Christians, should the welfare of the church or the salvation of men's souls hang on their courtesy?

(vi) The Questioning of the Royal Supremacy by Clergy within the Church

23. FROM E. DERING, *A Sermon preached before the Queen's Majesty . . . 25 of February, 1569,* n.d. sig. [E 4] – F1.

If I would declare unto your majesty all the great abuses that are in our ministry, I should lead you along in the spirit, as God did the prophet Ezekiel, and after many intolerable evils yet I shall still say unto you; behold, you shall see more abominations than these. I would first lead you to your benefices; and behold, some are defiled with impropriations, some with sequestrations, some laden with pensions, some robbed of their commodities; and yet behold more abominations than these. Look after this upon your patrons; and lo, some are selling their benefices, some farming them, some keep them for their children, some give them to boys, some to servingmen and very few seek after learned pastors; and yet you shall see more abominations than these. Look upon your ministry, and there are some of one occupation, some of another: some shakebucklers,[1] some ruffians, some hawkers and hunters, some dicers and carders, some blind guides and cannot see; some dumb dogs and will not bark: and yet a thousand more iniquities have now covered the priesthood. And yet you in the meanwhile that all these whoredoms are committed, you at whose hands God will require it, you sit still, and are careless, and let men do as they list. It toucheth not belike your commonwealth and therefore you are so well contented to let all alone. The Lord increase the gifts of his Holy Spirit in you, that from faith to faith you may grow continually till that you be zealous as good King David to work his will. If you know not how to reform from this, or have so little counsel (as man's heart is blinded) that you can devise no way, ask counsel at the mouth of the Lord and his holy will shall be revealed unto you.

To reform evil patrons your majesty must strengthen your laws that they may rule as well high as low. As Esdras said once, so may I say now; 'The hands of the princes and rulers are chief in this trespass.' If you will have it amended you must provide so that the highest may be afraid to offend. To keep back the ignorant from the ministry whom God hath not called to such a function, take away your authority from the bishops; let them not thus at their pleasure make ministers in their closet whomsoever it pleaseth them. To stop the incon-

[1] swashbuckler.

veniences that grow in the ministry by other, who say they are learned and can preach, and yet do not, that are, as I said, dumb dogs and will not bark, bridle at the least their greedy appetites, pull out of their mouths these poisoned bones that they so greedily gnaw upon. Take away dispensations, pluralities, totquots, nonresidences, and such other sins. Pull down the court of faculties, the mother and nurse of all such abominations. I tell you this before God that quickeneth all things, and before our Lord Jesus Christ that shall judge the quick and the dead in his appearance and in his kingdom: amend these horrible abuses, and the Lord is on your right hand, you shall not be removed for ever. Let these things alone, and God is a righteous God, he will one day call you to your reckoning. The God of all glory open your eyes to see his high kingdom, and inflame your heart to desire it.

24. B. M. Lans. Ms. 20. 60. Printed in J. Bruce and T. T. Perowne, eds. *Correspondence of Matthew Parker,* Parker Society, Cambridge, 1853, no. CCCLXIX.

11 April [1575] Archbishop Parker to William Cecil, Lord Burghley.

O Lord, I have to endure hostility, answer thou for me. I trust that this shall be one of the last letters which I shall write unto your lordship, the rather for that I am now stricken with mine old disease more sharply than ever I was. It may be that whereas I have a great while provided for death, yet God will peradventure have me continue a while to exercise myself in these contemplations of grief; *the Lord's will be done.* In your absence now from the court I have travailed with her majesty for the bestowing of the bishopric of Norwich. I have named unto her, at her commandment, three; that is, the dean of Westminster,[1] Dr Piers and Dr Whitgift. Amongst them all I have preferred for learning, life and governance the dean of Westminster, not because he is towards your lordship, whom I credibly hear that you named, or for any displeasure that I bear to my lord of Leicester's chaplains, or to her majesty's almoner, of any envy to his person; but surely, sir, I speak it afore God, seeing I see her majesty is affected princely to govern, and for that I see her in constancy almost alone to be offended with the Puritans, whose governance in conclusion will undo her and all others that depend on her, and that because I see him, and very few else, which mean to dull

---

[1] Gabriel Goodman, dean of Westminster 1561–1601. He was Cecil's chaplain. Despite this recommendation he received no higher preferment.

that lewd governance of theirs, I am therefore affected to him; whereof yet I make him not privy. For surely, my lord, I see and feel by experience that divers of my brethren partly are gone from me, partly working secretly against me, for the satisfying of some of their partial friends; but I see men be men.

Her majesty this other day when I was at Richmond at her commandment suddenly charged me for my visitation. I think I know from whence it came, and who did inform one nobleman to open it unto her: but I say, and say again, that my visitation in Winchester diocese (which was the device of the bishop) wrought such a contentation for obedience, that I do not yet repent of it, though the bishop be told that his clergy was sifted, and the thorn was put in his foot; but he will so pluck it out that it should be so in other men's feet that they should stamp again, as I am credibly informed. The Isle of Wight and other places of that diocese be now gone again from their obedience. If this be a good policy, well, then let it be so. If this be a good policy secretly to work overthwartly against the queen's religion stablished by law and injunction, as long as they so stand, I will not be partaker of it.

Her majesty told me that I had supreme government ecclesiastical; but what is it to govern cumbered with such subtlety? Before God, I fear that her highness' authority is not regarded, so that if they could, for fear of further inconvenience, they would change her government; yea, yours and mine, how cunningly soever we deal in it. And surely, my lord, whatsoever cometh of it, in this my letter I admonish you to look unto it in such sincerity as God may be pleased, or else he will rise one day and revenge his enemies. Does your lordship think that I care either for cap, tippet, surplice, or wafer-bread, or any such? But for the laws so established I esteem them, and not more for exercise of contempt against law and authority, which I see will be the end of it, nor for any other respect. If I, you, or any other named 'great Papists' should so favour the pope or his religion that we should pinch Christ's true gospel, woe be unto us all. Her highness pretendeth in the giving of her small benefices that for her conscience sake she will have some of us, the bishops, to commend them; and shall her majesty be induced to gratify some mortal man's request, *who moves the matter,* and be negligent in the principal pastor of so great a diocese, wherein peradventure her authority is utterly condemned? And yet we must reform such things as most part of gentlemen be against. As for my part, I set as much by my living, bigger or less, or nothing. But if this be not looked unto, I will plainly give over to strive against the stream.

This great number of Anabaptists taken on Easter day last may move us to some contemplation. I could tell you many particularities, but I cease, and charge your honour to use still such things as may make to the solidity of good judgement, and help her majesty's good government in princely constancy, whatsoever the policy of the world, yea, the mere world, would induce. To dance in a net in this world is but mere vanity. To make the governance only policy is mere vanity. Her princely prerogatives in temporal matters be called into question of base subjects, and it is known that her highness hath taken order to cease in some of them. Whatsoever the ecclesiastical prerogative is, I fear it is not so great as your pen hath given it her in the injunction, and yet her governance is of more prerogative than the head Papists would grant unto her. But I cease and refer all things to God, in whom I wish you continued to his pleasure. I am compelled thus to write, lying in my bed, by another man's pen, but I doubt not so chosen that you shall need to doubt. From my house at Lambeth, this 11th of April.

Sir, I am not much led by worldly prophecies, and yet I cannot tell how this old verse recourseth oft to my head; *A woman falls dead, and afterwards evils strike the land.*

Your lordship's assured friend in Christ,
Matthew Cant[erbury].

25. B. M. Lans. Ms. 23. 12. Printed in W. Nicholson, ed. *Remains of Edmund Grindal* Parker Society, Cambridge, 1843, pp. 376–390.

20 December, 1576. Edmund Grindal to the queen.

With most humble remembrance of my bounden duty to your majesty; it may please the same to be advertised that the speeches which it hath pleased you to deliver unto me, when I last attended on your highness, concerning abridging the number of preachers, and the utter suppression of all learned exercises and conferences among the ministers of the church, allowed by their bishops and ordinaries, have exceedingly dismayed and discomforted me. Not so much for that the said speeches sounded very hardly against mine own person, being but one particular man, and not much to be accounted of; but most of all for that the same might both tend to the public harm of God's church, whereof your highness ought by office to be *nurse,* and also to the heavy burdening of your own conscience before God, if they should be put in strict execution. It was not your majesty's pleasure then, the time not serving thereto, to hear me at any length concerning the said two matters then propounded: I thought it therefore my duty by writing to declare some part of my mind unto your highness; beseeching the same with patience to read over this that I now send, written with mine own rude scribbling hand; which seemeth to be of more length than it is indeed: for I say with Ambrose, *I write with mine own hand, for you alone to read it.*

And so, to come to the present case; I may very well use unto your highness the words of Ambrose above written, *I know thy piety [towards God, thy kindness towards men; I am bounden by thy benefits]* etc. But surely I cannot marvel enough, how this strange opinion should once enter into your mind, that it should be good for the church to have few preachers.

Alas, madam, is the scripture more plain in any one thing, than that the gospel of Christ should be plentifully preached; and that plenty of labourers should be sent into the Lord's harvest; which, being great and large, standeth in need, not of a few, but many workmen?

Now for the second point, which is concerning the learned exercise and conference amongst the ministers of the church: I have consulted with divers of my brethren the bishops, by letters; who think the same as I do: a thing profitable to the church, and therefore expedient to be continued. And I trust your majesty will think the like, when your highness shall have been informed of the manner and order thereof; what authority it hath of the scriptures; what commodity it bringeth with it; and what incommodities will follow, if it be clean taken away.

I trust, when your majesty hath considered and well weighed the premises, you will rest satisfied, and judge that no such inconveniences can grow of these exercises, as you have been informed, but rather the clean contrary. And for my own part, because I am well assured, both by reasons and arguments taken out of the holy scriptures, and by experience, the most certain seal of sure knowledge, that the said exercises, for the interpretation and exposition of the scriptures, and for exhortation and comfort drawn out of the same, are both profitable to increase knowledge among the ministers, and tendeth to the edifying of the hearers, I am forced, with all humility, and yet plainly, to profess, that I cannot with safe conscience, and without the offence of the majesty of God, give my assent to the suppressing of the said exercises: much less can I send out any injunction for the utter and universal subversion of the same. I say with St Paul, 'I have no power to destroy, but to only edify', and with the same apostle, 'I can do nothing against the truth, but for the truth'.

If it be your majesty's pleasure, for this or any other cause, to remove me out of this place, I will with all humility yield thereunto, and render again to your majesty that I received of the same. I consider with myself, *'That it is a fearful thing to fall into the hands of the living God'*. I consider also *'That he who acts against his conscience, resting upon the laws of God, builds for hell'.* 'And what should I win, if I gained' (I will not say a bishopric, but) 'the whole world, and lost mine own soul?'

Bear with me, I beseech you, madam, if I choose rather to offend your earthly majesty, than to offend the heavenly majesty of God. And now being sorry, that I have been so long and tedious to your majesty, I will draw to an end, most humbly praying the same well to consider these two short petitions following.

The first is, that you would refer all these ecclesiastical mattters which touch religion, or the doctrine and discipline of the church, unto the bishops and divines of your realm, according to the example of all godly Christian emperors and princes of all ages. For indeed they are things to be judged, as an ancient father writeth: *In the church, or a synod, not in a palace.* When your majesty hath questions of the laws of your realm, you do not decide the same in your court, but send them to your judges to be determined. Likewise for doubts in matters of doctrine or discipline of the church, the ordinary way is to refer the decision of the same to the bishops, and other head ministers of the church.

The second petition I have to make to your majesty is this: that, when you deal in matters of faith and religion, or matters that touch the church of Christ, which is his spouse, bought with so dear a price, you would not use to pronounce so resolutely and peremptorily, *as from authority,* as ye may do in civil and extern matters: but always remember that in God's causes the will of God, and not the will of any earthly creature, is to take place. It is the antichristian voice of the pope, *So I will have it; so I command: let my will stand for a reason.* In God's matters all princes ought to bow their sceptres to the Son of God, and to ask counsel at his mouth what they ought to do. David exhorteth all kings and rulers to serve God with fear and trembling.

Remember, madam, that you are a mortal creature. 'Look not only', (as was said to Theodosius) 'upon the purple and princely array, wherewith ye are apparelled; but consider withal, what is that that is covered therewith. Is it not flesh and blood? Is it not dust and ashes? Is it not a corruptible body, which must return to his earth again, God knoweth how soon?' Must not you also one day appear *'Before the fearful judgement seat of the Crucified, to receive there according as you have done in the body, whether it be good or evil?'*

And although ye are a mighty prince, yet remember that he which dwelleth in heaven is mightier. He is, as the psalmist sayeth, *Terrible, and he who taketh away the spirit of princes, and is terrible above all the kings of the earth.*

Wherefore I do beseech you, madam, *in the bowels of Christ,* when you deal in these religious causes, set the majesty of God before your eyes, laying all earthly majesty aside: determine with yourself to obey his voice, and with all humility say unto him, *Not mine, but thy will be done.* God hath blessed you with great felicity in your reign, now many years, beware you do not impute the same to your own deserts or policy, but give God the glory. And as to instruments and means, impute your said felicity, first to the goodness of the cause which ye hath set forth, I mean Christ's true religion: and, secondly, to the sighs and groanings of the godly in their fervent prayer to God for you; which have hitherto, as it were, tied and bound the hands of God, that he could not pour out his plagues upon you and your people, most justly deserved.

Take heed, that ye never once think of declining from God, lest that be verified of you, which is written of Ozetas[1] who continued a prince of good and godly government for many years together: and afterwards, *when he was strengthened,* (saith the text) *his heart was lifted up to his destruction, and he regarded not the Lord.* Ye have done many things well; but except ye persevere to the end, ye cannot be blessed. For if ye turn from God, then God will turn away his merciful countenance from you. And what remaineth then to be looked for, but only a terrible expectation of God's judgements, and an heaping up of wrath against the day of wrath?

But I trust in God, your majesty will always humble yourself under his mighty hand, and go forward in the zealous setting forth of God's true religion, always yielding due obedience and reverence to the word of God, the only rule of faith and religion. And if ye so do, although God hath just cause many ways to be angry with you and us for our unfaithfulness, yet I doubt nothing, but that for his own name's sake, and for his own glory's sake, he will still hold his merciful hand over us, shield and protect us under the shadow of his wings, as he hath done hitherto.

I beseech God, our heavenly Father, plentifully to pour his principal Spirit upon you, and always to direct your heart in his holy fear. Amen.

26. R. BANCROFT, *A Sermon preached at Paul's Cross the 9 of February . . . Anno 1588,* 1589, pp. 14–5, 16–20.

There are many causes set down by the said ancient fathers why so many false prophets do go out into the world, but I will only touch four, whereof I find the contempt of bishops especially to be one. For unto them, as St Jerome saith, ever since St Mark's time the care

[1] Joash.

of church government hath been committed. They had authority over the rest of the ministry.... 'That the seed of schisms might be taken away.' And again ... 'Lest everyone drawing to himself by a several way should rent in pieces the church of Christ'. For if bishops had not that authority.... 'There would be as many schisms in the church as there are priests.'

The second cause why so many false prophets are gone into the world I find to be ambition; or as Augustine saith, desire of glory. ... This will appear very evidently unto those who shall consider the histories of Arius coveting the bishopric of Alexandria ... Arius and Eustathius being scholars together in Pontus, and profiting in learning with like commendation at the last did sue one against another for a bishopric there. Eustathius obtained it: Arius is greatly offended. The bishop seeking carefully how to content him made him the master of an hospital. But herewithal Arius was not satisfied. The repulse he had taken greatly tormenting him, upon a stomach he gave over his hospital, and began to devise how to slander Eustathius, affirming him to be a proud man, and not the man he had been taken for; that now he abounded too much in wealth, and was declined ... to hording of money. Thereupon he entered into a schism, he departed from the church, and having allured unto him a multitude of men and women he fell into many absurdities. That he might likewise the rather (as he thought) pinch and vex Eustathius, as also for the advancement of his own credit, he affirmed himself (being but a priest) to be equal in honour and dignity with Eustathius a bishop; and that there was no difference by the word of God betwixt a priest and a bishop. He used for proof of these his assertions the very same arguments which now are used of those that maintain his opinions: as that the apostles sometimes writing to priests and deacons, and sometimes to bishops and deacons, should thereby signify that a bishop and a priest is all one. Which is an assertion (saith Epiphanius) ... full of folly. And thus you see what ambition accompanied with emulation wrought in Arius.

The course of which history I have the rather at large noted unto you, because Martin[1] would gladly have been as subtle to have deceived you, as he is malicious in depraving his superiors. Who taking upon him with Arius to prove an equality in the ministry, and that there ought to be no difference betwixt a bishop and a priest cometh at last to these words, 'There was never any but antichristian popes and popelings that ever claimed this authority', (he meaneth the superiority which bishops have over the clergy) 'especially when the matter was gainsaid etc.'

[1] Martin Marprelate.

Why? Doth man's allowance or disallowance make a matter anti-christian or not antichristian? Were they godly bishops which claimed this authority when it was not gainsaid, and are they become antichristian bishops for challenging the same, because some do mis-like it? But that you may yet farther see Martin's boldness (I might say either his malice or ignorance) it may please you to understand what account was made in the church of God in those days of Arius gainsaying and impugning of the superiority of bishops. For if then his opinion prevailed the favourers of the same cause now have some-what to boast of; but indeed it fell out far otherwise. For it appeareth in Epiphanius, after due trial and examination made by the learned fathers who then lived, of all his arguments and sleights which he used for the proof of his assertions, that with a general consent of the whole church his opinions were overthrown, and he himself persisting in them was condemned for an heretic. St Augustine like-wise beareth witness hereof, who in his book of heresies ascribeth this to Arius for one, in that he said. . . . 'That there ought to be no difference betwixt a priest and a bishop.'

Besides for all Arius gainsaying, the most of the godly, the best learned, and the most zealous of the fathers who spent themselves in the defence of religion against such heretics and schismatics as the church of God did then abound and flow withal did themselves take upon them the offices of bishops: and till this day there was never any but heretics, and such lewd persons, who did account them anti-christian.

27. B. M. Lans. Ms. 61. 54. Printed with errors in J. Strype, *Annals of Church and State . . .*, 1731, IV, 5–6.

4 August, 1589. Sir Francis Knollys to William Cecil, Lord Burghley.

I have received your lordship's letter of the first of August wherein I have received very small comfort, and small hope of the good main-tenance of her majesty's safety, consisting in the sincere maintenance of her majesty's supreme government against the covetous ambition of clergy rulers. For your lordship sayeth that the question is very disputable whereof I wrote unto your lordship: and I must needs confess that Campion's disputation against the humility of Christ's doctrine, and for the advancement of antichrist's doctrine was not only allowed to be disputable, but also it was very plausible in the minds of all those that favoured the worldly pompous rule of church government. For the nature of covetous ambition in church governors hath always despised the humble and base style of Christ's doctrine and government. . . .

And as touching the superiority of bishops to be disallowed as a false claim, it seems to me that Christ himself hath plainly decided the matter at what time as his apostles at two sundry times did seem to murmur and strive who should be the greatest after Christ's departure from them: where it seems to me that Christ condemned plainly all claiming superiority among the apostles. The which rule, if our bishops would follow, as no doubt they would if her majesty's supreme government were stoutly stand unto, then they would be contented to forbear their claimed superiority of government in the church, which Christ condemned in the apostles; and they would be satisfied with that equality that Christ left to his church among the apostles. But here you must not take me that I do deny that bishops may have any lordly authority or dignity that they have enjoyed, so that they claim it not from a higher authority than directly from her majesty's grant. But I do not mean hereby to contend with your lordship; through whose assistance I have always hoped that her majesty's safety (consisting in the true maintenance of her majesty's supreme government) should be jealously preserved. But yet your lordship must pardon me, although I do not think that her majesty's safety is anything the better preserved because our bishops dare not oppose themselves and their credit against her majesty's supreme government; for it is the Jesuits, and not our bishops, that must bring her majesty's safety into peril, if this maxim may be allowed unto the said Jesuits that our bishops of England are not under governors to her majesty over the clergy but they are superior governors over the said inferior clergy by God's own ordinance: whereupon it must needs follow that her majesty is not supreme governor over the clergy, if so be that our said bishops be not under governors to her majesty, but superior governors from a higher claim than directly from her majesty. But my trust is that the cause of your lordship's writing unto me that the question is very disputable is not for that your lordship is of that opinion, but rather for that your lordship would bridle and stay me from running too fast before your lordship in the matter of her majesty's safety. . . .

II. The Royal Supremacy in Practice

(i) Royal Intervention in the Church

28. FROM A. SPARROW, *A Collection of Articles, Injunctions, Canons . . . of the Church of England*, 1661, pp. 63–80.

Injunctions given by the queen's majesty as well to the clergy, as to the laity of this realm [1559].

The queen's most royal majesty, by the advice of her most honourable council, intending the advancement of the true honour of Almighty God, the suppression of superstition throughout all her highness' realms and dominions, and to plant true religion to the extirpation of all hypocrisy, enormities, and abuses (as to her duty appertaineth) doth minister unto her loving subjects these godly injunctions hereafter following. All which injunctions her highness willeth and commandeth her loving subjects obediently to receive, and truly to observe and keep, every man in their offices, degrees and states, as they will avoid her highness' displeasure, and the pains of the same hereafter expressed.

I The first is, that all deans, archdeacons, parsons, vicars, and all other ecclesiastical persons shall faithfully keep and observe, and as far as in them may lie, shall cause to be observed and kept of other, all and singular laws and statutes made for the restoring of the crown the ancient jurisdiction over the state ecclesiastical, and abolishing of all foreign power repugnant to the same. And furthermore all ecclesiastical persons having cure of souls shall to the uttermost of their wit, knowledge and learning purely and sincerely, and without any colour or dissimulation, declare, manifest and open four times every year at least in their sermons and other collations, that all usurped and foreign power having no establishment nor ground by the law of God, is for most just causes taken away and abolished; and that therefore no manner of obedience and subjection within her highness' realms and dominions is due unto any such foreign power. And that the queen's power within her realms and dominions is the highest power under God, to whom all men, within the same realms and dominions, by God's laws, owe most loyalty and obedience, afore and above all other powers and potentates in earth.

III Item, that they, the persons above rehearsed, shall preach in their churches, and every other cure they have, one sermon every month of the year at the least, wherein they shall purely and sincerely declare the word of God, and in the same exhort their hearers to the works of faith, as mercy and charity, especially prescribed and commanded in scripture; and that the works devised by man's fantasies, besides scripture, (as wandering of pilgrimages, setting up of candles, praying upon beads, or such like superstition) have not only no promise of reward in scripture for doing of them, but contrariwise great threatenings and maledictions of God, for that they be things tending to idolatry and superstition, which of all other offences God Almighty doth most detest and abhor, for that the same most diminish his honour and glory.

IV Item, that they, the persons above rehearsed, shall preach in their own persons once in every quarter of the year at the least, one sermon, being licensed especially thereunto, as is specified hereafter; or else shall read some homily prescribed to be used by the queen's authority every Sunday at the least, unless some other preacher sufficiently licensed, as hereafter, chance to come to the parish for the same purpose of preaching.

V Item, that every holy day through the year, when they have no sermon, they shall immediately after the Gospel openly and plainly recite to their parishioners in the pulpit the Pater noster, the creed, and the ten commandments, in English, to the intent the people may learn the same by heart; exhorting all parents and householders to teach their children and servants the same, as they are bound by the law of God and conscience to do.

VI Also, that they shall provide within three months next after this visitation at the charges of the parish, one book of the whole Bible of the largest volume in English; and within one twelve months next after the said visitation, the Paraphrases of Erasmus also in English upon the Gospel, and the same set up in some convenient place within the said church that they have cure of, whereas the parishioners may most commodiously resort unto the same, and read the same, out of the time of common service. . . .

VII Also, the said ecclesiastical persons shall in no wise at any unlawful time, nor for any other cause, than for their honest necessities, haunt or resort to any taverns or alehouses. And after their meats, they shall not give themselves to drinking or riot, spending their time idly by day and by night at dice, cards or tables playing, or any other unlawful game; but at all times, as they shall have leisure, they shall hear or read somewhat of holy scripture, or shall busy themselves with some other honest study or exercise; and that they always do the things which appertain to honesty, and endeavour to profit the commonwealth; having always in mind that they ought to excel all other in purity of life, and should be examples to the people to live well and Christianly.

VIII   Also, that they shall admit no man to preach within any their cures, but such as shall appear unto them to be sufficiently licensed thereunto by the queen's majesty, or the archbishop of Canterbury or the archbishop of York in either their provinces, or by the bishop of the diocese, or by the queen's majesty's visitors. . . .

XVI   Also, that every parson, vicar, curate and stipendiary priest, or elsewhere that is a letter of the word of God to be read in English, or sincerely preached, or of the execution of these the queen's majesty's injunctions, or a fautor of any usurped and foreign power, now by the laws of this realm justly rejected and taken away, they shall detect and present the same to the queen's majesty, or to her council, or to the ordinary, or to the justice of peace next adjoining.

XVI   Also, that every parson, vicar, curate and stipendiary priest, being under the degree of a master of art, shall provide and have of his own, within three months after this visitation the New Testament both in Latin and in English, with paraphrases upon the same, conferring the one with the other. And the bishops and other ordinaries by themselves or their officers, in their synods and visitations, shall examine the said ecclesiastical persons how they have profited in the study of holy scripture.

XXVII   Also, because through lack of preachers in many places of the queen's realms and dominions the people continue in ignorance and blindness, all parsons, vicars and curates shall read in their churches every Sunday one of the Homilies, which are and shall be set forth for the same purpose by the queen's authority, in such sort, as they shall be appointed to do in the preface of the same.

XXVIII   Item, whereas many undiscreet persons do at this day uncharitably contemn and abuse priests and ministers of the

church, because some of them (having small learning) have
of long time favoured fond fancies rather than God's truth;
yet forasmuch as their office and function is appointed of
God, the queen's majesty willeth and chargeth all her loving
subjects, that from henceforth they shall use them charitably
and reverently for their office and ministration sake, and
especially such as labour in the setting forth of God's holy
word.

XXIX Item, although there be no prohibition by the word of
God, nor any example of the primitive church, but that
the priests and ministers of the church may lawfully, for
the avoiding of fornication, have an honest and sober wife,
and that for the same purpose the same was by act of Parliament in the time of our dear brother King Edward VI made
lawful, whereupon a great number of the clergy of this realm
were then married, and so yet continue; yet because there
hath grown offence, and some slander to the church by lack
of discreet and sober behaviour in many ministers of the
church, both in choosing of their wives, and undiscreet living
with them, the remedy whereof is necessary to be sought: it is
thought, therefore, very necessary that no manner of priest
or deacon shall hereafter take to his wife any manner of
woman without the advice and allowance first had upon
good examination by the bishop of the same diocese, and
two justices of the peace of the same shire, dwelling next
to the place where the same woman hath made her most
abode before her marriage; nor without the goodwill of
the parents of the said woman, if she have any living, or
two of the next of her kinsfolks, or, for lack of knowledge
of such, of her master and mistress, where she serveth.
And before he shall be contracted in any place, he shall
make a good and certain proof thereof to the minister, or to
the congregation assembled for that purpose, which shall be
upon some holy day, where divers may be present. And if
any shall do otherwise, that then they shall not be permitted
to minister either the word or the sacraments of the church,
nor shall be capable of any ecclesiastical benefice. And for
the manner of marriages of any bishops, the same shall be
allowed and approved by the metropolitan of the province,
and also by such commissioners as the queen's majesty thereunto shall appoint. And if any master or dean, or any head
of any college, shall purpose to marry, the same shall not be
allowed, but by such to whom the visitation of the same

doth properly belong, who shall in any wise provide that the same tend not to the hindrance of their house.

29. Corpus Christi College, Cambridge, Parker Ms. CXXI, 381–386. Printed in J. Bruce and T. T. Perowne, eds. *Correspondence of Matthew Parker*, Parker Society, Cambridge, 1853, no. LXVIII.

c. October 1559. Parker, Grindal, Cox, Barlow and Scory to the queen.

Most humbly showeth your excellent majesty your lowly orators and loving subjects we underwritten that like as your most noble father of immortal memory, King Henry the VIIIth, and your most godly and noble brother, King Edward the VIth, in their princely zeal which they bare to the state of Christ's faith did much tender the advancement of learning by cherishing of students and encouraging of ministers, whereby they were the more able to do their duties to God, and to serve the necessity of the realm, by which their royal and princely affection they purchased perpetual fame and praise as well within their own realms as throughout all Christendom: so we trust undoubtedly that your grace, being endued with the benefits of knowledge far above any of your noble progenitors will be inclined no less to the maintenance of learning for the setting forth of Christ's true religion, now for want of sufficient ministers in great jeopardy of decay. In respect whereof we trust that your highness' gracious disposition will yet stay and remit this present alteration and exchange[1] (as we suppose in our consciences under reformation of your great wisdom), not meet to proceed for the inconveniences thereof now partly perceived like to ensue, and upon such good grounds and reasons as we could particularly describe in writing if your highness' pleasure were to admit us to the declaration of the same.

And yet, lest we should appear not to consider your highness' manifold and great charges daily sustained, in most humble wise we five underwritten, for us and the province of Canterbury, do offer to give unto the same yearly amongst us one annual pension of one thousand marks during our lives and continuance in the bishoprics for and in consideration of the exoneration of the said exchange.

How be it, most gravious sovereign, as most obedient subjects in true and lowly allegiance of our hearts we sue and pray that if this our said supplication shall not be thought meet to take place that yet your highness would condescend favourably to peruse these our petitions following, which we be persuaded to be grounded upon

---

[1] In 1559 Parliament had passed an act enabling the queen when a bishopric fell vacant to take the episcopal lands into her own hand and give in exchange impropriations, tithes etc.

natural equity, godly conscience, and good conformity, for most part
of them to the act passed.

1. First, that the vicarages of impropried benefices appointed in
    exchange may be made just livings for the incumbents of the
    same. And that the chancels and mansion houses decayed might
    be considered by survey to some reasonable proportion of
    allowance in the exchange.

2. Item, that yearly pensions payable may be reprised out of the
    parsonages set over in exchange and that yearly distributions,
    with the charges of church books etc. may be allowed, such as
    the injunctions bind the rectories withal.

3. Item, that where the manred with the manors is withdrawn from
    us, that we be not hereafter importably charged with the setting
    forth of men to war.

4. Item, that perquisites of courts and woods, sales and other such
    casual profits, may be parcels of the extent of the manors, and
    that consideration may be had for the equivalent recompense of
    the same, and that allowance may be made of procurations and
    synods payable at the visitations of parsonages impropriate, and
    also allowance for the mesne profits after the death of the
    incumbent to the next successor, so charged in the first fruits
    and tenths, which mesne profits were translated by act of Parlia-
    ment from the bishop to the successor of the benefice from the
    death of his predecessor.

5. Item, that fees to keepers of parks and woods not yet valued be
    not reprised out of the value of the manors, and that the said
    parks and woods may be also valued; and that corn, sheep, fowl
    and fish with carriages and other commodities may remain for
    hospitality to the bishops.

6. Item, that the patronage appendant to the manors exchanged may
    be reserved to the bishop's see, and that the bishops of the new
    erected churches may give the prebends of those churches as in
    other is used, the rather to maintain learned men and preachers.

7. Item, if any of the tenths and rectories be evicted from us by
    order of law, that then recompence may be made.

8. Item, that we may have remedy by law to recover the tenths
    denied or delayed, as well as when they were parcels of the
    revenues of the crown, before which assurance no exchange can
    reasonably pass.

9. Item, that no rents be returned for spiritual possessions which
    be paid into the Exchequer [nor] for annual rents temporal
    reserved *in the name of tithes*.

10. Item, that bishoprics may be discharged of all arrearages, of
    subsidies and tenths, and other incumbrances passed in the days

of the predecessors and in times of vacation, and that for the first year of our fruits-paying to be discharged of subsidy, as before time hath been used.

11. Item, that it may please your highness to continue the new erected sees founded upon great considerations by your noble progenitor the said King Henry, and that the benefice of Cliffe may be annexed to the see of Rochester, and from the see of Chester the benefice late annexed thereunto be not dismembered, in consideration of the exility of the bishoprics.

12. Item, we most humbly desire your majesty that in consideration of our chargeable expectation, and for the burden of necessary furniture for our houses, and for the discharge of the great fees paid before, and at the restitution of temporalities, to suffer us to enjoy the half year's rent last past at Michaelmas, and that our first fruits may be abated and distributed into more years, for the better maintenance of hospitality; and that we may be put to our own surety at the composition of our fruits. Which gracious favour in the latter premises if your highness do not show towards us, we shall not dare enter our functions whereto to your grace hath nominated us, being too importable else for us to bear. All which petitions, most redoubted sovereign lady, we make to your highness, not in respect of any private worldly advancement or temporal gain (as God knoweth our hearts) but in respect of God's glory, Christ's faith and religion, your grace's honour and discharge of your conscience to all the world, and for the honourable report of your nobility, and to the comfort of the realm.

> Your highness' most humble orators,
> Matthew [Parker] elect Canterbury,
> Edmund [Grindal] elect London,
> Richard [Cox] elect Ely,
> William [Barlow] elect *Chichester*,
> John [Scory] elect of Hereford.

30. Inner Temple, Petyt Ms. 538 vol. 47 f. 373. Printed with some errors in J. Strype, *Life and Acts of Matthew Parker*, 1711, p. 107.

9 August, 1561. Royal Injunction.

Elizabeth R.

By the Queen.

The queen's majesty, considering how the palaces and houses of cathedral churches and colleges of this realm have been both of ancient and late time builded and enclosed in severally, to sustain and keep societies of learned men, professing study and prayer, for the edification of the church of God, and so consequently to serve the commonweal; and understanding of late, that within the houses thereof, as well the chief governors, as the prebendaries, students and members thereof, being married, do keep particular households with their wives, children and nurses; whereof no small offence groweth to the intent of the founders, and to the quiet and orderly profession of study and learning within the same; hath thought meet to provide remedy herein, lest by sufferance thereof the rest of the colleges, specially such as be so replenished with young students, as the very rooms and buildings be not answerable for such families of women and young children, should follow the like example: and therefore expressly willeth and commandeth, that no manner of person, being either the head or member of any college or cathedral church within this realm, shall, from the time of the notification hereof in the same college, have, or be permitted to have, within the precinct of any such college, his wife or other woman, to abide and dwell in the same; or to frequent or haunt any lodging within the same college, upon pain, that whosoever shall do to the contrary shall forfeit all ecclesiastical promotions in any cathedral or collegiate church within this realm. And for continuance of this order, her majesty willeth, that the transcript hereof shall be written in the book of the statutes of every such college, and shall be reputed as parcel of the statutes of the same.

Given under our signet, at our town of Ipswich, 9th of August, the third year of our reign.

31. Inner Temple, Petyt Ms. 538 vol. 47 f. 374-5. Printed in J. Bruce and T. T. Perowne, eds. *Correspondence of Matthew Parker*, Parker Society, Cambridge, 1853, no. CXIV.

————1561. Matthew Parker to Sir William Cecil. Draft of a letter.

Sir, yesterday attending upon the queen's majesty to know if her highness had any especial matter to appoint me, I perceived her affection to be such toward the state of her clergy that I can but lament to see the adversary so to prevail, who either envieth the quiet government of her time, which is now at a good point, with some labour and diligence of our parties, or else, who, under colours of dissimulations, labour to undermine the state of religion, and to intervert, or rather subvert, the gospel of Christ and liberty of his holy word. Whose devices I doubt not but he *who dwells in heaven will in time deride and mock. For it is God who defends the truth to all eternity.*

I was in an horror to hear such words to come from her mild nature and Christianly learned conscience, as she spake concerning God's holy ordinance and institution of matrimony. I marvelled that our states in that behalf cannot please her highness, which we doubt nothing at all to please God's sacred majesty, and trust to stand before God's judgement seat in a good conscience therewith, for all the glorious shine of counterfeited chastity. And it is a wonder to me that her highness is so incensed by our adversaries, that all the world must understand her displeasure against us. Whereby our credits be little, our doings, (God's service and her's) shall take less effect among her subjects, to her own disquiet of government. I never heard or read, but that all manner princes, as well Christian as profane, did evermore cherish their ecclesiastical state, as conservators of religion, by the which the people be most strongly knit together in amity, their hearts stayed and won to God, their obedience holden under their governors, and we alone of our time openly brought in hatred, shamed and traduced before the malicious and ignorant people, as beasts without knowledge to Godward, in using this liberty of his word, as men of effrenate intemperancy, without discretion or any godly disposition worthy to serve in our state. Insomuch that the queen's highness expressed to me a repentance that we were thus appointed in office, wishing it had been otherwise. Which inclination being known at large to Queen Mary's clergy, they laugh prettily to see how the clergy of our time is handled, and what equity of laws be ministered to our sort. But by patience and silence we pass over etc. and leave all to God. In the meantime we have cause all to be utterly discomforted and discouraged.

Her majesty moreover talked of other manner injunctions that shall hereafter follow. I trust God shall stay her heart, as his grace hath moved her to begin godly this good work (which we take to be God's, and not *of this age*) and so to proceed, and so to finish. I doubt nothing, though these *human anxieties* conceived upon untrue reports, break sometime from her, that her majesty will well advise her doings, and will use Theodosius' days of deliberation in sentence giving, in matters of such importance. I would be sorry that the clergy should have cause to show disobedience with, '*it is better to obey God rather than men*'. And what instillers soever there be, there be enough of this contemned flock, which will not shrink to offer their blood to the defence of Christ's verity, if it be either openly impugned, or secretly suggilled.[1]

Alas, what policy is this? To drive out hospitality in cathedral churches, to drive out preachers in the head cities; which being well instructed, the rest of the country is better ruled in obedience. And to tarry in cathedral churches with such open and rebukeful separa-

[1] Defamed.

tions, what modest nature can abide it, or tarry where they be discredited? Horsekeepers' wives, porters', pantlers' and butlers' wives may have their cradles going, and honest learned men expulsed with open note, who only keep the hospitality, who only be students and preachers, who only be unfeigned orators in open prayers for the queen's majesty's prosperity and continuance, where others say their back pater nosters for her in corners. The extern discipline of this injunction might have been so ordered that both abuses might have been reformed or prevented, and yet our estimation preserved for our office sake; which for my part, I would I had never entered, and may rue the time to be the head to whom resorteth daily and hourly such complaints as I send you herewith, some copies having of this argument, divers others. I have neither joy of house, land or name, so abased by natural sovereign good lady; for whose service and honour I would not think it cost to spend my life; to the contentation of whose desire and commandment I have earnestly travailed, or else some things might peradventure have been worse. And where I have, for the execution of her laws and orders, purchased the hatred of the adversaries, and also, for moderating things indifferent, have procured to have the foul reports of some Protestants, yet all things thus borne never discomforted me, so I might please God and serve her highness. But yesterday's talk, with such earnest forcing that progress-hunting injunction made upon the clergy with conference of no ecclesiastical person, have driven me under the hatches, and dulled me in all other causes, mourning only to God, *in the bitterness of my soul so that I can say with Sarah, 'I beseech you, O Lord, free me from this reproach, or at least take me up from the earth'.* [Tobit. III. 13]. . . .[1]

To conclude infinite such places with St Hierome, *'The unmarried are not indispensible in the way that priests are indispensible',* whose affections with the honesty of the cause allowed in God's word, shall stablish my conscience with others, *that we may bear the disgrace of Christ with joy, looking to Jesus the author and perfector who for the joy which was set before him, endured the cross, despising the shame.*

32. B.M. Lans. Ms. 8. 6. Printed in J. Bruce and T. T. Perowne, eds. *Correspondence of Matthew Parker,* Parker Society. Cambridge, 1853, no. CLXX.

25 January, 1564/5. Queen Elizabeth to Matthew Parker.

Most reverend father in God, etc. We greet you well. Like as no one thing, in the government and charge committed unto us by the

---

[1] Here follow quotations from St Jerome, St Augustine and St Chrysostom in favour of a married clergy.

favourable goodness of Almighty God doth more profit and beautify the same to his pleasure and acceptation, to our comfort and ease of our government, and, finally, to the universal weal and repose of our people and countries, than unity, quietness and concord, as well amongst the public ministers having charge under us, as in the multitude of the people by us and them ruled; so, contrariwise, diversity, variety, contention and vain love of singularity, either in our ministers or in the people, must needs provoke the displeasure of Almighty God, and be to us, having the burden of government, discomfortable, heavy, and troublesome; and, finally, must needs bring danger of ruin to our people and country. Wherefore, although our earnest care and inward desire hath always been, from the beginning of our reign, to provide that by laws and ordinances agreeable to truth and justice, and consonant to good order, this our realm should be directed and governed, both in the ecclesiastical and civil policy, by public officers and ministers following, as near as possibly might be, one rule, form and manner of order in all their actions, and directing our people to obey humbly and live godly, according to their several callings, in unity and concord, without diversities of opinions or novelties of rites and manners, or without maintenance or breeding of any contentions about the same; yet we, to our no small grief and discomfort do hear, that where, of the two manner of governments without which no manner of people is well ruled, the ecclesiastical should be the more perfect, and should give example and be as it were a light and guide to allure, direct and lead all officers in civil policy; yet in sundry places of our realm of late, for lack of regard given thereto in due time, by such superior and principal officers as you are, being the primate and other the bishops of your province, with sufferance of sundry varieties and novelties, not only in opinions but in external ceremonies and rites, there is crept and brought into the church by some few persons, abounding more in their own senses than wisdom would, and delighting with singularities and changes, an open and manifest disorder and offence to the godly, wise and obedient persons, by diversity of opinions and specially in the external, decent and lawful rites and ceremonies to be used in the churches, so as except the same should be speedily withstand, stayed and reformed, the inconvenience thereof were like to grow from place to place, as it were by an infection, to a great annoyance, trouble and deformity to the rest of the whole body of the realm, and thereby impair, deface and disturb Christian charity, unity and concord, being the very bands of our religion; which we do so much desire to increase and continue amongst our people, and by and with which our Lord God, being the God of peace and not of dissension, will continue his blessings and graces over us and his people. And although we have now a good while heard to our grief sundry reports hereof, hoping that all cannot be true, but rather mistrusting that the adversaries of truth might of their evil disposition increase the reports of the same: yet we thought, until this present, that by the regard which you, being the primate and metropolitan would have had hereto according to your office, with the assistance of the bishops your brethren in their several diocese, (having also received of us heretofore charge for the same purpose), these errors, tending to breed some schism or deformity in the church, should have been stayed and appeased. But perceiving very lately, and also certainly, that the same doth rather begin to increase than to stay or diminish, we, considering the authority given to us of Almighty God for defence of the public peace, concord and truth of this his church, and how we are answerable for the same to the seat of his high justice, mean not to endure and suffer any longer these evils thus to proceed, spread and increase in our realm, but have certainly determined to have all such diversities, varieties and novelties amongst them of the clergy and our people as breed nothing but contention, offence, and breach of common charity, and are also against the laws, good usages and ordinances of our realm, to be reformed and repressed and brought to one manner of uniformity through our whole realm and dominions, that our people may thereby quietly honour and serve Almighty God in truth, concord, peace and quietness, and thereby also avoid the slanders that are spread abroad hereupon in foreign countries.

And therefore, we do by these our present letters require, enjoin and straitly charge you, being the metropolitan, according to the power and authority which you have under us over this province of Canterbury (as the like we will order for the province of York) to confer with the bishops your brethren, namely such as be in commission for causes ecclesiastical, and also all other head officers and persons having jurisdiction ecclesiastical, as well in both our universities as in any other places, collegiate, cathedral or whatsoever the same be, exempt or not exempt, either by calling to you from thence whom you shall think meet, to have assistance or conference, or by message, process, or letters, as you shall see most convenient, and cause to be truly understand what varieties, novelties and diversities there are in our clergy or amongst our people within every of the said jurisdictions, either in doctrine or in ceremonies and rites of the church, or in the manners, usages and behaviours of the clergy themselves, by what name soever any of them be called. And thereupon, as the several cases shall appear to require reformation, so to proceed by order, injunction or censure, according to the order and appointment of such laws and ordinances as are provided by act of Parliament, and the true meaning thereof, so as uniformity of order may be kept in every church, and without variety and contention.

And for the time to come we will and straitly charge you to provide and enjoin in our name, in all and every places in your province, as well in places exempt as otherwise, that none be hereafter admitted or allowed to any office, room, cure or place ecclesiastical, either having cure of souls, or without cure, but such as shall be found disposed and well and advisedly given to common order: and shall also, before their admittance to the same, orderly and formally promise to use and exercise the same office, room or place to the honour of God [and] the edification of our people under their charge, in truth, concord and unity; and also to observe, keep and maintain such order and uniformity in all the external rites and ceremonies, both for the church and for their own persons, as by laws, good usages, and orders are already allowed, well provided and established. And if any superior officers shall be found hereto disagreeable, if otherwise your discretion and authority shall not serve to reform them, we will that you shall duly inform us thereof, to the end we may give indelayed order for the same: for we intend to have no dissension or variety grow by suffering of persons which maintain dissension to remain in authority; for so the sovereign authority which we have under Almighty God should be violate and made frustrate, and we might be well thought to bear the sword in vain.

And in the execution hereof we require you to use all expedition that, to such a cause as this is, shall seem necessary, that hereafter we be not occasioned, for lack of your diligence, to provide such further remedy, by some other sharp proceedings, as shall percase not be easy to be borne by such as shall be disordered: and therewith also we shall impute to you the cause thereof.

33. B. M. Cot, Ms. Cleopatra F. 2. f. 278. Printed with some errors in W. Nicholson, ed. *Remains of Edmund Grindal*, Parker Society, Cambridge, 1843, pp. 467–9.

8 May, 1577. The queen to the bishops.

A letter from the queen's majesty sent to the bishops through England for the supplying [sic.] of the exercise called prophesying.

Right reverend father in God, we greet you well. We hear, to our great grief, that in sundry parts of our realm there are no small numbers of persons presuming to be teachers and preachers of the church, though neither lawfully thereunto called, no[r] yet fit for the same, which, contrary to our laws established for the public divine service of Almighty God, and the administration of his holy sacraments within this church of England, do daily devise, imagine, propound and put in execution, sundry new rites and forms in the church, as well by their preaching, readings, and ministering the sacraments, as well by procuring unlawful assemblies of a great number of our people out of their ordinary parishes, and from place far distant, and that also of some of good calling, (though therein not well advised) to be hearers of their disputations, and new devised opinions, upon points of divinity, far and unmeet of unlarge people: which manner of invasions they in some places call prophesyings, and in some other places exercises. By which manner of assemblies great numbers of our people, especially the vulgar sort, meet to be otherwise occupied with honest labour for their living, are brought to idleness, and seduced; and in manner schismatically divided among themselves into variety of dangerous opinions, not only in towns and parishes, but even in some families, and manifestly thereby encouraged to the violation of our laws, and to the breach of common order, and finally to the offence of all our quiet subjects, that desire to serve God according to the uniform orders established in the church: whereof the sequel cannot be but over dangerous to be suffered.

Wherefore, considering it should be the duty of the bishops, being the principal ordinary officers in the church of God, as you are one, to see this dishonours against the honour of God and the quietness of the church reformed; and that we see that by the increase of these through sufferance great danger may ensue, even to the decay of the Christian faith, whereof we are by God appointed the defender; besides the other inconveniences to the disturbance of our peaceable government. We, therefore, according to [the] authority we have, do charge and command you, as the bishop of that diocese, with all manner of diligence, to take order through your diocese, as well in places exempt as otherwise, that no manner of public and divine service, nor other form of administration of the holy sacraments, nor any other rites and ceremonies be in any sort used in the church, but directly according to the orders established by our laws. Neither that any manner of person be suffered within your diocese to preach, teach or read, or any exercise any function in the church, but such as shall be lawfully approved and licensed, as persons able for their knowledge, and conformable to the ministry in the rites and ceremonies of the church of England. And where there shall not be sufficient able persons for learning in any cures to preach or instruct their cures, as were requisite, there shall you limit the curates to read the public homilies, according to the injunctions heretofore by us given for like causes.

And, furthermore, considering for the great abuse that have been in sundry places of our realm, by reason of our foresaid assemblies, called exercises, and for that the same are not, nor have not been appointed nor warranted by us, or by our laws; we will and straitly charge you, that you do charge the same forthwith to cease, and not to be used: but if any shall attempt, or continue, or renew the same, we will you not only to commit the[m] unto prison as maintainers of disorders, but also to advertise us, or our council, of the names and qualities of them, and of their maintainers and abettors; that the[re]upon, for better example, their punishment may be more sharp for their reformation.

And in these things we charge you to be so careful and vigilant, as by your negligence, if we should hear of any person attempting to offend in the premises without your correction or information to us, we be not forced to make some example or reformation of you according to your deserts.

Given under our signet at our manor of Greenwich, the 7th of May, 1577.

34.   York. Borthwick Institute. R. VII. H.C. A.B. 10. f. 3–5.

The Northern High Commission in action against Recusants. 1580.

Monday 18th July, in the year of our Lord 1580. Before the reverend father in Christ, Edwin Archbishop of the diocese of York; and the illustrious gentleman, Henry Earl of Huntingdon, Lord President in the Northern Parts; and the worshipful gentlemen William Askquith, Lord Mayor of the city of York, Matthew Hutton, Professor of Sacred Theology, Dean of the cathedral church of York, and Robert Lougher, Doctor of Law; —— Rokeby, —— Hilyard, William Paler and John More, esquires; William Palmer, Edmund Bunny, Bachelors of Sacred Theology; Richard Percy, Doctor of Law and Henry Wright, Master of Arts, Commissioners of the Crown in Ecclesiastical Causes among others lawfully deputed.

In person The High Commissioners against Ann Cooke, *wife of Ambrose Cooke of the city of York.* [And sixteen others, named.]	All the said persons are prisoners for their obstinacy in religion in the Kidcote.
The High Commissioners against Katharine— [And twenty-one others, named.]	Prisoners in the Castle for their disobedience in refusing the church and communion.
The High Commissioners against Margaret Wright, wife of John Wright, apothecary of York.	She is suspected in religion and commanded to appear this day, etc.

The High Commis-
sioners against Lucy
Plowman.

John Wiseman and Alexander Howson of the city of York have undertaken for her appearance this day etc. to answer her contempt in refusing the church and communion.

In person The High Commis-
sioners against Eliza-
beth Wilkinson, wife of
William Wilkinson of
the same city.

The said Elizabeth is commanded to appear this day for the like offence etc. And bond is taken for her appearance.

Not pro- *The High Commis-*
ceeded *sioners against Ciciley*
with by *Fairfaxe, wife of Guy*
order of *Fairfaxe of Malton,*
the Lord *diocese of York.*
Arch-
bishop
19 *July*
1580.

A recognizance of £20 acknowledged by the said Guy for the appearance of his said wife on Friday last past is forfeited etc.

In person The High Commis-
sioners against Agnes
Wygan of the city of
York, widow.

John Jackson and Bryan Peerson of this city have undertaken to bring in the said Agnes this day to answer her contempt in refusing the church and communion. *On this day she appeared in person.* And being persuaded to go to church to hear divine service she promised to go to her parish church once monthly if she be able and her strength serve her and so was dismissed.

In person The High Commis-
sioners against Alice
Aldcorne, otherwise
Awdcorne, wife of
Thomas Aldcorne of
the city of York.

She refuseth the church and communion, and Rauf Iles of the said city hath judicially promised in this court to bring her in this day. *On this day she appeared in person.* And because she refused the church and to communicate she was committed to the Kidcote *until* [she conforms] etc.

N

In person The High Commissioners against Phillida Burdon, servant of the said Thomas.

She refuseth the church and communion and the said Iles hath undertaken for her appearance this day etc. *On this day she appeared in person* and promised to go to service to St Sampson's church upon Sunday next and so after as she is bound by law. She is a very simple poor woman.

In person The High Commissioners against Percival Geldarde of the Geldart *said city.*

Suspected in religion, and bound to appear this day. *On this day the said Geldart appeared in person* to whom the said commissioners offered an oath to answer to such interrogatories as he is bound by law; the which oath he refused to take divers times. And thereupon the said commissioners committed him to the castle to close prison *until etc.* And a bill of charges is taxed to 9s. 4d., the which he is to pay before his enlargement.

Appeared The High Commissioners against Ann Lyster, wife of Thomas Lyster of the said city.

She refuseth the church and communion and bond is taken for her appearance.

This man The High Commissioners against Henry Fairfaxe and Dorothy, his wife, of the parish of Bilbrough in the diocese of York.
3rd Oct.

Warrant sent out for apprehension of the said Henry and Dorothy against this day and place. On which day and hour and place the said Fairfax appeared in person and showed a bond to repair to the church and to receive the communion as by the laws he is bound and that his wife and his family shall do the like and to certify *on the first day of the next session after the feast of Michaelmas aforesaid.*

Not pro- The High Commis-
ceeded sioners against Agnes
Aygar, wife of
Thomas Aygar of
Huntington, diocese of
York.

Her husband is to bring her in
this day to answer her contempt
in refusing the church and communion. *On which day, hour
and place. . . .*

Hitherto The High Commis-
she did sioners against Mar-
not garet Thwaites, wife
appear of John Thwaites of
but now Marston, diocese of
she York, esquire.
*appeared
in person.*

*Warrant sent out for apprehen-
sion of the said Margaret to
answer why she refuses to go to
church and receive the holy
communion. On which day,
hour and place the said
Thwaites appeared in person
and was committed to the
custody of Mr. Maltby until. . . .
A warrant sent out etc.*

As above The High Commissioners against the
wife of Brian Palmes
of Naburn, diocese of
York.

As above The High Commissioners against Robert
Wright of Hunting-
ton in the diocese of
York, esquire.

A warrant was sent forth for the
said Robert Wright, and bond is
taken by the pursuivant for his
appearance upon two days warning to be given at his house or
abiding place, to answer his contempt in refusing the church
and communion.

In person The High Commissioners against Alice
Thorpe of Hunting-
ton aforesaid.

Bond is taken for her appearance this day to answer her contempt in refusing the church
etc. *On which day she appeared
in person.* And being interrogated what she misliked that is
now used in the church etc. she
said nothing. However, because
she refused to go to church to
hear divine service and to communicate etc. she was committed
to the castle *until etc.*

Great The High Commis-
with sioners against Katha-
child rine Browne, wife of
Robert Browne of Sut-

Bond is likewise taken for her
appearance this day to answer
for the like offence. But because
this court was certified that she

ton Grange, diocese of York.

Lawson   The High Commissioners against Ralf Lawson of Brough in the province of York, esquire.

was so great with child that she was not now able to appear, her appearance was excused at this time, the bond not withstanding. Suspected to be backward in religion, *appeared* and is sworn to answer truly to such interrogatories as he shall be asked of. And then being interrogated when he was at his parish church, by his oath he affirmed that he was there in Christmas last; and being likewise asked whether he was dissuaded by any person to abstain himself from the church; he answered none. Then being asked on what occasion he abstaineth he asked further respite till Easter next without other answer. He confessed, being interrogated, that his wife was delivered of child since Christmas last past, and that his said child was christened in his house according to the Book of Common Prayer, as his wife told him. And he further confessed that he misliked of nothing done now in the church of England. He confessed also that he had made no vow to absent himself from the church. Being asked whether his wife was purified or no, he said he knew not, neither knew he (as he affirmed) who was godfathers [sic] to his child.

The High Commissioners against Katharine Norton.

She appeared and being moved to conformity and to go to the church etc. she desired to have respite and that she might have time to confer with some learned preacher. Whereupon she was commanded to the custody of

The High Commissioners against Thomas Feilden, —— Feilden, Acryth and Acrig; and Stephen Hemsworth and Thomas Mudd, priests.

Alderman Broke for three days and licence granted her to repair to Mr. Dean or some other preacher in the mean time for conference in matters of religion. The said Thomas Feilden affirmed that he was persuaded not to come to the church because his conscience was so stayed: reason thereof he would give none saving that he said he believed the articles of faith etc. The other persons were not dealt withal saving Mudd. Mudd confesseth that the substance of baptism is now kept which was used heretofore, and licence is given him to set down in writing his opinion touching religion and account of his faith.

The High Commissioners against Agnes Clerk and Richard Ebden and Jane, his wife, and John Burghley of Whitwell Towers.

Burghley Monday after Michaelmas 3 Oct.

The said Agnes Clerk appeared and for that she refused the church she was committed to the castle etc. And the said Ebden entered into recognizance that he, his wife and family should resort to the church and become dutiful subjects. And to certify 3 October *next*. And the said Burghley is so bound for himself, and to certify the said third of October next.

35. FROM J. STRYPE, *Whitgift*, 1718, appendix, pp. 49–52.

A summary of the Twenty-four interrogatories administered by Whitgift and other High Commissioners under the *ex officio* oath at Lambeth, May, 1584.

The accused was asked, (and required to answer):

1. What his standing was in the church, and by whom he was ordained.
2. Whether he regarded his ordination and calling lawful and not repugnant to the word of God.

3. Whether at ordination he had sworn allegiance to the queen, and canonical obedience to his ordinary.

4. Whether he questioned the fact that the Book of Common Prayer was established by act of Parliament.

5. Whether he questioned that he was bound to say morning and evening prayer etc. as is set out in the Prayer Book, and not otherwise.

6. Whether he questioned the fact that by statute archbishops, bishops and ordinaries are charged to enforce the above act.

7. 'That you deem and judge the said whole Book to be a godly and a virtuous book, agreeable, or at the least, not repugnant to the word of God; if not we require and command you to declare wherein, and in what points.'

8. Whether within the last three years he had ministered communion in ordinary clothes and not in the surplice. He was required to state how often he had done so, and why.

9. Whether within the same period he had baptized any infant without using the sign of the cross.

10. Whether he had refused to baptize a weak child privately, and how many had so died unbaptized.

11. Whether he had celebrated matrimony without using the ring and words prescribed in the Prayer Book.

12. Whether he had neglected to use the form of thanksgiving for women after childbirth as prescribed in the Prayer Book.

13. Whether he had baptized infants not using the form prescribed in the Prayer Book, nor interrogatories to Godparents.

14. Whether he had refused to use all or any part of the Litany.

15. Whether he had refused to read any lessons prescribed in the Prayer Book.

16. Whether he had conducted any burial not using the form prescribed in the Prayer Book.

17. What other parts of Common Prayer he had neglected or refused to read and why.

18. Whether at communion he had altered the form prescribed in the Book of Common Prayer, and why.

19. Whether he had ever taught or written that the Book of Common Prayer or any part of it was repugnant to the word of God.

20. Whether he continued in his former opinions about the Book: whether he had used private conferences or assembled in conventicles.

21. Whether he had ever been presented before his ordinary for any of the above faults or opinions; if so, when and where had this been.

22. Whether he had subscribed to the following Three Articles:

i. 'That her majesty under God hath, and ought to have the sovereignty, and rule over all manner of persons born within her realm, dominions and countries, of what state, either ecclesiastical or temporal soever they be, and that none other foreign power, prelate, state or potentate hath or ought to have any jurisdiction, power, superiority, pre-eminence or authority ecclesiastical or spiritual, within her majesty's said realms, dominions or countries.

ii. That the Book of Common Prayer and of ordering of bishops, priests and deacons containeth in it nothing contrary to the word of God, and that the same may lawfully be used; and that you who do subscribe will use the form in the said book prescribed in public prayer, and administration of the sacraments, and none other.

iii. That you allow the book of Articles of Religion, agreed upon by the archbishops and bishops of both provinces, and the whole clergy in the Convocation holden at London in the year of our Lord God 1562, and set forth by her majesty's authority; and do believe all the articles therein contained to be agreeable to the word of God. . . .'

23. Whether he had preached or expounded scriptures not being licensed.

24. That all the premises, each and every one, had been truthfully answered.

36. B. M. Lans. Ms. 102. 111. Printed in J. Strype, *Whitgift*, 1718, appendix, pp. 63–4.

1 July, 1584. William Cecil, Lord Burghley to Archbishop Whitgift.

It may please your grace. I am sorry to trouble you so often as I do, but I am more troubled myself, not only with many private petitions of sundry ministers recommended from persons of credit for peaceable persons in their ministry, and yet by complaints to your grace and other your colleagues in commission greatly troubled; but also I am now daily charged by councillors and public persons to neglect my duty in not staying of these your grace's proceedings, so vehement and so general, against ministers and preachers; as the Papists are thereby generally encouraged, all ill disposed subjects animated and thereby the queen's majesty's safety endangered. With these kind of arguments I am daily assailed against which I answer that I think your grace doth nothing but being duly examined tendeth to the main-tenance of the religion established, and to avoid schisms in the church. I also have, for example, showed upon your papers sent to me how fully the church is furnished with preachers, and how small a number there are that do contend for their singularity. But these reasons do not satisfy all persons, neither do I seek to satisfy them, but with reason and truth.

But now, my good lord, by chance I am come to the sight of an instrument of 24 Articles of great length and curiosity, formed in a Romish style, to examine all manner of ministers in this time without distinction of persons; which articles are entitled, *At* Lambeth, May 1584, to be executed *ex officio mero* etc. And upon this occasion I have seen them. I did recommend unto your grace's favour two ministers, curates of Cambridgeshire, to be favourably heard: and your grace wrote to me they were contentious, seditious and persons vagrant to maintain this controversy. Wherewith I charged them sharply, and they both denied those charges and required to be tried and so to receive punishment. I answered that I thought your grace would so charge them; and then I should afterwards see what they should deserve, and advised them to resort to your grace, comforting them that they should find favourable proceeding. And so I hoped the rather upon my former commendation. What may be said to them I know not; nor whether they be so faulty as your grace hath been informed, do I know. Neither do I mean to entreat your favour for such men: for pardon I may speak upon their amendment. But now they coming to me, and I asking of them how your grace hath proceeded with them, they say they are commanded to be examined by the register at Lambeth[?]. And I asked them whereof? They said, of a great number of articles, but they could have no copies of them. I answered, then they might answer according to truth. They said they were so many in number, and so divers, as they were afraid to answer to them for fear of captious interpretation. Upon this I sent for the register who brought me the articles, which I have read; and find so curiously penned, so full of branches and circumstances as I think the inquisitors of Spain use not so many questions to comprehend and to trap their preys.

I know your canonists can defend these with all their perticels, but surely, under your grace's correction, this judicial and canonical sifting of poor ministers is not to edify or reform. And in charity, I think they ought not to answer to all these nice points, except they were very notorious offenders in Papistry or heresy. Now, my good lord, bear with my scribbling: I write with a testimony of a good conscience. I desire the peace of the church. I desire concord and unity in the exercise of our religion. I favour no sensual and wilful recusant. But I conclude, that according to my simple judgement this kind of proceeding is too much savouring of the Romish inquisition, and is rather a device to seek for offenders than to reform any. This is not the charitable instruction that I thought was intended. If these poor ministers should in some few points have any scrupulous conceptions, meet to be removed, this is not a charitable way to send them to answer to your common register upon so many articles at one instant, without any commodity of instruction by your register, whose office is only to receive their answers. By which the parties are first subject to condemnation before they be taught their errors.

It may be, as I said, the canonists may maintain this proceeding by rules of their laws: but though *all things are permitted,* yet *all things are not expedient.* I pray your grace bear this one (perchance a) fault, that I have willed them not to answer these articles, except their conscience may suffer them. And yet I have sharply admonished them that if they be disturbers in their churches they must be corrected. And yet upon your grace's answer to me I will leave them to your authority, as becometh me. *Let the cobbler stick to his last.* Neither will I put *my scythe in another's crop.* My paper teacheth me to end. *First July,* 1584.

Your grace's at commandment,
William Cecil.

Your grace must pardon my hasty writing, for I have done this *hastily* and without correction.

37. B. M. Lans. Ms. 42. 47. Printed in J. Strype, *Whitgift,* 1718, appendix, pp. 64–6.

3 July, 1584. Archbishop Whitgift to William Lord Burghley.

My singular good lord. In the very beginning of this action, and so from time to time, I have made your lordship acquainted with all my doings, and so answered the objections and reasons to the contrary, as I persuade myself that no just reply can be made thereunto. I have likewise, by your lordship's advice, chosen this kind of proceeding with them, because I would not touch any for not subscribing only, but for breach of order in celebrating divine service, administring the sacraments and executing other ecclesiastical functions according to their fancies and not according to the form by law prescribed, which neither your lordship nor others seemed to mislike, but to wish and require. And therefore I am much troubled at your last letters which seem so to be written as though your lordship had not been in these points already answered and satisfied.

The complaints which your lordship saith are made of me, and of other my colleagues, have been hitherto general and therefore cannot otherwise be answered than by a bare denial. But if any man shall charge me or them with particularities, I do wot not but we are and shall be ready to answer them and to justify our doings. My proceedings are neither so vehement, nor so general against ministers and preachers, as some pretend, doing me therein great injury. And I have sundry times satisfied your lordship therein. If I have any way offended it is in bearing too much with them, and in using of them too familiarly: which causeth them thus contrary to their duty to trouble the church, and to withstand me, their ordinary and lawful judge.

The objection of encouraging the Papists etc. hath neither probability nor likelihood. For how can Papists be animated by urging of men to subscribe against the pope's supremacy; or to the justifying of the Book of Common Prayers and of the Articles of Religion, both which they so greatly condemn? But indeed Papists etc. are animated because they see these kind of persons (which herein after a sort join with them) so greatly friended, so much born with, and so animated in their disordered doings against both God's law and man's law; and against their chief governors, civil and ecclesiastical. This, I say, encourageth the Papists and maketh them so malapert. The other is but a *fallacy*; a[n argument] *from a non-cause to a cause*. O, my lord, would to God some of them which use this argument had no Papists in their families, and not otherwise also countenance them, whereby indeed they receive encouragement. Assure yourself, that the Papists are rather grieved at my doings, because they tend to the taking away of their chief argument; that is, that we cannot agree among ourselves, and lack unity: and therefore are not of the church. And I am credibly informed that the Papists give encouragement to these men, and commend them in their doings, whereof I have also some experience. But if these reasons and sundry others will not satisfy some, I am sure your lordship will not think it convenient to yield to their wills without reason.

Touching the 24 Articles which your lordship seemeth so much to mislike, as written in a Romish style, smelling of the Romish inquisition etc. I cannot but greatly marvel at your lordship's vehement speeches against them (I hope without cause), seeing it is the ordinary course in other courts likewise, as in the Star Chamber, the Court of the Marches, and other places. And (without offence be it spoken) I think these articles to be more tolerable, and better agreeing with the rule of justice and charity, and less captious, than these in other courts. Because men are there often times examined at the relation of a private man concerning private crimes, *and concerning their own baseness*. Whereas here men are only examined of their public actions in their public calling and ministry. Whereunto in conscience they are bound to answer; and much more than in the case of heresy, because the one toucheth life, the other not. And therefore I see no cause why our judicial and canonical proceedings in this point should be misliked.

Your lordship writeth that the two for whom you speak are peaceable, observe the Book, deny the things whereof they are charged, and desire to be tried. Now they are to be charged why do they refuse it? *He who does evil hates the light.* I do minister these articles unto them, framed by the best learned in the laws (who, I dare say, hate both the Romish doctrine, and the Romish Inquisition) to the intent that I may truly understand whether they are such manner of men, or no, as they pretend to be, especially seeing by public fame they are noted of the contrary; and one of them presented by the sworn men of his parish for his disorders, as I am informed by the official there. I have written nothing to your lordship of them which their own behaviour doth not prove to be true. Therefore, I beseech your lordship not to believe them against me, either upon their own words or upon the testimony of such as animate them in their disobedience, and count disorder order, and contention peace, before they be duly and orderly tried, according to that law which is yet in force, and in my opinion, will hardly, in these judicial actions, be bettered; though some abuse may be in the execution thereof, as there is in other courts likewise; and that, peradventure, more abundantly.

Your lordship saith that these articles are devised rather to seek for offenders, than to reform any. The like may be said of the like orders in other courts also; but that should be the fault of the judge, not of the law: and I trust your lordship hath no cause to think so evil of me. I have not dealt as yet with any but such as have refused to subscribe, and give manifest tokens of contempt of orders and laws: my acts, remaining in record, will testify with me. And although the register doth examine them (as other officers do in other courts likewise, and the law doth allow of it) yet are they repeated before a judge, where they may reform, add or diminish as they think good. Neither hath any man thus been examined, which hath not before been conferred with: these two especially, even until they have had nothing to say. And, if they otherwise report to your lordship, *they assert a fable*; and they report untruly. A quality, wherewith this sect is marvellously possessed: as myself, of my own knowledge and experience can justify, against divers of them.

I know your lordship desireth the peace of the church: but how is it possible to be procured (after so long liberty and lack of discipline) if a few persons, so meanly qualified, as the most of them are, should be countenanced against the whole state of the clergy of greatest account, for learning, years, steadiness, wisdom, religion and honesty: and open breakers and impugners of the laws, young in years, proud in conceit, contentious in disposition, maintained against their superiors and governors, seeking to reduce them to order and to obedience? *These are the sources of heretics, and the origin and impulse of evil thinking schismatics, that they please themselves, that with swelling pride they condemn their superior: thus is a separation made from the church; thus is a profane altar set up from abroad; thus is war waged against the peace of Christ, against ordination and even against the unity of God.*

For my own part I neither do, nor have done anything in this matter, which I do not think myself in duty and conscience bound to do; which her majesty hath not with earnest charge committed unto me. And the which I am well able to justify to be most requisite for this state and church; whereof, next to her majesty, though most unworthy, or, at the least, most unhappy, the chief care is committed to me, which I may not neglect, whatsoever come upon me therefore. I neither esteem the honour of the place (which is to me *a very heavy burden*) nor the largeness of the revenues (for the which I am not as yet one penny the richer) nor any other worldly thing, I thank God, in the respect of doing my duty. Neither do I fear the displeasure of man, nor regard the wicked tongues of the uncharitable, which call me tyrant, pope, Papist, knave; and lay to my charge things which I never did nor thought upon. *I know this is the work of the devil who defames the servants of God with a lie, and dishonours the glorious name with false opinions, so that they who shine in the light of conscience are defiled by hostile rumours.* So was Cyprian himself used for the same causes, and other godly bishops to whom I am not comparable. The day will come when all men's hearts shall be opened and made manifest. In the meantime I will depend upon him who hath called me to this place; and will not forsake those that trust in him.

If your lordship do keep those two from answering according to the order set down, it will be of itself a setting at liberty of all the rest, and an undoing of all which hitherto hath been done. Neither shall I be able to do that which her majesty expecteth at my hands, and is now in very good towardness. And therefore, I beseech your lordship, to leave them unto me. I will not proceed to any sentence against them until I have made your lordship privy to their answers, and further conferred with you thereof; because I see your lordship so earnest in their behalf: whereof they have also made public boasts (as I am informed) which argueth of what disposition they are.

I heartily pray your lordship to take not only the length, but also the matter of this letter in good part, and to continue unto me as you have hitherto done. For if you now forsake me, and that in so good a cause (as I know you will not) I shall think my hap to be very hard that when I hope to deserve best, I should be worst rewarded. *But*

I hope for better things. And commit myself to the author of peace whom I beseech to bless and prosper your lordship.
From Croydon, the 3rd of July, 1584.

To your lordship most bound,
John *Canterbury.*

38. FROM J. STRYPE, *Whitgift,* 1718, p. 461.
The Lambeth Articles (translated from the Latin).

Articles approved by their reverend lordships John [Whitgift], Archbishop of Canterbury, D.D., and Richard [Fletcher], Bishop of London and other theologians, at Lambeth 20 November, 1595.

1. God from eternity predestined certain men to life and condemned others to death.
2. The moving or efficient cause of predestination to life is not foreseeing of faith, or of perseverance, or of good works, or of any other thing which is in the person predestined, but the will of the good pleasure of God alone.
3. The number of the predestined is prescribed and certain and it cannot be increased or diminished.
4. Those who are not predestined to salvation shall of necessity be damned on account of their sins.
5. A true, living and justifying faith and the sanctifying spirit of God is not extinguished, does not leave or disappear in the elect either finally or totally.
6. The man who has true faith, that is, the aforesaid justifying faith, is certain by the abundance of faith of the remission of his sins and of his eternal salvation through Christ.
7. Saving grace is not attributed, not communicated and not given to all men by which they may be saved if they so will.
8. No one can come to Christ except [grace] be given to him and except the Father draws him. And all men are not drawn by the Father to come to the Son.
9. It is not appointed that in his own will and power each and every man should be saved.

39. Trinity College, Cambridge. Ms. B/14/9. 117.

5 December, 1595. Sir Robert Cecil to Archbishop Whitgift.

May it please your grace. Her majesty having heard of Mr Whittacre's death, and of some business he came up about, hath commanded me to send unto your grace that she mislikes much that any allowance hath been given by your grace and the rest of any points to be disputed of predestination, being a matter tender and dangerous to weak, ignorant minds, and thereupon requireth your grace to suspend them. I could not tell what to answer, but do this as her majesty's commandment, and leave the matter for your grace who I know can best satisfy her in these things.

And thus I humbly take my leave. From the court this 5 of December, 1595.

> Your grace's to command,
> Robert Cecil.

40. Trinity College, Cambridge. Ms. B/14/9. 118–120.

8 December, 1595. Archbishop Whitgift to Mr Dr Neville.

Greetings in Christ. I have received your letters touching Mr Overall, and I very much rely upon your judgement in that case. Nevertheless, I am informed by some others that Mr Overall is something factious and inclined to that sect that loveth to pick quarrels to the present state and government of the church; which I hope not to be true because of your commendation. But I think you shall receive letters in her majesty's name for due care to be had in electing a person meet for that place. And therefore I do assure myself that you will be careful to provide such a one as shall be in all points conformable.

Mr Whittacre's death doth affect me exceedingly in many respects, he being a man whom I loved very well, and had purposed to have employed him in matters of great importance. At his last being with me he signified unto me what things he had in hand touching Stapleton. And therefore I am very desirous to have his notes and writings as well concerning that matter as other things. And therefore I pray you procure them unto me if you can. I will consider those that have the doing in these causes to their contentation. And although I may in some sort require them, yet I will forbear so to do, and hope that they will of courtesy not deny unto me this request. I am informed, and think it to be true, that her majesty intendeth to stay his library for herself, but his written books and papers are no part thereof.

At Mr Dean of Ely's and his last being here we agreed of certain propositions which are undoubtedly true, and not to be denied of any sound divine. But I know not how, or by what means the same hath been signified to her majesty in evil sense, and as though the same had been by me sent down to the university to be disputed upon, or (I know not how) published. It is the thing that I before something suspected etc. But you then refuse advertisements and think yourselves to have no need of advice; otherwise these things had never grown to this extremity. The foolery of Dr Some hath done no good to the cause. Her majesty is persuaded of the truth of the propositions, but doth think it to be utterly unfit that the same should any ways be publicly dealt with, either in semon or disputation, as I think you are like further to understand ere it be long. I pray you have me commended to Mr Vicechancellor, and let him understand so much from me: and desire him in the mean time so to use the said propositions as there be no publication thereof otherwise than in private. For indeed my meaning was only to let him and you understand that in these points I do concur with you in judgement, and will to the end; and mean not to suffer any man to impugn them openly, or otherwise. And when you shall have received the foresaid admonition from her majesty I do wish that you should return answer to your chancellor your willingness to observe her majesty's commandment: but with signification of your assured persuasion of the truth of the foresaid propositions. This advice I would have you to give privately to Mr Vicechancellor and to use it discreetly, but in no case to suffer these letters to go out of your own hands, but to keep them yourself, and either to burn them, or to bring them to me again at your coming hither.

You may also signifiy to Dr Baro that her majesty is greatly offended with him for that he being a stranger and so well used dare presume to stir up or maintain any controversies in that place, of what nature soever. And therefore advise him from me utterly to forbear to deal therein hereafter. I have done my endeavour to satisfy her majesty concerning him; but how it will fall out in the end I know not. *It is not fitting for a man, a foreigner, to be curious about a country not his own.* I write this to you as to my good and trusty friend, and as a feeling member of that body; and I cannot but commend very greatly her majesty's great care in these matters, being of the same mind myself. Farewell in Christ.

At Lambeth. 8 December, 1595.

Your assured loving friend,

(ii) Lay Intervention in the Church in Parliament

41. FROM S. D'EWES, *A Complete Journal of the Votes, Speeches and Debates, both of the House of Lords and House of Commons throughout the whole Reign of Queen Elizabeth*, 1693, pp. 166–7.

Saturday, 14 April, 1571.

The bill for reformation of the Book of Common Prayer was read the first time, after which (the bill being preferred by Mr Strickland) ensued divers long arguments . . . in manner and form following.

Mr Treasurer (of her majesty's household) reasoned to this effect: that if the matters mentioned to be reformed were heretical, then verily they were presently to be condemned; but if they are but matters of ceremony, then it behoveth us to refer the same to her majesty who hath authority, as chief of the church, to deal herein. And for us to meddle with matters of her prerogative (quoth he) it were not expedient. Withal, he said, what cause there might be to make her majesty not to run and join with those who seem to be most earnest. We are not to search whether it be for that in time and order she hopeth to bring them with her, or what other secret cause or scruple there may be in the heart of princes, it is not for all people to know.

Mr Comptroller argued to his effect as afore, commending the zeal but that the place and time were not fit. And since we knowledge her to be supreme head, we are not in these petty matters to run before the ball, which to do, and therein to offend, were great folly; how forewarned we were herein he did refer to our consideration, insinuating in some sort that our heady and hasty proceedings, contrary to and before the law, did rather hinder than help.

Hereupon one Pistor with a grave and seemly countenance, and good natural eloquence showed how conscience enforced him to speak; and rather to hazard his credit than to the offence of his conscience be silent. Albeit he would acknowledge willingly that many hundreds of that honourable and worshipful assembly were well able to teach him, and he indeed willing to learn of them all: the matter of his grief was that matters of importance standing us upon for our souls, stretching higher and further to every one of us than the monarchy of the whole world, were either not treated of, or so slenderly, that now after more than ten days continual consultation nothing was thereon concluded. This cause he showed to be God's, the rest are all but terrene, yea trifles in comparison; call you them never so great, or pretend you that they import never so much; subsidies, crowns, kingdoms, he knew not, he said, what they were in comparison of this: this, he said, I know, whereof he most thanked God, *'seek first the kingdom of God, and all the rest shall be added to you.'* This rule is the direction, and this desire shall bring us to the light, whereupon we may stay, and then proceed unto the rest: for in his word, and by him we learn, as saith St Paul, to correct, reform etc. Our true home certainly is not here, *'here we have no abiding city:'* and the justice of God moveth terror unto all, which he seemed to mean concerning the bill before mentioned of Strickland's propositions. And so did set it forth with vehemency, that there lacked no modesty; and with such eloquence, that it neither seemed studied nor too much affected, but grave and learned throughout, and no whit too long, but every well approved of.

And after him Mr Snagge, and far after him indeed, either for order, proof or matter; he entered into the discourse of Strickland's articles, and seemed to maintain them; this namely; not to kneel at the receiving of the communion, but rather, if a law hereof should be made, to lie prostrate to shun the old superstition; or otherwise to set every man at liberty, and in this behalf to do according to his conscience and devotion, he judged it to be nothing derogatory or contrary to the prerogative. And the directions he thought fit to be left out of the book, which should be a law etc.

After which arguments it was upon the question agreed, that a petition should be made by this House unto the queen's majesty for her licence and privity to proceed in this bill, before it be any further dealt in.

42. FROM *The Journals of the House of Commons*, I, p. 113.

9 March, 1576.

Mr Chancellor of the Exchequer touching the petition for reformation of discipline in the church doth bring word from the lords[1] that their lordships having moved the queen's majesty touching the said petition, her highness answered their lordships.

That her majesty, before the Parliament, had a care to provide in that case of her own disposition; and at the beginning of this session her highness had conference therein with some of the bishops, and gave them in charge to see due reformation thereof: wherein, as her majesty thinketh, they will have good consideration, according unto her pleasure and express commandment in that behalf. So did her highness most graciously and honourably declare further that, if the

[1] The lords of the Privy Council.

said bishops should neglect or omit their duties therein, then her majesty, by her supreme power and authority over the church of England, would speedily see such good redress therein, as might satisfy the expectation of her loving subjects to their good contentation.

Which message and report was most thankfully and joyfully received by the whole House with one accord.

43. FROM *The Journals of the House of Commons*, I, p. 131.
7 March, 1581.

Mr Chancellor of the Exchequer declareth that Mr Vicechamberlain, both Mr Secretaries and himself have according to their commission from this House conferred with some of my lords the bishops touching the griefs of this House for some things very requisite to be reformed in the church; as, the great number of unlearned and unable ministers, the great abuse of excommunication for every matter of small moment, the commutation of penance, and the great multitude of dispensations and pluralities, and other things very hurtful to the church: and in the name of this House desired their lordships to join with them in petition to her majesty for reformation of the said abuses. Declaring further that they found some of the said lords the bishops not only ready to confess and grant the said defects and abuses, wishing due redress thereof, but also very willing to join with the said committees in moving of her majesty in that behalf. Whereupon they afterwards joined in humble suit together unto her highness and received her majesty's most gracious answer.

That as her highness had, the last session of Parliament, of her own good consideration and before any petition or suit thereof made by this House committed the charge and consideration thereof unto some of her highness' clergy, who had not performed the same according to her highness' commandment. So now her majesty would eftsoons commit the same unto such others of them as with all convenient speed without remissness and slackness should see the same accomplished accordingly in such sort as the same shall neither be delayed or undone.

For the which, as they did all render unto her majesty most humble and dutiful thanks, so did Mr Chancellor further declare that the only cause why no due reformation hath been already had in the said petitions was only by the negligence and slackness of some others, and not of her majesty, nor of this House. Alleging withal, that some of the said bishops had yet done something in those matters delivered by her majesty to their charge, as in a more advised care of allowing and making of ministers; but yet, in effect, little or nothing to the purpose. And so concluding, moved this House to rest satisfied with her majesty's said most gracious answer, and to resolve upon some form of yielding thanks unto her highness, for her most gracious acceptation of the humble petition of this House unto her highness in that behalf; and also of putting her majesty in remembrance for execution thereof, at her highness' good pleasure.

44. FROM S. D'EWES, *A Complete Journal of ... both the House of Lords and House of Commons throughout the whole Reign of Queen Elizabeth*, 1693, pp. 328–9.

29 March, 1585. The queen's speech to both Houses of Parliament.

My lords and ye of the Lower House, my silence must not injure the owner so much as to suppose a substitute sufficient to render you the thanks that my heart yieldeth you, not so much for the safekeeping of my life for which your care appears so manifest, as for the neglecting your private future peril not regarding other way than my present state.

No prince herein, I confess, can be surer tied or faster bound than I am with the link of your good will, and can for that but yield a heart and a head to seek for ever all your best. Yet one matter toucheth me so near, as I may not overskip; religion, the ground on which all other matters ought to take root, and being corrupted, may mar all the tree. And that there be some fault finders with the order of the clergy, which so may make a slander to myself and the church, whose over-ruler God hath made me; whose negligence cannot be excused if any schisms or errors heretical were suffered. Thus much I must say that some faults and negligences may grow and be, as in all other great charges it happeneth: and what vocation without? All which if you, my lords of the clergy, do not amend, I mean to depose you. Look ye therefore well to your charges. This may be amended without heedless or open exclamations.

I am supposed to have many studies, but most philosophical. I must yield this to be true that I suppose few (that be no professors) have read more. And I need not tell you that I am so simple, that I understand not; nor so forgetful, that I remember not: and yet amidst my many volumes I hope God's book hath not been my seldomest lectures, in which we find that which by reason (for my part) we ought to believe; that seeing so great wickedness and griefs in the world in which we live but as wayfaring pilgrims, we must suppose that God would never have made us but for a better place and of more comfort than we find here. I know no creature that breatheth whose life standeth hourly in more peril for it than mine own, who entered not into my state without sight of manifold dangers of life and crown, as one that had the mightiest and greatest to wrestle with. Then it followeth that I regarded it so much, as I left my life behind my care; and so you see that you wrong me too much (if any such there be) as doubt my coldness in that behalf; for if I were not persuaded that mine were the true way of God's will, God forbid that I should live to prescribe it to you. Take you heed lest Ecclesiastes say not too true, 'They that fear the hoary frost, the snow shall fall upon them.'

I see many over-bold with God Almighty, making too many subtle scannings of his blessed will, as lawyers do with human testaments. The presumption is so great as I may not suffer it (yet mind I not hereby to animate Romanists, which what adversaries they be to mine estate is sufficiently known) nor tolerate new fangledness. I mean to guide them both by God's holy true rule. In both parts be perils; and of the latter I must pronounce them dangerous to kingly rule to have every man according to his own censure to make a doom of the validity and privity of his prince's government with a common veil and cover of God's word, whose followers must not be judged but by private men's exposition. God defend you from such a ruler that so evil will guide you.

Now I conclude that your love and care neither is nor shall be bestowed upon a careless prince, but such as but for your good will passeth as little for this world as who careth least: with thanks for your free subsidy, a manifest show of the abundance of your good wills, the which I assure you, but to be employed to your weal, I could be better pleased to return than receive.

(iii) Lay Intervention in the Church in the Localities

45. P.R.O. S.P. 12/78/38. Printed with some errors in J. C. Cox, ed. *Records of the Borough of Northampton,* Northampton, 1898, II, pp. 386–8.

The orders and dealings in the church of Northampton established and set up by the consent of the bishop of Peterborough, the mayor and brethren of the town there and others the queen's majesty's justices of peace within the said county and town taken and found the 5th day of June, 1571 *and* 13 *year* of Queen Elizabeth.

1. The singing and playing of organs before time accustomed in the choir is put down, and the common prayer there accustomed to be said is brought down into the body of the church amongst the people before whom the same is used according to the queen's book with singing psalms before and after the sermon.

2. There is in the chief church every Tuesday and Thursday from 9 of the clock until 10 in the morning read a lecture of the scriptures beginning with the confession in the Book of Common Prayer and ending with prayer, and confession of the faith etc.

3. There is in the same church every Sunday and holy day after morning prayer a sermon, the people singing the psalms before and after.

4. That service be ended in every parish church by 9 of the clock in the morning every Sunday and holy day to the end the people may resort to the sermon to the same church and that every minister give warning to the parishioners in time of common prayer to repair to the sermon there, except they have a sermon in their own parish church.

5. That after prayers done in the time of sermon or catechism none sit in the streets or walk up and down abroad or otherwise occupy themselves vainly, upon such penalty as shall be appointed.

6. The youth at the end of evening prayer every Sunday and holy day before all the elder people are examined in a portion of Calvin's catechism which by the reader is expounded unto them and holdeth an hour.

7. There is a general communion once every quarter in every parish church with a sermon which is by the minister at common prayer warned four several Sundays before every communion, with exhortation to the people to prepare for that day.

8. One fortnight before each communion the minister with the churchwardens maketh his circuit from house to house to take the names of the communicants and to examine the state of their lives, among whom, if any discord be found, the parties are brought before the mayor and his brethren, being assisted with the preacher and other gentlemen before whom there is reconcilement made, or else correction and putting the party from the communion which will not dwell in charity.

9. And immediately after the communion the minister etc. returneth to every house to understand who have not received the communion according to common order taken, and certifieth it to the mayor etc. who with the minister examineth the matter and useth means of persuasion to induce them to their duties.

10. Every communion day each parish hath 2 communions, the one for servants and officers to begin at 5 of the clock in the morning with a sermon of an hour, and to end at 8. The other for masters and dames etc. to begin at 9 the same day with a like sermon and to end at 12 at the uttermost.

11. The manner of this communion is, beside the sermon, according to the order of the queen's book, saving the people, being in their confession upon their knees, for the dispatch of many do orderly rise from their pews, and so pass to the communion table where they receive the sacrament and from thence in like order to their place, having all this time a minister in the pulpit reading unto them comfortable scriptures of the passion or other like pertaining to the matter in hand.

12. There is on every other Saturday, and now every Saturday, from 9 to 11 of the clock in the morning an exercise of the ministers both of town and country about the interpretation of scriptures, the ministers speaking one after another, doth handle some text, and the same openly among the people; that done, the ministers doth withdraw themselves into a privy place there to confer among themselves as well touching doctrine as good life, manners or others orders meet for them.

13. There is also a weekly assembly every Thursday after the lecture by the mayor and his brethren assisted with the preacher, minister and other gentlemen appointed to them by the bishop for the correction of discord made in the town as for notorious blasphemy, whoredom, drunkenness, railing against religion, or the preachers thereof, scolds, rybalds, and such like, which faults are each Thursday presented unto them in writing by certain sworn men appointed for that service in each parish, so the bishop's authority and the mayor's joined together being

assisted with certain other gentlemen in commission of peace, ill life is corrected, God's glory set forth and the people brought in good obedience.

14. The communion table standeth in the body of the church, according to the book, at the over end of the middle aisle, having three ministers, one in the middle to deliver the bread, the other two at each end for the cup. The ministers often times do call on the people to remember the poor which is there plentifully done, and thus the communion being ended, the people do sing a psalm.

15. The excessive ringing of bells at forbidden times by injunction, (whereby the people grew in disorder to the slaughter of some and unquieting of others given to hear sermons) is inhibited, allowing notwithstanding such orderly ringing as may serve to the calling of the people to church and giving warning of the passing and burial of every persons.

16. The carrying of the bell before cor[p]ses in the streets, and bidding prayers for the dead (which was there used till within these two years) is restrained.

17. There is hereafter to take place, ordered, that all ministers of the shire once every quarter of the year, upon one month's warning given, repair to the said town and there, after a sermon in the church heard, to withdraw themselves into a place appointed within the said church, and there privately to confer amongst themselves of their manners and lives, amongst whom if any be found in fault, for the first time exhortation is made to him amongst all the brethren to amend; and so likewise the second; the third time by complaint from all the brethren he is committed unto the bishop for his correction.

46. FROM P. COLLINSON, ed. *Letters of Thomas Wood, Puritan, 1566-77,* Bulletin of the Institute of Historical Research, Special Supplement 5, November, 1960, pp. 18-22. Hertfordshire Record Office. Ms. Gorhambury B/VIII/143.

[7 September, 1576] Thomas Wood to Robert Dudley, earl of Leicester.

I have received (right honourable and my singular good lord) your letter of the 19 of this last month, whereby I perceive to my great comfort that you are clear as touching the overthrow of the exercise of Southam, the contrary whereof I oft heard by sundry both wise and godly which I am fully persuaded wish well unto your lordship and that unfeignedly, as to their profession appertaineth. And that made me to affirm it more boldly in my letter to my lord your brother[1] than was meet, which fault I trust your lordship will pardon. And yet, if I should write unto you the words and protestations that your lordship's accuser made, you would think a wiser man than I might be abused, as divers others were which upon such reports thought it had been your lordship's fact indeed. But I hope ere it be long to put some of them out of that error. God amend them that have been the cause thereof, and grant that that exercise may be speedily set up again, the rather by your good means. Wherein I believe your lordship shall do one of the best services, both to God and your country, that ever you did, for it was undoubtedly without exception counted the best exercise in this realm, both for the number of the learned that repaired thither, as also of gentlemen and others more than the church could well hold. And for the ministers generally, I cannot learn of any disorder that hath been amongst them from the first day to the last, not the least that could be. For they kept precisely the same orders (as they affirm) which they received from the High Commissioners, as divers justices of peace can witness (for there were commonly three or four at every exercise) who according to their duties would have found fault if any had been. And this not with-standing, two of the chief preachers were sent for up, and being there neither could they know their accusers, nor, as they say, had not one word said to them touching the said exercise, but being examined of three or four points by the archbishop touching the book of service and surplice, were dismissed. Surely, my lord, this was hard dealing, whosoever was the cause thereof, and a great discouraging to those godly men who are much commended for God's great gifts bestowed upon them.

For your lordship's well deserving towards the learned ministers, especially those that of long time have been troubled about the un-profitable ceremonies (for the other could shift well enough for them-selves) I can be a witness when I was an humble suitor unto your lordship in the beginning of Mr Sampson's and Mr Goodman's first trouble, that you were their chiefest and in a manner their only patron, as in my former letters is mentioned, and that I never knew no man better bent to the setting forth of God's glory and help of such as were the unfeigned professors thereof than you showed yourself at many times when it pleased your lordship to talk with me. This both I have and will confess (God willing) so long as I live, as the truth is, and as I am in conscience bound, if I had never received benefit at your lordship's hands. As for the bishops whom your lordship hath commended, I know not. But there was one Young, preferred in the beginning to be one of the chiefest,[2] and of many thought to

---

[1] Ambrose Dudley, earl of Warwick.

[2] Thomas Young, archbishop of York 1560–1571.

be your lordship's doing, who was no divine but a simple civilian, and never preached at York but one sermon (as the report was) which he conned so ill by heart that he was forced to cut it off in the midst. I wrote to your lordship at the same time (if you remember) Mr Calvin's opinion out of his Institutions touching such bastard bishops. Touching the use of them, I will show your lordship a godly gentleman's opinion, now of very good calling, which he was wont oft merrily to utter, thus: 'Let the godliest man, and the best learned within this realm be chosen, and put once a rochet on his back, and it bringeth with it such an infection as that will mar him for ever.' I would experience had not taught this thing to be as true as it was merrily spoken. These are they that burden others to be disturbers of the peace of our church, where indeed they have been and are the doers of it. For if they had at the beginning sought a full reformation according to God's word, and an utter abolishing of all Papists' dregs, these controversies had never come into question. But every one sought how to catch a wealthy and rich bishopric, some paying well for it £40 pension to some one man during his life, as I have credibly heard. And thus neglecting God's glory, they sought their own, and therefore God never blessed their doings to this day, nor never will so long as they continue in this pomp and great wealth. Look upon Winchester, what large sums of money he hath given with his daughters, and how he hath matched them.[1] Look upon the rest, and for the most part your lordship shall find no better fruits, but everyone seeking to set themselves up a name. Thus with their covetous example they have done far more harm than they have done good by their preaching. But in this point, I have holden your lordship too long, and peradventure touched the quick too near if the bishops might be judge.

But now I will tell you of a good bishop indeed. There is not far from Ashby a poor town called Measham: the most part there are colliers. They have had one Peter Eglesall, a grave and godly man, to their minister not much above a year and half, who with his continual diligence in this time hath brought to pass that there is not one in his parish of lawful years but they are able by heart to make a good and godly confession of their faith, which they use to do before the receipt of the communion, besides the pains he hath taken with catechizing of their children. This man being of late cited before Bishop Bentham for the surplice as he had been oft before, two ancient old men above threescore years a piece would needs go with him, who coming to the bishop fell down upon their knees and besought him for the passion of Christ not to take from them their minister, confessing that at his coming to them they were ignorant

[1] Robert Horne, bishop of Winchester 1560–1580.

and obstinate Papists, and had been cast away for ever if God had not sent them that man by whose painful travail they had attained to a comfortable feeling of their salvation in Christ. Wherewith the bishop, being as it were astonied, turned his back and slipt away, and so, God be praised, they enjoy their minister still to their great comfort. And this man hath not of his parish (as I think) above £20 a year, besides a little farm of his own not far off. I do fear, my lord, that all they bishops, deans and chaplains in England are not able in these 19 years by past to show forth the like fruits. This is one of those men, my lord, that is counted precise and curious. The Lord increase the number of them to a thousand thousand, for such they be indeed that have been both the beginners and chief maintainers of all the godly exercises. And if the gospel has had any increase in England these years before named, it hath been chiefly by their preaching and godly example of life.

For deans, I never heard but that your lordship hath been too good to them in preferring some to two deaneries apiece, and others to more livings than they were able to discharge or can keep with good consciences. And till this be amended, let it never be said our ministry is reformed. For the universities, there is bruit of late that the chief and towardest young men and such as would have proved the fittest for the ministry are either gone or will go, for that the surplice and such like trifles are of late so urged as they must either receive them or lose their standing, which, if it be true, is lamentable, as was the driving away of some of the best and zealous preachers in Cambridge not long ago. Concerning the bishops' chaplains, I think there is scarce one maintained of the bishops' charges but they have one or two benefices abroad, and so live of the sweat of other men's brows, which perish for want of that spiritual food they ought to have at their hands. And shall not they that be preferrers and maintainers of such (far worse than cormorants) be partakers of their sins? No doubt of it. A bishop by St Paul's canon ought to rule his own house well, and in it is not so much as the name of a chaplain. Your lordship with many more are (no doubt) guilty in this most dangerous offence. For God's sake therefore rid your hands of such unnecessary chaplains, of whom assuredly the blood of all such as perish thorough their default shall be required. One man can but supply but one place at once, and therefore little enough for one flock, which no one man is able to discharge to the full. If your lordship will have a learned man or two to confer withal and so instruct your family, let them be maintained of your own purse, and suffer not the poor to be spoiled, nor your chaplains to keep more livings than one under pretence of your servant. Every one hath too many sins of their own, though they bear not the burden of others.

For our religion by law established as all good men praise God for it, so do many of good and sound judgement affirm that there be great wants in it; and that of such importance as neither ours nor any other church can be counted reformed without it, I mean discipline, which that godly learned Beza affirmeth to be one part of the word of God and the ordinance of Christ, without the which it is not possible but the whole building shall fall down. If this be true, as it is most true indeed, how can it be avouched that our reformation is good enough, seeing that the want of this discipline cannot be as is said but the overthrow of the whole building? And shall not then such godly ministers whose hearts the Lord hath touched with an unfeigned zeal of his glory cry out still for the obtaining of it, and abolishing of that popish discipline yet retained for the gain of a few, which do far more harm than good, as many good men think? Strive, saith Solomon, for the truth to the death. And no doubt there be no small number that by all good means will prosecute this so good a cause, as also the reformation of divers other things, so long as God giveth them liberty and life; who give to your honour and all other that fear him zeal and courage boldly to join with them in this behalf to the perfect building up of Sion. And if in this attempt you be ill spoken of or frowned upon, remember it is the Lord's work you have in hand, who both is able and will maintain his own cause, though all the world should bend itself against it. And forget not that it is the portion of all God's faithful servants to hear evil for well doing, which ought to be a sufficient comfort to you against all enemies. The Lord direct you by his Holy Spirit to do that in all your enterprises which may please him, for that is praiseworthy indeed. If that do come to pass which your lordship and many others fear, that is, not only the taking away of the exercises, but of the rest, too, it is, my lord, for that men will be wiser than God and will not submit themselves to his word in all points, but willingly, or rather stubbornly, refuse and reject Christ's ordinance, being, as is said before, a part of God's word, without the which religion never flourished in any city or country; and therefore they do great injury to God that shall put fault in those his most faithful servants, which only labour to obtain that which would be the preservation of all, namely that nothing be wanting in our religion which God's word requireth, nor anything allowed which that word doth not warrant. And this, my lord, is the mark they shoot at.

47. Leicester Museum. BR/II/18/1. 157. Printed with some errors in J. Thompson, *History of Leicester*, 1849, pp. 288–9.

12 April, 1586. The corporation of Leicester to Henry Hastings, third earl of Huntingdon.

Right honourable, our very good lord, our duty humbly premised. May it please your honour favourably to accept of this our humble suit, which we presently make both for our private good, and for the public benefit of the inhabitants of this town of Leicester. So it is, our very good lord, that being deprived by the just judgement of God for our sins of our faithful, godly and learned preacher, Mr Johnson, as your honour full well knoweth, we have been destitute ever sithence of the blessed benefit of a resident preacher faithfully to divide unto us the everlasting bread of our salvation. And understanding that the godly preacher, Mr Travers, a man, as we are credibly informed, of singular godliness and approved learning, now resteth uncharged with any cure,[1] and, hearing besides of his godly travails bestowed in other places, with the good success that it hath pleased God to give him in them, we have emboldened ourselves to acquaint your lordship with our extreme want of a resident preacher, and with our special liking of this man: humbly beseeching your honour with convenient speed to help to relieve the one, and to effect and further the accomplishment of the other. And we shall, as for all other your honour's benefits conferred on this town, so especially for this, most humbly pray to God for your honour's long life and good preservation, and rest ourselves most dutifully at your lordship's command. Thus humbly recommending unto your honour's godly disposition this our present grievous want, and to your favourable approbation this our nomination of Mr Travers, beseeching your good lordship to remember us herein, as occasion shall be offered your honour, and as your other serious businesses shall permit you, we humbly take our leave, and commit your honour to the protection of the Almighty.

Leicester, the 12th of April, 1586.

Your honour's humbly at command,

James Clarke, mayor,	John Eyrick,
Richard Parkyns,	Thomas Sampson,[2]
William Mortun,	John Tatam,
George Tatam,	William Noryce,
Philip Freake,	John Myddleton,
Thomas Clarke,	James Ellys,
Robert Heyricke,	William Ludlam.

[1] Walter Travers had been deprived of his lectureship at the Temple for his pulpit controversy with Hooker earlier in the year.

[2] Almost certainly Thomas Sampson, the former dean of Christ Church, Oxford, deprived for his nonconformity in 1565 and since 1567 master of Wyggeston's Hospital. Although he had long been crippled by a stroke he did not die until 1589.

48. Huntington Library, San Marino, California. Hastings Ms. H A 5093. To be printed in C. Cross, ed. *The Letters of Sir Francis Hastings, 1574–1609,* Somerset Record Society, LXIX, 1969.

28 February, 1592. Francis Hastings to Mr Price.[1]

Emmanuel.

Master Price, pardon me and take this lovingly that I write of love, for as I have found you most loving and kind to me in all civil and neighbourly friendships so truly I acknowledge all your kindnesses with thankfulness and am and ever will be ready to requite the same in anything wherein I may stead you or do you pleasure: and this that I now write proceedeth from the very inward affection and love of my heart to you.

Finding in myself, Mr Price, many foul faults by which I blemish the profession that I show to make of the glorious truth of the Almighty, and being led by the gracious goodness of my God to look into them, and in some measure to feel the weight and burthen of them, to the touch of my conscience and the grief of my heart, I have decreed with myself (through the help of my good God) to bend my whole forces to the amending of these my faults, and to carry a watch of myself in such sort as never hereafter to offend as I have done, and to cease from those evils wherein I have been over deeply plunged. And surely, Mr Price, the consideration of these mine own particular sins have drawn me to wish not only mine own reformation but also the amendment of all others wandering out of the way of a right course necessarily required in every Christian calling: and the rather because the longer we hold on to a custom in sinning the more perilous is our estate, being in danger to grow so benumbed in our spiritual senses as to become void of all feeling: and adding hereunto the uncertainty of our life not being able to promise to ourselves one half hour, being subject to death at every moment even in the turning of an hand; and in weighing withal the miserable estate we stand in if we take not hold of unfeigned repentance in time, I cannot but persuade both myself and all others to fall into a speedy reckoning how grievously we have offended the Lord, our good God, either by omitting the performance of any necessary duty imposed upon us, and expected from us, or by committing any sin to the slander of our profession and dishonour of his most holy name, that we may see into it with sorrow of heart: and so taking hold of true repentance may meet this most mighty and just God before he come in the heat of his anger and judgement, who yet of his unspeakable mercy will[s]

[1] This may be Cadwallader Price instituted to the living of Newton St Loe in Somerset in 1585. F. W. Weaver, *Somerset Incumbents,* Bristol, 1889, p. 278.

not the death of a sinner but rather that he be converted and live. And this moveth me to write these few following unto you at this time.

There be three things, Mr Price, which I will make bold to lay down unto you as faults, in my judgement, necessarily to be reformed in your function and calling. The first is your not instructing of your people in some measure; the second is your admitting them to the Lord's Table without examination, being so far unable to give a reason of their faith as some of them can scarcely say the articles of their belief; the third is your want of care in visiting and instructing those that be sick, that if they live they may learn to glorify God by amending their former evils, and if they die they may learn with courage and comfort to leave this wretched vale knowing that death is but their passage to a better life. I neither do nor will take upon me to prescribe you what particular course you shall take herein, I only offer to your consideration what you ought in duty and conscience to have a care of, that God may be glorified by you in your calling, your people may be edified, and your conscience in some measure discharged.

And that you may think I have some ground in mine own small understanding to lead me to persuade you to look into this, I beseech you weigh well with me the words of the prophet Ezekiel, or rather of the spirit of God poured down by the prophet wherein you shall find the prophet complaining against the shepherds of Israel that they feed themselves and not the sheep, and proceedeth in reproving and saith that, 'The weak they have not strengthened, the sick they have not healed: they have not bound up the broken, nor brought again that which was driven away, nor sought out that which was lost': and so proceedeth in his reproof very largely. But if all these parts be looked for in every shepherd, as no doubt they are, or else the prophet would not have reproved the shepherds of Israel for omitting them, I pray you, Mr Price, consider well your own case herein, for whatsoever is written it is written for our learning. And know this for truth that the day is not far off, and it will come, wherein all flesh must hear these words and obey them; 'Arise you dead and come to judgement'. At which time both minister and people, master and servant, prince and people, and all without exception must *give an explanation of their evil doing*; unto the which the God of mercy so prepare us, as we may be freed from the sentence of condemnation and receive mercy at his heavenly hands. To this our good God and most gracious Father I commend and commit you both now and ever.

49. Cambridge University Library. Mm. 1. 43. (Baker Ms. 32) 426.

5 July, 1593. Henry Hastings, third earl of Huntingdon to Arthur Hildersham.

Since that it hath pleased the Lord to call Thomas Wyddowes to his mercy, who was (in my opinion) both faithful, careful and diligent in his function according to his talent, I do wish with all my heart, the supply of that place to be such as that which good father Gilby and he by the good providence and mercy of God have planted in and about Ashby may be continued and increased. Therefore I choose to present you unto that pastoral charge of Ashby which I trust by that time I have finished my long intended purpose, shall be a sufficient place for any learned preacher. And with this letter I send you my presentation to the vicarage with a letter to the bishop of Lincoln, who, I hope, will easily accept of you, with all honour. Yet let this be your care, to advance the glory of God by exercise of your ministry, which you shall do best when you are in the pastoral charge. I am forced to end. God ever direct you, and ever assist you with all necessary graces.

At York, hastily, 5 July, '93.

Henry Huntingdon.

To the comfort of the poor widow I will take some care.

50. B. M. Egerton Ms. 2614. 9. D. M. Meads, ed. *Diary of Lady Margaret Hoby*, 1930, pp. 73–5.

Extract from the diary of Margaret wife of Sir Thomas Posthumous Hoby.

Saturday, the 22 [Sept. 1599]
After a private prayer I brake my fast and then talked with Mr Lister:[1] then I took my coach and went to Bishopthorpe to the bishop: there I dined, and talked with Mrs Hutton of religion till I came from thence: then I came to York to Mr Skidmore's house, where, after I had prayed, I went to supper to my cousin Bowser's house where I had conference with a religious gentlewoman, and thence returning went to bed.

The Lord's day, 23 [Sept.]
After private prayer I walked and did eat my breakfast: then I read a chapter of the Bible to my mother, and repeated the doctrines which from thence I had heard Mr Rhodes[2] collect: then I went to

[1] Lady Hoby's doctor.

[2] Richard Rhodes, Lady Hoby's chaplain. He acted as preacher at Hackness, and eventually received the benefice.

the church where I heard Mr Palmer speak, but to small profit to any: thence I returned and privately prayed, lamenting the misery of God's visible church, and praising his goodness to myself above others: then, soon after, I went to dinner: after that I talked with Mr Hoby, and so went to my cousin Bowser's child['s] christening, and heard a sermon, something better than that in the morning: which ended, with all ceremonies, I returned to my lodging, and examined myself and prayed: then I went to supper to Mr Nevil's, and after I went to my lodging, and so went to bed.

Thursday, the 27 [Sept.]

After I had prayed privately I went to breakfast: I took my coach and came home to Hackness safe, I thank God, and, after I had prayed privately and supped I heard Mr Rhodes catechize and soon after went to bed.

Friday, the 28 [Sept.]

In the morning after private prayer I took order for things about the house and at 8 I did eat my breakfast: then I heard Mr Rhodes read till almost dinner time: after dinner I talked with Thomas Addeson about the purchasing his own farm: then I wrought till almost supper time, and, after I had privately prayed, I went to supper: after that I walked till lector[1] time, and after that I heard one of the men read of the Book of Martyrs, and so went to bed.

Saturday, the 29 [Sept.]

After private prayer I did take order for things in the house, then I brake my fast and went to church. Then I came home and privately prayed. After I had dined I wrote to my mother and Mr Hoby, and dispatched one away to him, then I saw some things done in the house. After I wrote notes in my Bible, then I prayed with Mr Rhodes, and then walked till almost supper time, and then examined myself and prayed.

The Lord's day, 30 [Sept.]

After private prayer I went to church where I heard the word preached and received the sacraments to my comfort. After I had given thanks and dined I walked a while and then went to church, whence, after I had heard catechizing and sermon I returned home and wrote notes in my Bible, and talked of the sermon and good things with Mrs Ormston: then I went to prayer, after to supper, then to repetition of the whole day's exercise and prayers, heard one of the men read of the Book of Martyrs, and so went to bed.

---

[1] A devotional reading or exhortation.

ALLEN, J. W. *History of Political Thought in the Sixteenth Century*, 1928.

ALLEN, W. *A True, Sincere and Modest Defence of English Catholics*, 1584. And also see Kingdon, R. M.

AVELING, H. *Northern Catholics: the Catholic Recusants of the North Riding of Yorkshire 1558–1790*, 1966.

AYLMER, J. *An Harborow for Faithful and True Subjects against the Late Blown Blast concerning the Government of Women*, 1559.

AYRE, J. ed. *The Works of John Jewel*, I–III, 1845–1850.

AYRE, J. ed. *The Sermons of Edwin Sandys*, 1841.

AYRE, J. ed. *The Works of John Whitgift*, I–III, 1851–1853.

BABBAGE, S. B. *Puritanism and Richard Bancroft*, 1962.

BALD, R. C. ed. *Robert Southwell, An Humble Supplication to her Majesty*, 1953.

BANCROFT, R. *A Sermon Preached at Paul's Cross the 9 of February, being the First Sunday in the Parliament, Anno 1588 . . .*, 1589.

BARROW, H. *Writings*, see Carlson, L. H.

BILSON, T. *The True Difference between Christian Subjection and Antichristian Rebellion*, 1585.

BIRT, H. N. *The Elizabethan Religious Settlement*, 1907.

BOOTY, J. E. *John Jewel as Apologist of the Church of England*, 1963.

BOOTY, J. E. ed. *An Apology of the Church of England*, 1963.

BOSSY, J. 'The Character of Elizabethan Catholicism', *Past and Present*, XXI, 1962, pp. 39–59.

BROWNE, R. *Writings*, see Peel, A. and Carlson, L. H.

BRUCE, J. ed. *The Letters of Queen Elizabeth and King James VI*, Camden Society, First Series, XLVI, 1849.

BRUCE, J. and PEROWNE, T. T. eds *The Correspondence of Matthew Parker*, 1853.

BURRAGE, C. *The True Story of Robert Browne*, 1906.

BURRAGE, C. *The Early English Dissenters in the Light of Recent Research, 1550–1641*, 2 vols, 1912.

CAMDEN, W. *The History of the most Renowned and Victorious Princess Elizabeth, late Queen of England . . .*, 1688.

CARAMAN, P. ed. *John Gerard: the Autobiography of an Elizabethan*, 1951.

CARAMAN, P. ed. *William Weston: the Autobiography of an Elizabethan*, 1955.

CARGILL THOMPSON, W. D. J. 'Anthony Marten and the Elizabethan Debate on Episcopacy', Bennett, G. V. and Walsh, J. D. eds *Essays in Modern English Church History in Memory of Norman Sykes*, 1966, pp. 44–75.

CARLSON, L. H. ed. *The Writings of Henry Barrow 1587–1590*, 1962.

CARLSON, L. H. ed. *The Writings of John Greenwood 1587–1590*, 1962.

Cartwrightiana, see Peel, A.

CECIL, W. *The Execution of Justice* ... see Kingdon, R. M.

CHERUBINI, L. *Magnum Bullarium Romanum*, II, 1727.

CLANCY, T. 'English Catholics and the Papal Deposing Power', *Recusant History*, VI, 1961–2, pp. 114–140, 205–227; and VII, 1963–4, pp. 2–8.

COLLINS, W. E. *Queen Elizabeth's Defence of her Proceedings in Church and State*, Church Historical Society, LVIII, 1899.

COLLINSON, P. *The Elizabethan Puritan Movement*, 1967.

COLLINSON, P. ed. *The Letters of Thomas Wood, Puritan, 1566–1577*, Bulletin of the Institute of Historical Research, Special Supplement, no. 5, 1960.

COLLINSON, P. *A Mirror of Elizabethan Puritanism: the Life and Letters of 'Godly Master Dering'*, 1964.

COLLINSON, P. 'The Elizabethan Puritans and the Reformed Churches in London', *Proceedings of the Huguenot Society of London*, XX, no. 5, 1964.

COLLINSON, P. 'The Role of Women in the English Reformation illustrated by the Life and Friendships of Anne Locke', Cuming, G. J. ed. *Studies in Church History*, II, 1965, pp. 258–272.

COLLINSON, P. 'Episcopacy and Reform in England in the later Sixteenth Century', Cuming G. J. ed. *Studies in Church History*, III, 1966, pp. 91–125.

COLLINSON, P. 'The Godly: Aspects of Popular Protestantism in Elizabethan England', *Past and Present* Conference Papers, July 7, 1966.

Commons Journals, I.

COOPER, T. *An Admonition to the People of England*, 1589.

COX, J. C. ed. *The Records of the Borough of Northampton*, II, 1898.

CROSS, C. *The Puritan Earl: the Life of Henry Hastings, Third Earl of Huntingdon, 1536–1595*, 1966.

CROSS, M. C. 'Noble Patronage in the Elizabethan Church', *Historical Journal*, III, 1960, pp. 1–16.

CROSS, M. C. 'The Third Earl of Huntingdon and Elizabethan Leicestershire', *Transactions of the Leicestershire Archaeological and Historical Society*, XXXVI, 1960, pp. 6–21.

DAVIES, E. T. *Episcopacy and the Royal Supremacy in the Church of England*, 1950.

D'ENTRÈVES, A. P. *Medieval Contribution to Political Thought*, 1939.

DERING, E. *A Sermon Preached before the Queen's Majesty. By E. Dering, the 25. of February, 1569*, [c.1570].

D'EWES, S. *A Complete Journal of the Votes, Speeches and Debates both of the House of Lords and House of Commons throughout the whole reign of Queen Elizabeth*, 1693.

ELTON, G. R. *The Tudor Constitution*, 1960.

FIGGIS, J. N. *The Divine Right of Kings*, 1914.

FIGGIS, J. N. 'Political Thought in the Sixteenth Century', *Cambridge Modern History*, III, 1907, pp. 736–769.

FRERE, W. H. and DOUGLAS, C. E. eds *Puritan Manifestoes*, 1954 reprint.

GEE, H. *The Elizabethan Clergy and the Settlement of Religion 1558–1564*, 1898.

GEE, H. *The Elizabethan Prayer Book and Ornaments*, 1902.

GERARD, J. *Autobiography*, see Caraman, P.

GREENWOOD, J. *Writings*, see Carlson, L. H.

GRINDAL, E. *Remains*, see Nicholson, W.

HALL, B. 'Puritanism: the Problem of Definition', Cuming, G. J. ed. *Studies in Church History*, II, 1965, pp. 283–296.

HARRISON, R. *Writings*, see Peel, A. and Carlson, L. H.

HAUGAARD, W. P. *Elizabeth and the English Reformation*, 1968.

HICKS, L. ed. *Letters and Memorials of Father Robert Persons, S. J.* Catholic Record Society, XXXIX, 1942.

HILL, C. *Economic Problems of the Church from Archbishop Whitgift to the Long Parliament*, 1956.

HILL, J. W. F. *Tudor and Stuart Lincoln*, 1956.

HILL, J. W. F. 'The Beginnings of Puritanism in a Country Town', *Transactions of the Congregational Historical Society*, XVIII, no. 2, 1957, pp. 40–49.

HOBY, M. *Diary*, see Meads, D. M.

HOOKER, R. *Of the Laws of Ecclesiastical Polity*, 1666.

HOOKER, R. *Works*, 1888.

HOUK, R. A. ed. *Hooker's Ecclesiastical Polity, Book VIII*, 1931.

HUGHES, P. *Rome and the Counter Reformation in England*, 1942.

HUGHES, P. *The Reformation in England*, III, 1954.

HUME, M. A. S. ed. *Calendar of State Papers, Spanish, 1558–1567*, 1892.

JEWEL, J. *An Apology or Answer in Defence of the Church of England*, 1564.

JEWEL, J. *The Works of the very learned Father in God, John Jewel*, 1611.

Jewel's Works, see Ayre, J.

KINGDON, R. M. ed. *Cecil, Execution of Justice: Allen, Modest Defence*, 1965.

KNOX, J. *The Appellation*, 1558.

KNOX, J. *The First Blast of the Trumpet against the Monstrous Regiment of Women*, 1558.

LAMONT, W. M. *Marginal Prynne, 1600–1669*, 1963.

LAMONT, W. M. 'The Rise and Fall of Bishop Bilson', *Journal of British Studies*, V, 1966, pp. 22–32.

LEATHERBARROW, J. S. *The Lancashire Elizabethan Recusants*, Chetham Society, New Series 110, 1947.

LEWIS, C. S. *English Literature in the Sixteenth Century Excluding Drama*, 1954.

MAITLAND, F. W. 'Elizabethan Gleanings: Supremacy and Uniformity', *English Historical Review*, XVIII, 1903, pp. 517–532.

MATTINGLY, G. 'William Allen and Catholic Propaganda in England', *Travaux d'Humanisme et Renaissance*, XXVIII, 1957.

McGINN, D. J. *The Admonition Controversy*, 1949.

McGRATH, P. *Papists and Puritans under Elizabeth I*, 1967.

MEADS, D. M. ed. *Diary of Lady Margaret Hoby*, 1930.

MEYER, A. O. *England and the Catholic Church under Elizabeth*, 1967 reprint.

MORRIS, C. *Political Thought in England: Tyndale to Hooker*, 1953.

MORRIS, J. ed. *The Troubles of our Catholic Forefathers*, Third Series, 1877.

MUNZ, P. *The Place of Hooker in the History of Thought*, 1952.

NEALE, J. E. *Elizabeth I and her Parliaments*, 2 vols 1953, 1957.

NEALE, J. E. 'Elizabethan Acts of Supremacy and Uniformity', *English Historical Review*, LX, 1950, pp. 304–332.

NICHOLSON, W. ed. *Remains of Edmund Grindal*, 1843.

O'CONNELL, M. R. *Thomas Stapleton and the Counter Reformation*, 1964.

OWEN, H. G. 'London Parish Clergy in the reign of Elizabeth I', Unpublished London Ph.D. thesis, 1957.

OWEN, H. G. 'Lectures and Lectureships in Tudor London', *Church Quarterly Review*, CLXII, 1961, pp. 63–76.

OWEN, H. G. 'The Liberty of the Minories: a Study in Elizabethan Radicalism', *East London Papers*, VIII, no. 2, 1965, pp. 81–97.

OWEN, H. G. 'A Nursery of Elizabethan Nonconformity 1567–1572', *Journal of Ecclesiastical History*, XVII, 1966, 65–76.

Parker Correspondence, see Bruce, J. and Perowne, T. T.

PARSONS, R. *Letters*, see Hicks, L.

PAUL, J. E. 'Hampshire Recusants in the time of Elizabeth I, with special reference to Winchester', *Proceedings of the Hampshire Field Club*, XXI, pt II, 1959, pp. 61–81.

PEARSON, A. F. S. *Thomas Cartwright and Elizabethan Puritanism*, 1925.

PEARSON, A. F. S. *Church and State: Political Aspects of Sixteenth Century Puritanism*, Cambridge, 1928.

PECK, F. *Desiderata Curiosa*, I, 1779.

PEEL, A. *The Brownists in Norwich and Norfolk about 1580*, 1920.

PEEL, A. *The First Congregational Churches*, 1920.

PEEL, A. 'William White: an Elizabethan Puritan', *Transactions of the Congregational Historical Society*, VI, 1913–15, pp. 4–19.

PEEL, A. and CARLSON, L. H. eds *Cartwrightiana*, 1951.

PEEL, A. and CARLSON, L. H. eds *The Writings of Robert Harrison and Robert Browne*, 1953.

PORTER, H. C. *Reformation and Reaction in Tudor Cambridge*, 1958.

PRICE, F. D. 'The Abuses of Excommunication and the Decline of Ecclesiastical Discipline under Queen Elizabeth', *English Historical Review*, LVII, 1942, pp. 106–115.

PROTHERO, G. W. *Select Statutes*, 1913.

RENOLD, P. ed. *The Wisbech Stirs 1595–1598*, Catholic Record Society, LI, 1958.

RICHARDS, M. 'Thomas Stapleton', *Journal of Ecclesiastical History*, XVIII, 1967, pp. 187–199.

ROBINSON, H. ed. *Zurich Letters*, First and Second Series, Parker Society, 1842 and 1845.

RUSSELL, C. 'Arguments for Religious Unity in England 1530–1650', *Journal of Ecclesiastical History*, XVIII, 1967, pp. 201–226.

SANDYS, E. *Sermons*, see Ayre, J.

SCARISBRICK, J. J. *Henry VIII*, 1968.

SHIRLEY, F. J. *Richard Hooker and Contemporary Ideas*, 1949.

SISSON, C. J. *The Judicious Marriage of Mr Hooker and the Birth of the Laws of Ecclesiastical Polity*, 1940.

SOUTHERN, A. C. ed. *An Elizabethan Recusant House*, [1954].

SOUTHGATE, W. M. *John Jewel and the Problem of Doctrinal Authority*, 1962.

SOUTHWELL, R. *An Humble Supplication*, see Bald, R. C.

SPARROW, A. *A Collection of Articles, Injunctions, Canons, Orders, Ordinances and Constitutions Ecclesiastical, with other Public Records of the Church of England . . .*, 1661.

Statutes of the Realm, IV.

STRYPE, J. *Life and Acts of Edmund Grindal*, 1710.

STRYPE, J. *Life and Acts of Matthew Parker*, 1711.

STRYPE, J. *Life and Acts of John Whitgift*, 1718.

STRYPE, J. *Annals of the Reformation and Establishment of Religion . . . in the Church of England*, 4 vols 1725–31.

SYKES, N. *Old Priest and New Presbyter*, 1956.

THOMPSON, J. *History of Leicester*, 1849.

THOMPSON, J. V. P. *Supreme Governor*, 1940.

TRAVERS, W. *A Full and Plain Declaration of Ecclesiastical Discipline out of the Word of God and of the declining of the Church of England from the same*, 1574.

TRIMBLE, W. R. *The Catholic Laity of Elizabethan England 1558–1603*, 1964.

TYLER, P. 'The Ecclesiastical Commission for the Province of York 1561–1641', Unpublished Oxford D.Phil. thesis, 1965.

TYLER, P. 'The Significance of the Ecclesiastical Commission at York', *Northern History*, II, 1967, pp. 27–44.

USHER, R. G. *The Rise and Fall of High Commission*, 1968 reprint.

WALKER, F. X. 'The Implementation of the Elizabethan Statutes against Recusants, 1581–1603', Unpublished London Ph.D. thesis, 1961.

WALKER, R. B. 'The Growth of Puritanism in the County of Lincoln in the reign of Queen Elizabeth I', *Journal of Religious History*, I, no. 3, 1961, pp. 148–159.

WESTON, W. *Autobiography*, see Caraman, P.

Whitgift's Works, see Ayre, J.

WOOD, T. *Letters*, see Collinson, P.

Zurich Letters, see Robinson, H.

DATE DUE

JA 1 4 '96			
	NO 23 82		
		DE 14 82	
GAYLORD			PRINTED IN U.S.A.